MANDATES AND MISSTEPS
AUSTRALIAN GOVERNMENT SCHOLARSHIPS TO THE PACIFIC – 1948 TO 2018

MANDATES AND MISSTEPS

AUSTRALIAN GOVERNMENT SCHOLARSHIPS
TO THE PACIFIC – 1948 TO 2018

ANNA KENT

ANU PRESS

PACIFIC SERIES

ANU PRESS

Published by ANU Press
The Australian National University
Canberra ACT 2600, Australia
Email: anupress@anu.edu.au

Available to download for free at press.anu.edu.au

ISBN (print): 9781760466152
ISBN (online): 9781760466169

WorldCat (print): 1403846248
WorldCat (online): 1403846180

DOI: 10.22459/MM.2024

This title is published under a Creative Commons Attribution-NonCommercial-NoDerivatives 4.0 International (CC BY-NC-ND 4.0) licence.

The full licence terms are available at
creativecommons.org/licenses/by-nc-nd/4.0/legalcode

Cover design and layout by ANU Press.

Cover photograph: National Archives of Australia, A1501, A5054/3, Fijian and Tongan students staged a spectacular 'Festival of the South Seas' in Brisbane, which attracted a capacity house of 500 guests, mostly Australians, to Brisbane's Chinese Club. Photographer, R W Nicol, 1964.

This book is published under the aegis of the Pacific editorial board of ANU Press.

This edition © 2024 ANU Press

Contents

Acknowledgements   vii
Foreword   ix
Nayahamui Michelle Rooney
Acronyms   xv
Notes on geography and language   xvii
Introduction   1

Part 1: 1948–1957
1. Before the beginning   27
2. Administrative labyrinths   43

Part 2: 1958–1970
3. Uncertain decolonisation   55
4. Gradual development   79

Part 3: 1971–1983
5. Radical subsidies   93
6. Independence for Papua New Guinea   109

Part 4: 1984–1996
7. Goldring, Jackson and the fight for the future of international education   123
8. Centring the power   149

Part 5: 1997–2018
9. Multiple objectives for scholarships and aid   177
10. Diplomacy or development?   203
Conclusion   219
Bibliography   227
Index   247

Acknowledgements

The bulk of this book was written on the lands of the Wurundjeri people of the Kulin Nation. I pay my respects to their elders, past and present. Sovereignty was never ceded.

I would like to acknowledge the students that have made the difficult decision to move away from their homes in the South Pacific for study. Their stories are the backbone of, and the reason for, this study. I would also like to thank all the alumni that I have spoken to over the course of this project, who have shared their experiences with me. These conversations have enriched this work and my own understanding.

This book started its life as a PhD thesis, supported by a scholarship connected to the Australian Research Council–funded Discovery Project, 'Australia's foreign aid since 1945'. My continued thanks go to my supervisor, David Lowe, for his guidance, support, understanding, empathy and knowledge. Thanks also to Helen Gardner and Carolyn Holbrook, who were excellent and supportive associate supervisors. Thanks also to my excellent PhD examiners.

I am also indebted to the other historians of the Centre for Contemporary Histories at Deakin. In particular, Sarah Pinto, Bart Ziino, Clare Corbould and Jon Ritchie have provided advice and collegiality that is a wonderful representation of possibilities of a supportive academic community. I was also fortunate to test out many of the ideas of this book at conferences over the years, and I am grateful for the interest, questions and comments that many colleagues made.

I am grateful for the archivists at the National Archives of Australia, National Archives of Fiji (NAF), the National Archives of Papua New Guinea and the National Archives and Records Administration in the United States of America. In particular, I would like to thank Amelia Waqamailau at the NAF and Asena Dame, Emily Rasoqosoqo and Amaili Vakanawa at the

NAF Library. I also appreciate the collegiality of staff at the University of the South Pacific, especially Nic Halter. Thanks also go to staff at the Australian High Commissions in Suva and Papua New Guinea who reaffirmed the need for research like this.

To my ECR (Early Career Researcher) colleagues, Brad, Deb, Jacqui, Fiona, Celeste and more, thank you so much for your support and encouragement, and for tolerating my ramblings and enthusiasm with kindness. Thanks to Matt Mawer, Joan Dassin and Anne Campbell for showing the global potential of my research, to Jemma Purdey for encouraging me into this, and to Joanne Barker for joining the scholarship research caper. To my colleagues, mentors and friends in the international education world, I hope to repay your support by translating this research into a broader understanding of international education history in Australia.

Special acknowledgements and thanks go to my friends, who have encouraged me in this madcap scheme from the beginning, consoling me and celebrating with me throughout.

Finally, thank you to my family. To my parents, for showing us the world as it is and the ways it can be better. To my sisters, Elly and Kate and their families for their support, and special thanks to Elly for paving an academic pathway (and for a place to stay in Canberra). To my kids, Adele and Quinn, whose encouragement and curiosity fill me with joy and love. Thanks also to the best office buddy, Grover. And to Peter, thank you.

Foreword

Nayahamui Michelle Rooney

On Wednesday 24 October 1990, when I was in my final year of high school in Port Moresby, and with about two weeks before the final Year 12 exams, I woke up one morning to my mother crying as she entered into my room. During those times, every morning either her or our father would walk in and wake me up for school. This morning, our father was away in Manus. He was then working between Mendi, Kavieng, Port Moresby and Manus and had taken one of his regular trips to Manus to check on their lodge, Lorengau Kohai Lodge. He called home regularly to check on us and when we spoke over the phone the night before he asked me how my exam preparation was going. I had told him things were okay and I asked when he would return home. His response was something along the lines of a lighthearted tiredness of being on the road so often; 'Maybe never' or 'God only knows'. I remember those words and his voice because it was our last conversation. Through her crying, and my confusion about why she was crying as she entered my room, I also remember her words becoming clearer. 'He is dead. They killed him'. I sat up abruptly, awake, and asked, 'Who?' or 'What?'. She repeated 'They killed him. They killed Papa'. I knew he was in Manus. He must have been killed in Manus.

I screamed and got out of bed and followed her to their bedroom where we made a phone call to my brother's friend to ask him if he could go and pick my brother who was at work. Mama had already begun making calls to let people know. Mama was a political figure in Papua New Guinea and the news about our father's death spread rapidly. The house began filling up with streams of friends, relatives and my parents' colleagues arriving in shock to confirm the news or to mourn and offer condolences. My world was turned upside down, into a big fast-moving blurry place with a lot of wailing and moving people. I knew we would be going to Manus, and I thought that I would never return back to Port Moresby.

That day, amid the turmoil, a phone call came in and my mother took it. I recall her sitting in the corner speaking on the phone and waving me over to her. She was saying to the person on the line, 'It is best you tell her, and she hears it directly from you.' Curious, I took the phone from her hand. On the other end of the line, a female voice explained that she was a staff member from AIDAB (the Australian International Development Assistance Bureau, later called AusAID). She told me that my application for an Equity and Merit Scholarship Scheme (EMSS) had been successful. I had been selected for a scholarship to study economics at The Australian National University (ANU). At that moment, leaving our Port Moresby home in the direction of Australia, instead of Manus, was the last thing on my mind. I tried to explain that my father had just died and that I was returning to Manus for the funeral and did not know when I would return. The voice on the other end of the call informed me that they had already heard the news and she proceeded to calmly tell me to go to Manus and to contact them when I returned. My scholarship would be held for me. I cannot remember her name. At that time, I was Papua New Guinean. With our father being a former Australian citizen and with his family in Australia, our family had always lived between the two countries. Mama had made it clear to Papa when they got married that, if he married her, he was marrying her entire family and so PNG was the home they chose to live and raise us in. With our mother's family in PNG, her political career and our father's decision to become a Papua New Guinean citizen, we also held PNG citizenship. Both our parents were very proud Papua New Guineans, and they made this clear. When I reflect on my, and my siblings', education, each of our journeys seems to reflect our parent's juggling between life realities for each of our specific situations, their aspirations to educate us, year-to-year strategies for affording different forms of education, while supporting a large extended family. In my case, this included spending around three years living with my paternal uncle and aunt in Australia attending a public school. I think because of this, my parents never raised my expectations and nor did I entertain the idea that they would pay for me to attend university in Australia. I was encouraged to look for scholarships and to apply to what was available in PNG. They encouraged me in certain ways that, now on hindsight, I think also reflected their worries at that time. For example, in high school my favourite subject was art. However, my mother encouraged me to think about other career options. In any case, even after two years of art, I never saw my art portfolio because it got lost during the Year 12 examination process and the tumult when my father died. Despite scoring top marks for art and under average in maths, that day in 1990 set my life's pathway on a different direction so perhaps any ideas I had about pursuing art were never meant to be. As a PNG citizen exploring options to pursue tertiary education, I was aware of the restrictions and costs of studying in Australia. There were not many scholarships around and I applied for the EMSS when it was advertised. At home, I applied and received an offer to do an arts degree at the University of PNG. I was also accepted to another Australian university; a nice but impossible dream for our mother to even consider supporting after our father died.

Both those events on that fateful day – the death of my father and the phone call informing me about the scholarship – changed the course of my life and marked the beginning of the life I came to know; defining my entry into adulthood, setting the course for my professional and scholarly journey. As we journeyed to Manus to bury our father there was a kind of darkness that comes when you combine sorrow, confusion and apprehension about the nature of his death itself and the unknown details of his murder and the investigation that followed. In the sea of faces of people present for his funeral and burial, someone or some people knew what happened. That phone call gave me an alternative world to imagine as my world slipped into that darkness of grief and uncertainty. After our father's burial in Manus and the customary five days mortuary ceremony, I returned to Port Moresby still dazed, and sat my Grade 12 exams. Now back in Port Moresby with the exams over and my imminent departure to Canberra, I resisted our mother's plans for us to return to Manus for the Christmas holidays. The way our father had died and with a scholarship to look forward to, Manus had become a sad place for me; I did not want to return. However, Mama was a strong woman and insisted that I return with everyone to Manus. It was an important return; beautiful and sad at the same time; it helped to keep me grounded.

By early 1991, I was on my way to Canberra. At the Port Moresby international airport departure area, I recall very shyly giving an interview to one of the national radio stations. The interview might have been arranged by the EMSS Australian scholarship officials because I recall the question seemed to focus on what I thought I would do with the education I was to receive in Australia. I recall responding along the lines of using the education to help the development of Papua New Guinea. A few hours later I was on a plane arriving into Canberra with a small cohort of other scholarship recipients. I stayed at the Ursula Hall college to commence an economics degree with the College of Economics. At ANU I met other Papua New Guinean students. In Canberra, family and friends formed an important social support net as I immersed into life as an ANU Bachelor of Economics student. My mother came to visit Canberra soon after I arrived. I remember one conversation when she and I were walking from ANU to Canberra's city centre. I was feeling so sad and homesick for family and friends. I told her that I wanted to give up the studies and return home to PNG. I mentioned that perhaps I could return and take up the UPNG offer to study for an arts degree. But she did not want to hear a word of it. In no uncertain terms, she sternly told me I was to focus on my studies and complete the degree at ANU.

The scholarship must have been a great relief for our mother and other family who tried to fill in the gap our father left. In all the sorrow that arrived with that news that day, that phone call was like a light through a pinhole in the darkness. I could see some hope and relief in my mother's eyes. As she grieved and cried, she would also mention this good news. Reading some of the letters she sent to me and her diarised notes during those years after our father died, it is evident that she was grieving deeply and under immense pressure to try to figure out, along with other family members, how to cope after his death. I know that under the circumstances and with her knowledge of the challenges PNG women face, and what had just happened to her husband, our father, she must have been very worried about the kinds of challenges we faced ahead of us. At the age of 18, she and our father had already provided an excellent foundation for me, but without him around she would need support. The scholarship to ANU was a unique opportunity for me to study while relieving her of one worry.

I put my head down and completed my degree between 1991 and 1994 and graduated with a Bachelor of Economics with second class honours. I stayed at Ursula Hall college in 1991, Burton and Garran Hall in 1992, then moved off campus for 1993 and 1994. In 1993, my younger brother lived with me as he attended school in Canberra. In 1994, he would visit me over weekends in Canberra from boarding school in Goulburn. The scholarship enabled me to provide small but important support to other family and loved ones. It enabled me to return home to visit during those years.

I returned home to PNG in 1994 with my degree in hand and returned straight to Manus where I stayed and waited for responses to my job applications. I returned to Port Moresby in early 1995 after I received a job offer from the Bank of PNG to work as a monetary policy officer. I have always been drawn to social and development issues, and in 1996 I successfully applied for a job as a National Program Officer with the

FOREWORD

United Nations Development Programme (UNDP). I spent over 10 years as a national officer with the UNDP and then just under a year with the World Bank. In 2009, facing challenges in life and after our daughter fell very ill, I made the decision to migrate to Australia when I found out that I was eligible for Australian citizenship by descent because of my father's citizenship before he took up PNG citizenship. I took up Australian citizenship and moved to Australia in 2010. Under PNG laws at the time, I had to forfeit my PNG citizenship. I cried so much when I lost my PNG citizenship. But now as a mother myself, I was making decisions for my family. In Australia, after some time looking for work, including working in casual childcare, I commenced my PhD in 2012 with the ANU State, Society and Governance in Melanesia program, which is now known as Department of Pacific Affairs. My PhD was very much motivated by my own questions about how we create social safety in our life, and how we balance life between the customary obligations and our aspirations for education, good health, motherhood and so on.

My career has been a journey since that phone call telling me that I had been awarded a EMSS scholarship to do economics. It has defined my professional life, my scholarly journey and my entire life since my father died. My mother's response to me when I told her I wanted to give up also taught me about being humble and pragmatic about life choices. Even if I was not sure if I wanted to do this course, or if I was more passionate about doing something more creative, at that moment in our lives she was very constrained in how she could support me. It was better for me to take what was available and follow the course of where it would take me, rather than return home to an uncertain future ahead of us. I have held this approach in my life. We don't always get to choose what we study or what life deals out, but when presented with opportunities, we can try to make the best of these opportunities. The EMSS to study economics at ANU was my opportunity and I have no regrets taking it. Even today, when some of my work is critical of the Australian government's approach to Papua New Guinea, I am always grateful to the Australian and PNG governments for creating the opportunity in that scholarship.

Anna Kent's book provided me with historic context and gave me an insight into the official side of the scholarship schemes and the various iterations of the Australian government's scholarship schemes through themes like decolonisation, national interests, Australian aid, foreign relationships, education policies and Australia's domestic political environment. A key argument of the book is that scholarship policies are characterised by incremental iterative policy changes. I was intrigued to learn that the EMSS scholarship, which I was a recipient of, was a short-lived scholarship scheme which, according to Kent, was a compromise between the two major reports – Goldring and Jackson reports – commissioned by the Australian government. According to this book, the EMSS was another departure from the trend of iterative change and was an experiment in redefining the role of recipient government's decisions over scholarships.

I read this book as a 1991 recipient of the Australian EMSS. I have sometimes wondered about the selection process and what and how decisions were made that led to that specific phone call being made on that day. How was the decision made for me to do economics at ANU? It is so long ago, and perhaps it does not really matter now. I have simplified my story for the purposes of reflecting on the importance of this book because I believe that it will be of interest to a wide audience within and beyond academia and the policy space. The case studies drawn from the official records of scholarship recipients were an excellent way to introduce the key themes and underlying policy and political considerations at the time. The case studies also help to bring the book closer to readers who have either directly been recipients of scholarships or have been a family member of a scholarship recipient. Like me, I know the book will prompt many scholarship recipients to reflect on the questions of how the Australian scholarships shaped their lives. What specific iteration of Australia's scholarship policy did their scholarship come under, and how and why were they selected for the scholarship? How did each of our experiences, individually and collectively contribute, or not, to the goals of those policies? Each scholarship recipient has our unique story to tell about the ways the Australian scholarship shaped our lives and careers. All our stories are rich with multiple relationships that mean that the actual reach and influence of the scholarships extend far beyond recipients of scholarships and the state bilateral relationship.

Given the changing geopolitical context that we find ourselves in, international students, including recipients of Australian scholarships, will remain crucial to the Australian tertiary sector and Australia's engagement with the Pacific region. Importantly, the experiences and relationships formed as part of the experiences of scholarship recipients will remain important threads in the fabric of Australia's relationship with the region. This book provides an important baseline study to understand how the past shapes Australia's current and future policies on scholarships. It will also open new conversations and points of inquiry about Australia's scholarship policy discourse and recipients' experiences both in Australia and the region.

Acronyms

AA	Australia Awards
ADAA	Australian Development Assistance Agency
ADAB	Australian Development Assistance Bureau
ADCOS	Australian Development Cooperation Scholarship
ADS	Australian Development Scholarships
AIDAB	Australian International Development Assistance Bureau
ALAS	Australian Leadership Award Scheme
ANAO	Australian National Audit Office
ARDS	Australian Regional Development Scholarship
ASTAS	Australian Sponsored Training Assistance Scheme
AusAID	Australian Aid Agency
AVCC	Australian Vice-Chancellors' Committee
CAA	Community Aid Abroad
CD&W	(British) Colonial Development and Welfare
COE	Commonwealth Office of Education
CSFP	Commonwealth Scholarship and Fellowship Plan
DEA	Department of External Affairs
DFA	Department of Foreign Affairs
DTS	Development Training Scholarships
EMSS	Equity and Merit Scholarship Scheme
HECS	Higher Education Contribution Scheme
IDP	International Development Program
ITC	International Training Courses
JCSS	John Crawford Scholarship Scheme

MELCOS	Melbourne Council for Overseas Students
ODA	Overseas Development Assistance
OECD DAC	Organisation for Economic Co-operation and Development, Development Assistance Committee
OSC	Overseas Student Charge
PNG	Papua New Guinea
RAMSI	Regional Assistance Mission to Solomon Islands
SSSP	Secondary School Students' Project
STP	Sponsored Training Program
TPNG	Territory of Papua and New Guinea
UK	United Kingdom
UNSC	United Nations Security Council
UPNG	University of Papua New Guinea
USA	United States of America
USP	University of the South Pacific
USSR	Union of Soviet Socialist Republics

Notes on geography and language

The Pacific can be a difficult geographic concept to define. It is complicated by a range of ideas about the Pacific as a region. Historian Matt Matsuda wrote that defining what 'the Pacific' means is a 'daunting challenge'.[1] Matsuda goes on to discuss the difficulty of 'history drawn from such a complex set of boundaries, nested temporalities, and geographies'.[2]

In this book 'the Pacific' is used to describe the south-westerly area of the Pacific Ocean, often known as the South Pacific. This area stretches from Papua New Guinea in the west, and the Cook Islands and French Polynesia to the east. These areas are often described as Melanesian and Polynesian cultural areas – which are themselves constructions. To the north of the equator – what Crocombe and Meleisea describe as a 'big geographical and cultural divider',[3] lies Micronesia. Kiribati is the most northerly nation that features in this research; other Pacific Island states north of the equator tend to be more closely linked to the United States of America and have attracted less attention from the Australian Government in relation to aid. This focus aligns closely with British imperialism; many of the states and territories in the Pacific that the Australian Government has been concerned with over the period covered in this book are former British colonies.

---

1   Matt K Matsuda, 'The Pacific', *The American Historical Review* 111, no. 3 (2006): 758, doi.org/10.1086/ahr.111.3.758.
2   Matsuda, 'The Pacific', 759.
3   Ron Crocombe and Malama Meleisea, 'Higher Education in the Pacific Islands: Spheres of Influence, Trends and Developments', *International Journal of Educational Development* 9, no. 3 (1989): 164, doi.org/10.1016/0738-0593(89)90044-8.

This book also discusses the nation now known as Papua New Guinea, and the former territories that make it up (in the timeframe of this book) – the Territory of Papua and the Trust Territory of New Guinea. The legal distinctions between these territories are important, and affect the status of their residents as part of the Australian state.

As Hank Nelson has written, 'the names for the east of the island of New Guinea are confusing'.[4] In 1906, Australia was granted control of the south-eastern half of the island that had been British New Guinea, which became the Territory of Papua. The north-eastern half was German New Guinea, until 1921 when it became 'officially' Australian New Guinea, a mandate territory under the League of Nations and later a trust territory under the United Nations. Both territories were administered together by the Australian Government, becoming officially known as the Territory of Papua and New Guinea. They are not, however, the same territory. There are key administrative differences that change the status of the individual residents of these territories. The impact of these administrative differences will be discussed across this book.

This book discusses international education at length. The terms used for the globally mobile student cohort that is part of what is now known as international education have varied over the decades covered in this book. In the early postwar years students were generally referred to as 'Asian students'. Later they were known as 'overseas students' and in contemporary times they are referred to as 'international students'. All of these terms are used at times in this book, and they all refer to the same grouping: students who have travelled from one country to another for study.

---

4   Hank Nelson, 'Liberation: The End of Australian Rule in Papua New Guinea', *The Journal of Pacific History* 35, no. 3 (1 December 2000): 269–80, doi.org/10.1080/00223340020010562.

Introduction

There is a long history of student mobility across land and sea to access higher education.[1] For the people of the islands of the South Pacific during much of the twentieth century, travelling overseas was the only option to access higher education. And for many of these students, a scholarship was the only way to access such opportunities. For more than 70 years, the Australian Government has been providing scholarships to Australian universities for aspiring students from across the Pacific and the rest of the world.

For much of that time, scholarships have been considered part of the Australian nation's obligation to provide aid to developing countries in its own region, including the Pacific. Despite changes in governments, aid and foreign policy approaches and the conditions in the recipient territories and nations, scholarships have persisted. This longevity, through changing national interests and shifting government priorities, through (and in spite of) reviews that have sought to reshape aid and scholarships, is remarkable. It is also instructive. This book explains what both the persistence and the longevity of international scholarships can tell us about Australian foreign and aid policy over the last 70 years, particularly in relationship to the Pacific region. This is particularly relevant today given the current Australian Government's focus on engagement with the Pacific.

There are three key themes running within this book. The first is the flexible but powerful notion of national interest, and in particular Australian national interest. The second is the decolonisation of territories and colonies in the South Pacific, and the related British Empire and Commonwealth,

---

1 Travel was often, although not exclusively, within the borders of empires. For example, there is travel around what Herrera refers to as the 'fluid borders that made up the Islamic Empire' from the ninth century. Linda Herrera, 'Higher Education in the Arab World', in *International Handbook of Higher Education*, ed. JJF Forest and PG Altbach, 409–21, Springer International Handbooks of Education, vol. 18 (Dordrecht: Springer, 2007), 410.

especially the Australian Territory of Papua and New Guinea. The final is the concept of incrementalism, of un-radical, iterative policy change in scholarships, and why that iterative change has occurred.

The concept of national interest is nebulous, difficult to pinpoint and changes over time. Political scientist Scott Burchill wrote that at the 'very basis of claims for the national interest is an assumption that a political community can speak with a common voice'.[2] What this book, and these scholarships, demonstrate is that this common voice is assumed, but not necessarily present in the community involved in the planning and implementation of international development scholarships. Political scientist Thomas Davis has noted that the relationship between effective development assistance and Australia's national interest should not be assumed.[3] National interest is an umbrella term that can contain particular interests at different times. By understanding these scholarships through the prism of the 'national interest' that different departments and individuals were seeking to defend, one can see the differing interpretations, ideological and otherwise, of national interest. It is a contention of this book that this quality, the malleability of purpose and approach in framing the national interest, helps to explain the longevity of international development scholarships in the Australian foreign aid approach.

The bilateral relationships between Australia and Pacific nations, and earlier Pacific colonial administrations, are central to the book. In some cases, such as the administration prior to 1975 in what for simplicity will be referred to as the Territory of Papua and New Guinea (TPNG), this relationship is intragovernmental. This Pacific lens allows for an in-depth analysis of the colonial and decolonising relationships that the Australian Government had with these Pacific administrations and postcolonial governments. These relationships have changed since 1948, when the first awards were made, as one would expect. However, the presence and the role of scholarships have remained relatively constant.

Domestic policies, immigration policies and politics also played a significant role in the provision of these scholarships. This was particularly acute in relation to scholarships for TPNG, where the White Australia Policy affected

---

2   Scott Burchill, *The National Interest in International Relations Theory* (New York: Palgrave MacMillan, 2005), 13, doi.org/10.1057/9780230005778.
3   Thomas Davis, 'Does Australia have an International Development Assistance Policy? National Interest and Foreign Aid Policy Making', in *Proceedings, Second Oceanic Conference on International Studies* (Australia: University of Melbourne, 2006).

the ability of non-European students from the colony to travel to mainland Australia for study. However, it also affected the design of subsequent schemes as equal opportunity and racial discrimination legislation was introduced in Australia. This book argues national interest, and domestic policies, play such a dominant role in these international development scholarships that these programs are more a reflection of Australia, and its perception of itself as a nation in the Pacific, than they are reflective of the needs of Pacific Island nations.

This is also evident because, while the relationships between the Australian Government and Pacific Island governments are central to the implementation of scholarships, these relationships were seldom a priority for Australian governments. The spotlight of the Australian foreign policy community was rarely focused on the Pacific region, and when it was, it was often with colonial or paternalistic intentions, and usually with a security and military lens.

This is also true for scholarships. The Pacific has never been the driver of scholarship policy; it was more often a secondary consideration.[4] In 1948 the Department of External Affairs (DEA) convinced the Chifley Cabinet of the value of a small scholarship, the South-East Asian Scholarship Scheme, to counter some of the negative perceptions of Australia being generated by the White Australia Policy. Decisions about where the six awards were to be allocated were fraught, and debate between DEA, the Prime Minister's Department and the Director of Education was intense. Each department, and each individual, brought to these debates their own ideas about what the goals of the scholarship program should be, and who ought to be its primary beneficiaries.

The South-East Asian Scholarship Scheme was offered, as the name suggests, firstly to nations from South-East Asia. It was later offered to Pacific nations, which did cause some confusion, with the *Pacific Islands Monthly* magazine noting in 1955 that the offer of scholarships under the scheme wasn't because 'someone in Australia had confused his geography'.[5] This sense of confusion in nations and territories outside South-East Asia

---

4 In contemporary times, the lack of foreign policy focus on the Pacific has been matched by an ambivalence within the Australian tertiary education sector about engagement with the Pacific.
5 'Australian Scholarships for Fiji', *Pacific Islands Monthly*, 1 January 1955, 59.

led to a name change, to the Australian International Awards Scheme.[6] There was also discussion in the 1960s of a 'Pacific Colombo Plan', drawing on a policy developed – the Colombo Plan – for South and South-East Asia. The scheme was never implemented for a number of reasons that will be discussed in a later chapter.

These brief examples help to illustrate that the Pacific region was rarely the centre of policy thinking. It is also clear that the leaders of the Pacific were aware of this status. In the early years covered by this research, it showed itself in requests for scholarships far exceeding the small number offered. In later decades it played out in expansions in non-Pacific scholarship programs and little focus on the 'smaller' scholarship programs in the Pacific. Australian governments, both conservative and Labor, have taken the Pacific for granted.[7] Prime ministers and foreign ministers have not needed to ensure the Pacific nations share Australia's foreign policy goals, they have assumed it. The book will argue that this assumption of shared policy goals was a continuation of colonial patterns of thinking. These patterns of behaviour and thinking have been recognised in Senate Committee reports, by academics and Pacific governments, but the approach continued.

Australia's colonial approach to Pacific administrations and governments is clear and is part of a broader story of decolonisation in the Pacific. Australia was itself a colonial power in TPNG, and shared administrative responsibility with the United Kingdom and New Zealand for Nauru. Scholarships played a role in both the colonisation of the Pacific, and the decolonisation.

Early scholarships were often granted in an effort to support a colonial administration, with men (and it was nearly always men) sent to the metropolitan or colonial power for training to fulfil the civil administration roles required to maintain a colony. This 'hub and spoke' model of movement, from the periphery to the centre, was acute in colonial scholarship programs, but continued as the territories of the Pacific decolonised. The connections between colonialism and the broader field of development, where international development scholarships fit, are also worth noting. As Ferns

---

6   There is some question as to whether the Australian International Awards Scheme was a separate scheme or merely a renaming of the South-East Asian Scheme, but most of the archival evidence points to it being a change in name only.
7   Stephen Henningham noted that most Australians, including those in 'senior positions, have only a vague "picture postcard" image of the Pacific island states and territories'. Stephen Henningham, 'No Easy Answers: Australia and the Pacific Islands regions', *Parliamentary Research Service*, no. 5 (1995): iii.

notes in his 2017 thesis on Australian foreign aid, viewing decolonisation through the 'development lens' shows that the efforts of former colonisers and metropolitan powers were 'in many cases a continuation of the colonial project'.[8] This view is supported by Stephen Browne, who noted that aid programs were a 'sequel to … colonial obligations'.[9] In most cases multiple motivations play a role in aid policy decision-making. As the Australian Government began to frame itself as a middle power, the growth in the planning and delivery of aid in the postwar period of rapid decolonisation was predominantly motivated by development and strategic concerns.[10] The actions of the Australian Government in its own colonial territory, the TPNG, in the 1950s and 1960s demonstrated an unwillingness by many politicians and bureaucrats to grapple with the inevitability of decolonisation. Racist and paternalistic beliefs were fundamental to the policy decisions of the TPNG Administration.

The place of race and racism is inevitably tied up in this colonial discourse. It is also clear in the privileging of a Western-style education, which is fundamental to the provision of the scholarships discussed in this book. While this book does not linger on the effectiveness of scholarships in a conventional sense, it does discuss the role of scholarships in promoting the 'ideals' of Australia and its social and political structures. Effectiveness is a malleable concept, as this book will show. The idea that education would perform a civilising role in TPNG was fundamental to Australian education policy in the territories and is discussed in this work. Ideas of equity and access are also tied to race; exclusion and inclusion based on race was fundamental to the operation of a number of scholarships in the Pacific.

As noted earlier, the final broad theme that emerges from this book is that of iterative change. Since the South-East Asian Scholarship Scheme began in 1948, few governments or bureaucrats have been prepared to make substantial changes to scholarship schemes that are in place. The subsidy scheme of the 1970s and the Equity and Merit scheme of the late 1980s are notable exceptions, but in general small tinkering changes are the story of Australian Government scholarships. However, as noted above, this incrementalism does not diminish the important role that scholarships have played in foreign aid and foreign policy over the past 70 years.

---

8   Nicholas Ferns, 'Beyond Colombo: Australian Colonial and Foreign Policy in the Age of International Development, 1945–1975' (PhD thesis, Monash University, 2017), 8.
9   Stephen Browne, *Aid and Influence: Do Donors Help or Hinder?* (London: Earthscan, 2006), 19.
10 Ferns, 'Beyond Colombo'; Daniel Oakman, *Facing Asia: A History of the Colombo Plan* (Canberra: Pandanus Books, 2004).

This book covers a significant period of time, and a large number of policies and schemes. The longevity of international development scholarships as a framework for development assistance, and diplomatic investment, do allow for this longer-term analysis. This book also aims to shift the conversation about the history of international development in Australia away from the Colombo Plan. While the Colombo Plan remains as a constant policy shadow, by moving the focus to the Pacific (where the Colombo Plan was not offered) we are able to see scholarships, aid and international education in a broader context.

Why is it important?

Despite the status of international education in Australia's current social and economic system, there remains little research into the history of international education, and the way the mobility it encourages has shaped Australia's relationships with its regional neighbours. Even less of this small amount of research has focused on the nations of the Pacific, despite Australia's various roles as coloniser, trustee and geographic neighbour. Both Australia and Pacific Island countries are the product of the colonialist project of Europe, settled by the British (Australia and New Zealand are understood as settler colonies; by contrast many Pacific Island territories were colonised for their resources or strategic importance), Germans, Dutch and French. But the trajectory of each of these nations after their 'independence' from colonial rule is different, and this history influences and shapes the relationship between the states – as cultural theorists Ien Ang and John Stratton note, 'colonial legacies in particular … remain powerful determinants in the present-day trajectories of cultural flows'.[11] Understanding these coloniser–colony shared histories is important, and scholarships are an enduring element of that history.

While this is not an evaluation of the scholarships awarded by the Australian Government between 1948 and 2018, understanding the goals and motivations of scholarships is important to understanding how they have evolved, and the important role they have played in a period of decolonisation in the Pacific. Recognising the influence of education, and in particular, movement from a Pacific Island state to a metropolitan

---

11   Ien Ang and John Stratton, 'Asianing Australia: Notes Toward a Critical Transnationalism in Cultural Studies', *Cultural Studies* 10, no. 1 (1996): 28, doi.org/10.1080/09502389600490441.

nation such as Australia, helps to assess the contribution of scholarships in the decolonisation process across the Pacific. This work does not centre on the journeys and currents followed by Pacific Islanders, as is so clearly articulated in the work of Tracey Banivanua-Mar, who highlighted the role of transnational connections across the Pacific in the development of a process of active decolonisation.[12] By its nature, it is a history of the policies of the Australian Government, and not a student-tracing project. Nevertheless, as is clear from the foreword to this book by Nayahamui Rooney, the stories of the students who came to Australia do offer a different lens through which to view Australian foreign policy and the scholarship policies the students were subjected to. Therefore, each part of this book contains a small selection of stories of students who travelled to Australia from TPNG and the Pacific during the period being examined. These anecdotes have been found in the archives, in marketing material and other sources. The purpose of these vignettes is to provide the voice of those for whom these journeys were life-changing. As Banivanua-Mar wrote: 'we have seen from West Papua to Samoa, to Tahiti and New Caledonia, [that] access to education and a counter-imperial literacy gave subject peoples an international voice'.[13] The voice of students and alumni is important to this work, and is often lost in discussions of scholarship and international education policy. There is a fundamental asymmetry of power between the actors involved in scholarships, the privileging of certain forms of knowledge. This book does not argue that by including the voices of students and alumni this power imbalance will be corrected, but it does put these stories on record in ways that are not always present in other works. It is also of note that in general the histories of scholarships have often had, as historians Tamson Pietsch and Meng-Hsuan Chou noted, 'a hagiographic focus on a small cohort of "familiar suspects"'[14] rather than a broader view. These vignettes walk a line between these two extremes, the absence of a student voice and a hagiographic focus on individuals.

---

12 See Tracey Banivanua-Mar, *Decolonisation and the Pacific: Indigenous Globalisation and the Ends of Empire*, Critical Perspectives on Empire, Cambridge University Press (Cambridge, 2014) and Tracey Banivanua-Mar, 'Shadowing Imperial Networks: Indigenous Mobility and Australia's Pacific Past', *Australian Historical Studies* 46, no. 3 (2015): 340–55, doi.org/10.1080/1031461X.2015.1076012, among other work.
13 Banivanua-Mar, *Decolonisation and the Pacific*, 221.
14 Tamson Pietsch and Meng-Hsuan Chou, 'The Politics of Scholarly Exchange: Taking the Long View on the Rhodes Scholarships', in *Global Exchanges: Exchange Programs, Scholarships and Transnational Circulations in the Modern World*, ed. Ludovic Tournès and Giles Scott-Smith, 33–49 (Oxford: Berghahn Books, 2017), 36, doi.org/10.2307/j.ctvw04fqt.7.

Another crucial outcome of scholarships is the financial contribution to the host universities by the host government.[15] This indirect funding plays a role in the regional Pacific scholarships discussed in this book, but is also important to consider in the context of Australian universities and institutions. This support comes in the form of fees (scholarships are most often 'full-fee' students – meaning the Australian Government is paying full fees on behalf of the student) and support to the community via the spending of stipend funds (on rent, food and other essential items). This is an important factor in the broad support for development scholarships by universities and other domestic stakeholders.

Even though scholarships are broadly understood to be a continuation of the colonial project, they remain popular across developing and developed nations. Understanding their historical form, their use and misuse, is relevant to contemporary conversations about scholarships. Using the prism of scholarships to view the intentions of the Australian Government in the Pacific also provides a different understanding of what role the Australian Government and the Australian bureaucracy saw for itself in the Pacific, and how Australia's national interest could be protected or advanced. This is clear in the many decisions about scholarships to the Pacific that reflect domestic (Australian) considerations; it is often domestic imperatives that are the most visible in decision-making about international aid and scholarships. It is because scholarships have been so popular with recipient nations and domestic stakeholders, and allow governments to satisfy foreign and domestic imperatives, that they have remained in place. Their 'success' does not encourage radical change or action. Iterative changes have been sufficient to meet evolving needs.

Higher education and mobility

International students have been coming to study in Australia since the establishment of universities in the country, however it was not until the end of the Second World War that they appeared in any great numbers. Australia's geographic position ensured that students from South-East Asia began arriving in large numbers, despite the hurdles put in place by the Department of Immigration (seeking to maintain the White Australia Policy). In 1951 the Australian Government agreed on some general rules

---

15   Anna Kent, 'Australian Development Scholarships and their place within diplomacy, development and education' (Masters thesis, The University of Melbourne, 2012).

around the entry of 'non-European students' into Australia for study. This policy codified a process that had been applied in an ad hoc manner up to that point, without seriously challenging the White Australia Policy.[16] It also formalised the settings for the thousands of students who would come to Australia over the next decades as what is termed 'private' students. In most contexts this means those not sponsored by the Australian Government. Students would also come to Australia under other scholarship programs, for example the Colonial Development and Welfare Scholarships (CD&W) (UK), and sponsored by their own national governments. Private students, however, far outnumbered those sponsored by the Australian Government. In fact, the very first scholarship scheme, the South-East Asian Scholarship Scheme, provided fewer than six awards per year. The Colombo Plan, which began in the early 1950s, had a far greater number of awards, but nevertheless sponsored students were outnumbered five to one[17] by their privately funded peers.

So great has been the increased international mobility of students since the Second World War that the number of globally mobile students (in higher education) was estimated, prior to the Covid-19 pandemic, to be 4.5 million in 2020.[18] As Dassin, Marsh and Mawer explained, 'countries and communities that were isolated from global educational systems only a few decades ago are now significant contributors to the movement of students and skilled professionals across borders'.[19] China is the most prominent example of this phenomenon. International education is, in government circles at the very least, recognised as an important part of foreign policy; both the sending and receiving of students is consequential.[20]

---

16   'Non-European Students | Policy Information', F28/7/79, 1951, Fiji National Archives (FNA).
17   Oakman, *Facing Asia*, 179.
18   Joan Dassin, Robin Marsh and Matt Mawer, 'Introduction: Pathways for Social Change?', in *International Scholarships in Higher Education: Pathways to Social Change*, ed. Joan Dassin, Robin Marsh and Matt Mawer, 3–21 (New York: Palgrave Macmillan, 2017), 9, doi.org/10.1007/978-3-319-62734-2.
19   Dassin, Marsh and Mawer, 'Introduction', 9.
20   There is a growing body of research into the role of government scholarships and globally mobile students as a form of diplomacy or foreign policy. Other examples not discussed include Kongkea Chhoeun, 'Australian and Chinese Scholarships to Cambodia: A Comparative Study' (PhD Thesis, Australian National University, 2019); Lily Dong and David W Chapman, 'China's Scholarship Program as a Form of Foreign Assistance', in *Crossing Borders in East Asian Higher Education*, ed. DW Chapman, WK Cummings, GA Postiglione, 145–66, CERC Studies in Comparative Education, vol. 27 (Dordrecht: Springer, 2010), 145–66, doi.org/10.1007/978-94-007-0446-6_7; Morgan McMaster, Alejandra Guevara, Lacey Roberts and Samantha Alvis, *USAID Higher Education: A Retrospective 1960–2020* (Washington DC: United States Agency for International Development, 2019); Caitlin Byrne and Rebecca Hall, 'Realising Australia's International Education as Public Diplomacy', *Australian Journal of International Affairs* 67, no. 4 (2013): 419–38, doi.org/10.1080/10357718.2013.806019; Natalie Laifer and Nicholas Kitchen, 'Making Soft Power Work: Theory and Practice in Australia's International Education Policy', *Politics and Policy* 45, no. 5 (2017): 813–40, doi.org/10.1111/polp.12219.

Scholarships form part of this great student mobility, albeit a small part. In scholarships we are able to see a microcosm of student mobility and government policy.

Understanding scholarships

This is a history of Australian Government scholarships. But that history cannot be told without an understanding of the history of scholarships more broadly. Scholarships have existed for centuries, but they proliferated in the postwar period, often related to Cold War influence operations.[21] A typology of international scholarships written by Laura Perna and others in 2014 goes some way to breaking down their purposes, with four main 'types' of international scholarship programs. These are: development of basic skills, acquisition of advanced knowledge in developing nations, improvement of advanced knowledge in developed nations and promotion of short-term study abroad.[22] Recent work by scholarship researchers Anne Campbell and Emelye Neff reviews the purposes behind a broad range of scholarships offered to students from the Global South. These rationales include human capital development, diplomacy, social change, sustainable development, the internationalisation of universities and access to higher education.[23] That there are multitudes of scholarships, each with multitudes of purposes, both stated and unstated, is clear from the work of Perna, Campbell and Neff. But despite this, international scholarships like those considered in this book are more alike than they are different.

Histories of scholarships often exist in their own worlds, that is as the history of a specific scholarship scheme.[24] This research deviates from that approach slightly, in that it covers a number of scholarship schemes over a period of

---

21　For example see Julie Hessler, 'Third World Students at Soviet Universities in the Brezhnev Period' (202–15) and Lonnie R Johnson, 'The Fulbright Program and the Philosophy and Geography of US Exchange Programs Since World War II' (173–87), both in Tournès and Scott-Smith, *Global Exchanges*.
22　Laura W Perna et al., 'Promoting Human Capital Development: A Typology of International Scholarship Programs in Higher Education', *Educational Researcher* 43, no. 2 (2014): 63–73, doi.org/10.3102/0013189X14521863.
23　Anne C Campbell and Emelye Neff, 'A Systematic Review of International Higher Education Scholarships for Students from the Global South', *Review of Educational Research* 90, no. 6 (2020) (online publication), doi.org/10.3102/0034654320947783.
24　For example, Tamson Pietsch, 'Many Rhodes: Travelling Scholarships and Imperial Citizenship in the British Academic World, 1880–1940', *History of Education* 40, no. 6 (2011): 723–39, doi.org/10.1080/0046760X.2011.594096; Alice Garner and Diane Kirkby, *Academic Ambassadors, Pacific Allies: Australia, America and the Fulbright Program*, Key Studies in Diplomacy (Manchester: Manchester University Press, 2019), doi.org/10.7228/manchester/9781526128973.001.0001; and Oakman, *Facing Asia*.

several decades. It also focuses on one geographic region, a region that has not received significant scholarly attention in the context of scholarships or international education. This focus on one donor with multiple programs and one geographic region with multiple countries sets this book apart from existing scholarship in this field.

One of the pre-eminent and most well-known scholarships, certainly across the Anglosphere, is the Rhodes Scholarship. Established in 1901 according to terms outlined in the Will of Cecil Rhodes, the scholarship was designed as 'a scheme of travelling scholarships that he hoped would foster good imperial citizens'.[25] This scholarship quickly became a symbol for elite education and training, and is mentioned often in discussions about scholarship programs from that point on, as a goal of what scholarships could or should become, or what they do not wish to become (in terms of an elite/non-elite approach). What is less understood is the extent of the influence the scholarship program had on the development of other scholarship programs around the world. Pietsch and Chou point to the influence of the Rhodes Scholarship on the Fulbright Scholarship,[26] and another clear example demonstrating this point is the Morris Hedstrom Scholarship Scheme in Fiji. Morris Hedstrom Limited is a department store, long established as a trader in colonial Fiji (and still in business today). In 1944 the board of the company made a decision to create a scholarship program for Fijian students, 'with a tenure of three years, for the persons wholly or partly of the Fijian race … [which] will enable the fortunate youths who gain the prize to have an approved University course for a period of three years'[27] (at the time there was no university in Fiji). A request was made of the Governor of Fiji for a copy of the Rhodes Trust Deed. The Trust Deed was duly sent, and formed the basis of the Morris Hedstrom Scholarship.[28] Further research into these connections between scholarship programs is likely to find other connections, either as clear as the Rhodes – Morris Hedstrom link or more subtle connections.

Also important is the temporal aspect of these scholarships. While the Rhodes Scholarship began in 1901, the 1940s saw an explosion in the number of awards on offer, influenced both by postwar reconstruction and the emerging polarities of the Cold War. The Morris Hedstrom award was

---

25 Pietsch, 'Many Rhodes', 723.
26 Pietsch and Chou, 'The Politics of Scholarly Exchange', 35.
27 'Fiji Scholarship – Proposal by Morris Hedstrom | Newspaper Clipping from 26 July 1944', F28/265, 1944, FNA.
28 'Morris Hedstrom Trust Deed Draft', F28/265, FNA.

created in 1944, with an aim to support Fijians to 'hold their own in postwar years' and to encourage the 'Government to make better provision for primary and secondary education of Fijian children … to take advantage of the opportunity of completing their education'.[29] Leaving aside the rather unrealistic goal of influencing all levels of education via the provision of one scholarship per year, this scholarship was aimed at supporting the development of Fijians in an environment wherein they were being expected to become more independent in the postwar years. The CD&W Scholarships, funded by the UK, had a similar mandate: while part of a broader Colonial Development and Welfare Act, the scholarships were, by the late 1940s, a £1,000,000 effort to support colonies that were on a path to independence and were to be spread across the British Empire.[30] No doubt this scheme, in its breadth and ambition, influenced the Colombo Plan in 1950, and it is certain that it played a part in the Commonwealth Scholarship and Fellowship Plan developed later in the 1950s.

Why, then, was there such an increase in the number of scholarship programs offered, particularly by developed nations, during this period of accelerating decolonisation across the world? Was it because, as Mark Bray writes, most 'departing colonial powers also sought structures in which to maintain political linkages in the post-colonial era'?[31] Scholarships were used extensively as a tool of influence during the Cold War.[32] In one Australian example, a Kenyan minister mentioned the existence of scholarships from 'beyond the Iron Curtain' to a group of Papua New Guinean men, causing the opening of a Confidential file and concern from Australian authorities.[33]

Even as the Cold War was ending, scholarships remained a key element of the foreign aid budgets of developed countries around the world. Scholarships, and tertiary education more broadly, were not included in the Millennium Development Goals of the 2000s, but significant spending on

---

29 'Fiji Scholarship – Proposal by Morris Hedstrom | Newspaper Clipping from 26 July 1944'.
30 'C.D&W Scholarship – Applications and Recommendations', 28/277/4, 1951, FNA.
31 M Bray, 'Decolonisation and Education: New Paradigms for the Remnants of Empire', *Compare: A Journal of Comparative and International Education* 24, no. 1 (1994): 38, doi.org/10.1080/0305792940240104.
32 Julie Hessler notes that one of the goals of the Soviet international education scheme was the 'inculcation of socialist values and political empathy for the USSR', in Hessler, 'Third World Students at Soviet Universities in the Brezhnev Period'. Other examples include Paul A Kramer, 'Is the World Our Campus? International Students and U.S. Global Power in the Long Twentieth Century', *Diplomatic History* 33, no. 5 (2009): 775–806, doi.org/10.1111/j.1467-7709.2009.00829.x; Garner and Kirkby, *Academic Ambassadors, Pacific Allies*.
33 'Offer of Scholarships from Iron Curtain Countries to Papua and New Guinea', A1209, 1965/6088, 1965, National Archives of Australia (NAA).

scholarships continued. As this book shows, enthusiasm for scholarships has rarely waned over the twentieth century, or into the twenty-first. And while scholarships are most certainly linked to broader theoretical and practical conversations about modernisation and development, no amount of critical review has dampened their appeal.

Scholarships and decolonisation

Education itself is intertwined with the processes of colonisation and decolonisation. For many states in the Pacific, the schooling structure that was left in place after the departure of the colonial power remained in place. This was, in part, a deliberate effort of the former colonising powers to ensure ongoing influence in the postcolonial period.[34] The lack of universal secondary schooling in many Pacific Island colonies and then countries, and the lack of universities in the region until the mid-1960s, ensured that despite their move towards self-government and independence, decolonising states remained reliant on donors, including Australia, for supporting education systems, and providing higher education options for a limited number of students. This continued to be the case across the second half of the twentieth century.[35] Fijian academic and politician Tupeni Baba mounts a convincing case against the policies of education that use Australian experts and Australian training to support Pacific education needs. He described some academics as buccaneers, winning lucrative contracts to deliver education and training in the Pacific.[36] Elsewhere Baba describes Australia's involvement in education in the Pacific as patronising[37] and neo-colonial.

---

34 Bray, 'Decolonisation and Education'. Bray also discusses these concepts in an earlier work, Mark Bray, 'Education and the Vestiges of Colonialism: Self-Determination, Neocolonialism and Dependency in the South Pacific', *Comparative Education* 29, no. 3 (1993): 333–48, doi.org/10.1080/0305006930290309. Evangelina Papoutsaki and Dick Rooney also discuss the concept of developing countries inheriting their coloniser's education system, and the adoption of Western models of higher education in their work. Evangelia Papoutsaki and Dick Rooney, 'Colonial Legacies and Neo-Colonial Practices in Papua New Guinean Higher Education', *Higher Education Research and Development* 25, no. 4 (2006): 421–33, doi.org/10.1080/07294360600947434.
35 Churches also played a significant role in the provision of education across the Pacific, including in Papua and New Guinea, with much schooling provided by Mission Schools across the late nineteenth and twentieth centuries. Churches were often involved in sponsoring students to travel to developed countries for tertiary or further study. Nevertheless, given the focus of this work on government-funded scholarships, church scholarships will not be addressed in any depth.
36 Tupeni L Baba, 'Academic Buccaneering Australian Style: The Role of Australian Academics in the South Seas', *Directions: Journal of Educational Studies* 9, no. 1 (1987): 3–11.
37 Tupeni L Baba, 'Australia's Involvement in Education in the Pacific: Partnership or Patronage?', *Directions: Journal of Educational Studies* 11, no. 2 (1989): 43–53.

The relationship between education systems and colonialism is a backdrop to this book, implicit in so many of the decisions that have been made by Australian and Pacific governments across decades, and intimately linked to concepts of race and citizenship that were part of Australia's colonial engagement with Papua New Guinea (PNG) and other Pacific territories.

Sources

A significant element of the literature for this book is government reports, policy statements, reviews and the like, often referred to as grey literature. These serve in part as primary source documents. In later chapters covering recent decades, grey literature, reports from the Australian National Audit Office (ANAO) and other reviews, make up the bulk of the primary source material analysed. This is necessary because the archives for that period were not open at the time of writing. A number of reviews and reports remain within the closed archival collection. This is in part because a significant amount of the research conducted or commissioned by the Australian Government about scholarships is never released to the public. There have been notable exceptions, such as a 2011 Freedom of Information release that saw a large swathe of review reports and other documents released after a request by a *Canberra Times* journalist.[38] Markus Mannheim's 2011 article, based on the FOI request, pointed to the problems that were commonly discussed within AusAID, but not more widely. This includes the use of scholarships as patronage and the misgivings within AusAID about the development impact of the scholarships.[39]

---

38 Markus Mannheim, 'Doubts Raised over Aid Scholarships', *The Canberra Times*, 27 April 2011; and 'FOI Disclosure Log – Australian Aid Related Requests (before 1 November 2013)', Department of Foreign Affairs and Trade, www.dfat.gov.au/about-us/corporate/freedom-of-information/Pages/foi-disclosure-log-australian-aid-related-requests.aspx, accessed 22 May 2016.
39 These issues were particularly acute in Pacific Island nations – Jack Corbett and John Connell have discussed the issues of small island states in retaining citizens (and especially public servants) who have received high-level training via a scholarship. They also noted that this issue is more acute where 'recruitment to the public service may be linked to nepotism and patronage'. Jack Corbett and John Connell, 'All the World is a Stage: Global Governance, Human Resources, and the "Problem" of Smallness', *Pacific Review* 28, no. 3 (2015): 446, doi.org/10.1080/09512748.2015.1011214.

Outline

This book is arranged into five parts. Each part consists of two chapters, and a vignette with stories of the students who have come to Australia over the 70 years this book covers. Each part covers between 10 and 20 years, and the book is written chronologically. Each part covers the schemes or scholarships that were in place at the time, and addresses the themes and policies of the period.

Part One covers the period from 1948 to 1957, beginning with the stories of Cyril Chan and a group of students sent to high school in Charters Towers, Queensland, from the Territory of Papua and New Guinea (TPNG). The first chapter, 'Before the beginning', addresses the South-East Asian Scholarship Scheme, which was subsequently renamed the Australian International Awards Scheme, reflecting a recurring desire among bureaucrats and politicians to ensure that scholarship titles give adequate recognition to their benefactor. The second chapter discusses Australia's colonial obligations in TPNG, and is titled 'Administrative labyrinths'. This was a period of confusion within the bureaucracy about the responsibilities of education and scholarships for residents of TPNG. The labyrinths that students like Cyril Chan had to navigate in order to study in Australia have given this chapter its title. These chapters also analyse interdepartmental debates about responsibilities and power to make decisions. These were conflicts and contestations that persisted for decades.

Part Two covers the period from 1958 to 1970. Chapter Three, 'Uncertain decolonisation', begins with the Oxford Conference in 1959, and discusses the Commonwealth Scholarship and Fellowship Plan (CSFP). The CSFP helped to demonstrate how governments around the world were using scholarships as a form of aid and postcolonial development support. This was a period when the geopolitical structures held in place by the British Empire fell away to become the Commonwealth. This new structure reflected, in part, a less hierarchical structure between the colonisers and the decolonising states. This influenced the way in which the CSFP developed and was supported by Australia and other Commonwealth nations.

Chapter Four, 'Gradual development' addresses the complexities and complications that students from PNG faced in accessing Australian Commonwealth Scholarships and other educational opportunities.

Part Three covers the period of sweeping change from 1971 to 1983. Chapter Five, 'Radical subsidies', analyses the significant change and reform that occurred in the 1970s, including the introduction of free tertiary education. These subsidies, which allowed for fee-free university education for both domestic and international students, had a profound impact on Australia's education sector, and the relationships between Australian governments and the newly decolonised (or still decolonising) states of the Pacific. This was the most substantial reform to the international education sector in Australia during the period discussed in this book. Chapter Six, 'Independence for Papua New Guinea', is devoted to what was also a period of radical change in TPNG, with independence in 1975. This chapter also discusses the ways in which Australia's colonial education policies intersected and conflicted with emerging international education policies.

Part Four covers the period from 1984 to 1996. Chapter Seven is titled 'Goldring, Jackson and the fight for the future of international education'. Subsidising higher education was expensive, so by the early 1980s the Fraser and then Hawke governments were reviewing their commitments. This chapter analyses the Goldring and Jackson reviews, two important government reviews that reported in 1984. These reviews set the framework for changes to the policy settings for education and aid in the coming decades. These two reports are the foundation on which much subsequent international education and international scholarship policy was based. The synthesis of these two reviews provided the Hawke Government with an opportunity to shape the future of international education in Australia, and set in train significant changes that have continued to affect the funding of higher education in Australia.

The second chapter in Part Four is Chapter Eight, 'Centring the power'. This chapter centres on the Equity and Merit Scholarship Scheme (EMSS), which was introduced in 1989. This scheme represented a substantial shift in scholarship design and ambition, and took the place of the subsidy scheme that had been so popular in the Asia-Pacific region. A key element of the EMSS was a change in the locus of control. Control over selection was shifted from the recipient government to the Australian Government, and course selection control was shifted to the student, upending decades of scholarship practice. This was challenging for recipient governments to accept, and their dissatisfaction with the scheme played a large role in its short lifespan.

INTRODUCTION

The final part of the book, Part Five, covers the period from 1997 to 2018. Chapter Nine is titled 'Multiple objectives for scholarships and aid' and discusses the Australian Development Scholarships Scheme (ADS). This scheme was introduced in 1998. The late 1990s and 2000s were a time of political instability in the Pacific, and Australia's approach to scholarship provision clearly reflects the most pressing Australian Government concerns at the time. Security and governance became the central themes around which scholarships were framed.

Chapter Ten, 'Diplomacy or development?', is focused on the Australia Awards. A huge increase in the number of scholarship awardees reflected a diplomatic goal: a temporary seat on the United Nations Security Council (UNSC). And while the provision of scholarships declined suddenly after the UNSC vote, the scholarships continued to play a role in Australia's aid delivery in the Pacific. Their contribution to Australia's diplomatic ambitions, and the way in which they were cut as soon as that goal was achieved allows for a thorough investigation of the importance of a scholarship scheme in the context of a modern bilateral relationship, albeit one of uneven power dynamics.

PART 1: 1948–1957

The first scholarship to be considered in this book is the South-East Asian Scholarship Scheme, which commenced in 1948. As the name suggests, the scheme was intended for South-East Asia and was closely tied to Australian diplomatic efforts in that region, addressing the nationalist and anticolonial movements that were coming to the fore as the impacts of the end of the Second World War became apparent. The beginning of this scholarship has determined the starting point of this book, but this period in Australian Government scholarship policy was not driven by the South-East Asian Scholarship Scheme, but rather by the Colombo Plan, which was agreed upon in 1950. It was the Colombo Plan concept and model that dominated thinking in Australian aid and scholarships over the 1950s.

While the Colombo Plan model dominated the thinking of Australia's international aid policymakers, bureaucrats and politicians considered the development needs of the Territory of Papua and New Guinea as being at a different stage. Access to senior secondary education was limited to those able to travel to continental Australia (with or without a scholarship), and there were no specific tertiary scholarships available for residents of TPNG.

This part of the book ends at the beginning of a new scholarship, the Commonwealth Scholarship and Fellowship Plan, which again challenged Australia's understanding of itself within the British Empire in the twentieth century.

Cyril Chan and Charters Towers

The Australian Government was mandated by the United Nations to work towards development in Papua and New Guinea. In relation to education the approach was, in many ways, in line with the concurrent Colombo Plan approach to training citizens of countries in the region. However, non-European Territorians were subjects, rather than citizens, and access to higher levels of education in Papua and New Guinea was difficult if not impossible. This ensured that the policy formula based on the Colombo Plan could not work in practice. Matters of immigration, citizenship and rights of entry tangled the administrators and the Australian Government in knots.

The confusion in the Australian policy and legislation was personified in the case of Cyril Chan. Chan was born in Rabaul, but his parents had emigrated to the Territory of Papua and New Guinea (TPNG) from China before his birth. This ensured his citizenship status was complicated by several factors, including race. Chan was sponsored by the Territory Administration (via a scheme to support non-European students to complete secondary school in Australia) to undertake his secondary schooling in Australia, along with around 300 other 'non-European' students from Papua and New Guinea.[1] In 1954, Chan was attending high school in Bowral, New South Wales. The headmaster held 'a very high opinion of this lad's ability'.[2]

Chan and his supporters had sought a Commonwealth Scholarship for Cyril Chan through the University of Sydney, but university officials had told him that because his parents were resident in New Guinea, he was ineligible for a scholarship designed for Australian citizens. The first proposed solution was to broaden eligibility for public service cadetships to

---

1 This figure is changeable depending on the date and source. A report in 1957 notes 99 students having been sponsored since 1954 (JA Lee, 'Review of the Native Secondary Scholarship Scheme, 14 March 1958', A452, 1961/2382, National Archives of Australia (NAA)). A newspaper article in 1959 discusses the 118 students having been sent to Australia for Secondary School ('Most Students Now Have Jobs', *South Pacific Post*, 13 March 1959). In 1956 the cohort was 291 students – '56 natives, 28 mixed race and 207 Asian students', 'Notes on Discussion on Guidance and Supervision of Papua and New Guinea Students in Australia, Director of Education, Port Moresby, 1956', A452, 1961/2382, NAA.
2 'Letter from HR Cooper Regarding Cyril Chan', A452, 1958/743, NAA.

British citizens and 'protected persons' in the territories.³ The Department of Territories sought advice from the Commonwealth Office of Education in Sydney, writing:

> our Minister is interested in this case and has asked if it is a fact that any resident of Papua and New Guinea is debarred from the Commonwealth Scholarship Scheme?⁴

The Commonwealth Office of Education confirmed that residents of Papua and New Guinea were in fact eligible, although they noted that the circumstances of Mr Chan's case were still being investigated. This related to his Chinese heritage – there was significant uncertainty as to whether his parents were considered resident or subjects of Australia 'enough' for eligibility for the scholarship program – highlighting the complex interplay of race-based immigration policies, Territory Administration policies and education policies that students like Cyril Chan had to negotiate in order to access higher education in Australia. The decision regarding the eligibility of residents of Papua and New Guinea had been decided two years previously, when the government accepted a recommendation from the Universities Commission that these students could apply for a Commonwealth Scholarship, and would compete against students in the state in which they completed their matriculation exam. Officials at the time considered providing Papua and New Guinea with a quota of Commonwealth Scholarship places, but they decided that:

> Should the Territory authorities provide education at the secondary level, there could perhaps be a case for reviewing the present position either with the objective of considering the practicability of adopting a special scheme, or of providing a special quota of places within the Commonwealth's scholarship scheme.⁵

---

3   'Briefing Note for Minister Hasluck', A452, 1958/743, NAA. Cyril Chan may have been considered a British citizen or subject because his parents had migrated to Papua and New Guinea from another British colonial territory. Nevertheless, Chan was eventually considered a citizen of an Australian territory. These complications were caused by Australia's race-based immigration policies and the problems that this caused for an understanding of Australian citizenship. A similar confusion was also experienced by the United States of America when considering its own territories outside of the 'mainland' such as the Philippines. This is discussed at length by Daniel Immerwahr in *How to Hide an Empire: A History of the Greater United States* (London: The Bodley Head, 2019).
4   'Letter to Commonwealth Office of Education', A452, 1958/743, NAA.
5   'Acting PM Fadden to Minister Hasluck Letter, 1952', A452, 1958/743, NAA.

The confusion of the administration in Port Moresby and the Department of Territories about the eligibility of students from Papua and New Guinea is clear from the archival material. It is highly likely that this confusion at senior levels of decision-making stymied the attempts of other students to access the Commonwealth Scholarship, particularly if they did not have the persistence that Cyril Chan and his supporters showed.

Cyril Chan was eventually offered a Commonwealth Scholarship, and completed Arts and Law degrees at the University of Sydney. The Minister for Territories, Paul Hasluck, took great interest in Chan's progress, and the student kept the minister apprised of his progress until his graduation.[6] Chan's case was not plain sailing once he received a scholarship; he lost his scholarship after repeatedly failing an English class. This led to a proposal being put to the Territory Administrator that non-European territory students required additional support during their university studies, support similar to that provided to secondary school students from the territories.[7] Chan was nevertheless considered a success story by the administration in the territories, and featured in the *Rabaul Times* after he graduated with a Bachelor of Arts.[8]

The experiences of Cyril Chan demonstrate how the scholarship policies of the Australian Government were impacted by and tied to other policies, especially those relating to TPNG. The colonial subject status of Papuans and New Guineans reflected a confusing collection of ideas around race, residency and entitlement. His was certainly not the first case from Australia's territories that challenged the White Australia Policy. The Australian bureaucracy had been asked to address this issue in the early 1950s when seeking to take over the administration of the Cocos Islands from the United Kingdom. Section Three of the Immigration Act created a loophole that allowed non-mainland territories other than Tasmania to be excluded from the standard rights of travel associated with citizenship. In the Cocos Islands the Australian Government had agreed on a specific solution, after much negotiation, but it was very clear that the Immigration Department would not allow for exceptions from TPNG.[9]

---

6   'Letters from Cyril Chan to Minister Hasluck (Various)', A452, 1958/743, NAA.
7   'Letter, Administration to Department of Territories', A452, 1958/743, NAA.
8   'Graduated in Sydney – Extract from Rabaul Times', A452, 1958/743, NAA.
9   David Goldsworthy, 'British Territories and Australian Mini-Imperialism in the 1950s', *Australian Journal of Politics & History* 41, no. 3 (1995): 356–72, doi.org/10.1111/j.1467-8497.1995.tb01266.x.

PART 1

Cyril Chan was only able to access his entitlement (to a Commonwealth Scholarship) because of the support of high-status individuals in Australia. His entitlement was constantly questioned, based on his Chinese ethnicity, his birthplace and, during the term of his scholarship, the wealth of his family. Access to the Australian mainland was restricted for non-European (or non-white) residents and citizens, making the entitlements of Australian citizenship impossible. Despite a requirement under the trusteeship obligations that the Australian Government work towards the development of TPNG in preparation for independence, administrators and politicians decided that independence was so far away that access to higher education could be extremely limited.

Papuan and New Guinean students like Cyril Chan began their schooling in Australia at secondary level. These students, often in their late teens or early twenties, were often placed with much younger classmates, because of the lack of access to senior secondary education in the territories. This created problems for many students. In one circumstance, 10 students (all male) were placed in secondary school in Charters Towers, Queensland in 1957, and resided in a boarding house managed by a Mr McCulloch. Events in Charters Towers became a demonstration of the problems faced by students, teaching staff, scholarship administrators and territory administrators. JA Lee, Acting Senior Guidance Officer in the Territory Administration, wrote about the students in his report of his Tour of Duty (his visit to students in Australia in 1957). He noted the problems with the accommodation:

> It is quite evident that the real difficulty at Charters Towers has been the hostel accommodation and supervision ... management appears to be quite hopeless and I recommend that all students now at the hostel be removed at the end of the year.[10]

Despite these warnings, the situation soon deteriorated in Charters Towers, with a group of four students sent back to Port Moresby having been stripped of their scholarships. The incident was reported in the *Daily Telegraph* with the headline: 'Natives Taken from School', noting that the students were drinking with a sailor. The Territories Assistant Administrator is quoted in the article as blaming the behaviour on lax attitudes by hostel managers.[11] This view was supported by Minister Hasluck, who was quoted

---

10   JA Lee, 'Mr JA Lee – Tour of Duty in Australia – April 25th – June 13th', A452, 1961/2382, NAA.
11   'Natives Taken from School', *Daily Telegraph*, 24 July 1957.

in an article in the Melbourne *Herald* blaming those who led the boys astray, rather than the boys themselves.[12] The Territory Administrator DM Cleland was compelled to explain the decision to return the students to TPNG after stories of the incident were published in metropolitan newspapers. He wrote that despite the four students being warned about their 'attitude', their behaviour was not meeting expected standards. Cleland noted that 'all four students were well above the age of their class and below the intellectual norm for Australian students. They showed no promise of success in the Junior Certificate'.[13] This assessment was paired with news that on their return to the territory, the four students would be placed in employment.

These students, returned home for poor behaviour, were different to Cyril Chan in another important way. Even within the territory, treatment and rights were related to ethnicity. Expectations of academic success were linked to ethnicity – a Melbourne psychologist, Dr Alex Sinclair, visited the territory for three months in 1958 and it was his view that 'while the Asian students were doing well, the natives appeared likely to present a picture of dismal failure'.[14] Dr Sinclair objected to the fact that students from the territory were treated like other students coming from South-East Asia – 'without any realisation that the Papua New Guinea background was considerably more primitive'.[15]

The students of Papua New Guinean background did not have universally poor experiences. Many students were supported well through their studies, aided by the structures put in place by the Rotary Club, Apex and other organisations to support Colombo Plan students. The *South Coast Bulletin*, a newspaper printed in Southern Queensland, carried a photo in August 1959 of students from New Guinea and New Britain – calling them a 'happy group' of boys unable to return home for the holidays.[16] The boys were listed as attending secondary schools in Brisbane, and it was noted that they were all 21 years old. This would make the boys significantly older than their fellow students. This links the experience of these students to both the psychologist's report and the administrator's report regarding the

---

12   'Don't Blame Native Boys Says Minister', *Melbourne Herald*, 24 July 1957.
13   'Papuan Students – Charters Towers, Letter from DM Cleland, 31 July 1957', A452, 1961/2382, NAA. A more flattering assessment of the capabilities of students from the territories describes them as having 'inadequate intellectual equipment'; A452, 1961/2382, NAA.
14   'Report Does Not Satisfy Director', *South Pacific Post*, 3 October 1958.
15   'Report Does Not Satisfy Director'.
16   'Happy Group of New Guinea and New Britain Secondary Students', *South Coast Bulletin*, 28 August 1959.

students from Charters Towers – these students were expected to enter into Australian schools despite having little educational preparation, being older than their year level peers and coming from immensely different cultural and social backgrounds.

As has been noted, one of the reasons for students coming to Australia for secondary schooling was the lack of secondary schools in Papua and New Guinea. This created a situation where 'native' students in Papua and New Guinea were asked to travel to Australia for schooling, and expected to perform at an Australian senior secondary level, despite no preparation for that level of schooling, or forced into newly established 'secondary schools' that were not teaching at the secondary school standard. The inequity of access was made very clear in a newspaper article published in the *South Pacific Post* in September 1958, discussing the higher standards to be imposed on 'native' students in Australian secondary schools in the future. In the article, the Director of Education, DGT Roscoe, noted that the administration intended opening two secondary schools in the territory early next year: 'These will be of European type and will be attended by European children and children of mixed race, but a number of selected native students will also be admitted'.[17] That schools were being established in the territory to cater to non-native students, while academic standards were also being increased for those same students while they were in Australia, seems a contradiction not recognised by the administrators. Asking students to conform to an entirely foreign concept of education, and then frustrating their access to that education marked this period of Australian administration in TPNG.

---

17   'Natives' Exams to Be Made Tougher', *South Pacific Post*, 16 September 1958.

1

Before the beginning

In the late 1940s Australia found itself in a strange predicament. Although it was on the side of the victors of the Second World War, the nation had once again become acutely aware of its own geography. The Pacific Ocean and Pacific Islands had been the site of much conflict, and the neighbours to Australia's north and north-west in South and South-East Asia had begun a process of decolonisation that the Chifley Government, and many Australians, viewed as potentially dangerous. Australia had an existing race-based immigration system that effectively excluded any large-scale immigration from neighbouring countries other than New Zealand, a scheme that also made travel to Australia for study difficult for those considered non-European. These policies did not go unnoticed by regional governments and administrators. So, while the White Australia Policy 'protected' Australia, it also drew attention to it. The Chifley Government wanted to keep the wall of the White Australia Policy in place, but it was aware that it needed good relations with the newly emerging nations of South and South-East Asia.

This chapter outlines the first of Australia's international scholarship schemes. These scholarships have continued, in various iterations, for the decades since – which, as noted in the Introduction to this book, shows remarkable permanence. This story of policy and program constancy began in 1948 with a Cabinet decision to create the South-East Asian Scholarship Scheme, part of a deliberate effort by the government to foster good relations with elites in Asia, particularly those showing nationalist ambitions.[1]

---

1   Chris Waters, 'The MacMahon Ball Mission to East Asia 1948', *Australian Journal of Politics & History* 40, no. 3 (1994): 351–63, doi.org/10.1111/j.1467-8497.1994.tb00109.x.

This effort also included a mission to Asia by the diplomat and academic William MacMahon Ball, also in 1948, to promote both the scholarships and other aid and engagement efforts. As Chris Waters and Garry Woodard have explained, the MacMahon Ball mission was plagued by distrust, both within the Australian camp and between the Australians and their hosts.[2] However, as this chapter will explain, the very small nature of the award may have had something to do with the less than welcome reception that the MacMahon Ball mission received.

In 1948, the Chifley Cabinet decided to offer scholarships, called the South-East Asian Scholarship Scheme, to nations around the region. Cabinet approved the granting of scholarships to 'nationals of South-East Asia' in January 1948.[3] The scheme was small, with less than 10 awards offered per year, rising to 12 by the end of the 1950s.[4] In general, offers were made to a country or territory not under Australian control[5] – with the government or administration asked to nominate an appropriate candidate.

This small scheme was soon joined by a much larger scholarship program – the Colombo Plan. While the Colombo Plan was far more than just a scholarship program, it has become an anchor point in Australian understanding of aid, scholarships and international education. The Colombo Plan also became, in part due to its high profile and size, a template for government engagement with regions – in practice, in policy and in the imaginations of bureaucrats and politicians. The Colombo Plan played an important role in opening up the communities within Australia to the presence of overseas students in Australian universities and colleges. It continues to dominate in the foreign policy imagination of Australian politics, evidenced by the introduction of the New Colombo Plan in 2014.

Beginning in 1951, the Colombo Plan brought students from participating countries (mostly Commonwealth countries, but other participant countries included Indonesia) into Australian tertiary institutions across the country. These students, along with thousands more privately supported students, have had a lasting impact on Australia. These scholarship programs offered

---

2   Waters, 'The Macmahon Ball Mission'; Garry Woodard, 'Macmahon Ball's Goodwill Mission to Asia 1948', *Australian Journal of International Affairs* 49, no. 1 (May 1995): 129–34, doi.org/10.1080/10357719508445151.
3   'Draft Submission for Cabinet Approval – Proposals for an Australian Overseas Scholarship Scheme', A1838, 2047/1, 1957, National Archives of Australia (NAA).
4   'Draft Submission for Cabinet Approval – Proposals for an Australian Overseas Scholarship Scheme', A1838, 2047/1, 1957, NAA.
5   For example, awards were offered to Fiji, New Hebrides and New Caledonia – at the time all colonial territories.

a different view of Australia in the region to the one created by the White Australia Policy. And importantly, they offered Australians a different view of Asia. They were also a visible element of the policy response to the perceived threat of impending communist takeover as communist-led revolutionary movements challenged authorities in places such as Malaya, Vietnam, Philippines, China and Indonesia. The idea of influencing the hearts and minds of young people from across South-East Asia was attractive to politicians and policymakers alike. In the Pacific region, this period was a time of recovery from the war. It was also a period where the metropolitan powers that had previously carved up the Pacific region to their liking were having their status and dominance, with the exception of the USA, reduced. These metropolitan powers were not limited to the United Kingdom, Germany, France, the Netherlands and the USA; they also included Australia and New Zealand. Through Australia's responsibilities as the trustee of New Guinea, and as co-trustee of Nauru, the government was required to address the needs of development and education in these territories. The Australian Government was also part of broader conversations about the development of Pacific Island territories with fellow metropolitan powers.[6] These obligations challenged the Australian Government's understanding of citizenship, access to opportunities and international development.[7] This chapter investigates the first Australian Government development scholarship, placing it in its temporal, political and geographic context. It also addresses the political and bureaucratic machinations behind the scholarship, and Australia's education policy in the Territory of Papua and New Guinea.

Australian Government policymakers, and the wider community, were very concerned about the spread of communism in Asia. As Alex Auletta notes, the context in which the Colombo Plan was conceived was particularly complicated for a nation only recently developing its independent approach to foreign affairs.[8] The Cold War was pitting the United States (and its

---

6   Christopher Waters, '"Against the Tide": Australian Government Attitudes to Decolonisation in the South Pacific, 1962–1972', *The Journal of Pacific History* 48, no. 2 (2013): 195, doi.org/10.1080/00223344.2013.794576.
7   The connections between colonial obligations and international development are discussed by a number of scholars including Nicholas Ferns ('Colonialism as Foreign Aid: Australian Developmental Policy in Papua New Guinea, 1945–75', *Australian Historical Studies* 51, no. 4 (2020): 459–76, doi.org/10.1080/1031461X.2020.1808689) and Charlotte Lydia Riley ('"Tropical Allsorts": The Transnational Flavor of British Development Policies in Africa', *Journal of World History* 26, no. 4 (2016): 839–64, doi.org/10.1353/jwh.2016.0065) and others.
8   Alex Auletta, 'A Retrospective View of the Colombo Plan: Government Policy, Departmental Administration and Overseas Students', *Journal of Higher Education Policy & Management* 22, no. 1 (2000): 47–58, doi.org/10.1080/713678129.

allies) against the USSR (and its allies), and this was playing out in conflicts in Asia. The defence pact negotiated between Australia, New Zealand and the United States – ANZUS, signed in 1951 – was in part Australia's way of addressing this risk of conflict.[9]

The Chifley and then Menzies governments had watched India and Indonesia claim their independence, and states in Africa[10] and Asia pushed rapidly towards decolonisation and independence from colonial powers. Nevertheless, the Pacific was considered differently. For the Australian Government, as Chris Waters puts it, 'the 1950s, far from being a precursor to decolonisation in the South Pacific, had seen serious consideration of the expansion of Australia's imperial responsibilities in the region'.[11] Australia, rather than embracing the global move towards decolonisation in the aftermath of the Second World War, worked to manipulate the system to ensure its dominance in the Pacific region. This ambition was not new, as Marilyn Lake has noted, 'the Commonwealth of Australia was founded in dreams of a Pacific empire'.[12] Australia was, by the 1950s, giving 'serious consideration of the expansion of Australia's imperial responsibilities'[13] in the Pacific region, including Papua New Guinea (PNG). This was in contrast to the public efforts made by some European powers to decolonise their empires, or at the very least reduce the cost of those empires to the metropole. These global events put pressure on the Australian Government, which belatedly accepted that it could not avoid the global movement towards decolonisation.

Australia's general sense of unease with Asia continued to plague policymakers across the 1950s. The sense of a role in the South Pacific was better developed over the period, as can be seen in a briefing note to the Secretary of the Department of External Affairs in August 1957:

> Australia's interest in the Pacific area is primarily strategic. Our concern is to ensure that the social and political development of the British territories Pacific islands remain linked with the West and particularly the Commonwealth.[14]

---

9   Andrew Kelly, *ANZUS and the Early Cold War* (Cambridge: Open Book Publishers, 2018), doi.org/10.11647/OBP.0141.
10 Such as Ghana, which became independent in 1957.
11 Waters, '"Against the Tide"', 195.
12 Marilyn Lake, 'The Australian Dream of an Island Empire: Race, Reputation and Resistance', *Australian Historical Studies* 46, no. 3 (2015): 410, doi.org/10.1080/1031461X.2015.1075222.
13 Waters, '"Against the Tide"', 195.
14 'Australian Overseas Scholarship Scheme – Briefing Note to the Secretary (of External Affairs) – Annexe A –23 August 1957', A1838, 2047/1, NAA.

The note goes on to explain the role that education, or more specifically scholarships, could play in supporting that strategic interest: 'education ties would be a valuable means of strengthening such links and countering Communist and other disruptive influences which have already appeared, for example, in Fiji'.[15] The certainty expressed in this briefing is instructive; foreign policy bureaucrats were very clear of the role that Australia could play in the Pacific.

The oceanic Pacific territories were, as mentioned earlier, the subjects of various colonial powers. By the 1950s, the USA, France and the United Kingdom[16] were the dominant colonial powers of the Pacific; territories held by other imperial powers were now governed as trustee territories, under the auspices of the United Nations Trusteeship System. The trustee system required trustees to 'promote the political, economic, social, and educational advancement of the inhabitants of the trust territories' and support 'progressive development towards self-government or independence'.[17] This was, in part, a process of structured decolonisation. Of the 11 territories under the trusteeship system, Australia was the Administering Authority for New Guinea and was jointly, with New Zealand and the United Kingdom, the Administering Authority for Nauru. Other trust territories in the Pacific were Micronesia, Marshall Islands, the Northern Mariana Islands and Palau (together administered by the USA as the Trust Territory of the Pacific Islands) and Western Samoa. Those nations with trustee responsibilities were able to write the rules of the process, and the process itself was voluntary, a factor that Tracy Banivanua-Mar contended ensured that 'the spirit of the Charter was effectively unenforceable'.[18] However the system did mandate regular visiting missions and resulted in significant pressure on the Australian Government in relation to the development of Territory of Papua and New Guinea (TPNG), in particular in relation to educational progression.

The problematic elements of the trusteeship system highlighted by Banivanua-Mar can be seen in the case of Australia and Nauru. Just after independence, in late 1968, historian James Davidson described the

---

15 'Australian Overseas Scholarship Scheme – Briefing Note to the Secretary (of External Affairs) – Annexe A –23 August 1957', A1838, 2047/1, NAA.
16 Australia and New Zealand also had territorial claims in the Pacific.
17 'Chapter XII: International Trusteeship System', in *Charter of the United Nations* (New York: United Nations, 1945). www.un.org/en/about-us/un-charter/chapter-12#:~:text=The%20United%20Nations %20shall%20establish,referred%20to%20as%20trust%20territories, accessed 26 September 2020.
18 Tracey Banivanua-Mar, *Decolonisation and the Pacific: Indigenous Globalisation and the Ends of Empire*, Critical Perspectives on Empire (Cambridge: Cambridge University Press, 2014), 122.

arrangements that decided the future for Nauruans as being 'unfavourable', with Australia, New Zealand and the United Kingdom each coming into the process as joint trustees with their own motivations and approaches.[19] As Nancy Viviani pointed out, during the interwar period 'Australia assumed its role as political administrator and became the chief beneficiary of the immense amounts of phosphate on the island'.[20] Phosphate, and its role in developing the agricultural sector of Australia, was significant in Australia's interactions and ambitions in the Pacific region during the 1950s. Australian investments in Nauru were limited, and Nauruans were unable to serve in the island's administration because of a lack of educational qualifications, and the opportunities that led to those qualifications.[21] Official meetings to discuss ownership of phosphate by Nauruans were frustrated by the failure of the British Phosphate Commission representatives to explain the pricing structures. Australian officials were happy, however, to encourage Nauruans to move off the island because of the environmental degradation caused by phosphate mining.[22]

Viviani noted that there was 'conflict between Australia's economic interests and her duties as an Administering Authority under the United Nations Charter',[23] and that this conflict was not only limited to relations with Nauru. Under the trusteeship system, agreements had to be made in accordance with the Trusteeship Charter, but Banivanua-Mar argues that 'administering governments, in the end, could devise their own trust agreements, effectively making their own rules subject only to approval by the General Assembly'.[24] Across the 1950s, Australia and other trust powers continued to utilise the trustee system to justify development spending that was intended to protect strategic and economic interests, not always in the best interests of the trust territories.[25]

The exploitation of physical land and resources was not counteracted by significant investment in the improvement of the social, economic and educational positions of the inhabitants of the trustee territories of the

---

19 James W Davidson, 'The republic of Nauru', *The Journal of Pacific History* 3, issue 1 (1968): 146, doi.org/10.1080/00223346808572131.
20 Nancy Viviani, *Nauru, Phosphate and Political Progress* (Canberra: Australian National University Press, 1970), 2.
21 Roger C Thompson, *Australia and the Pacific Islands in the Twentieth Century* (Australian Scholarly Publishing, 1998), 141.
22 Thompson, *Australia and the Pacific Islands*, 142–43.
23 Viviani, *Nauru, Phosphate and Political Progress*, 2.
24 Banivanua-Mar, *Decolonisation and the Pacific*, 123.
25 Banivanua-Mar, *Decolonisation and the Pacific*, 124.

1. BEFORE THE BEGINNING

Pacific. However, as trust territories were moving towards independence, even at a slow pace, the Department of External Affairs recognised that these trust territories and other colonies in the Pacific would at some time become self-governing or independent. Thus, human resource development, and the possibilities of influence offered through scholarships, became a useful tool of seeking leverage while undertaking the work of 'development'. The tool was small – in the South-East Asia/Australian International Awards scheme there were only six to twelve scholarships available per year. The way in which those awards were to be allocated, and the decisions around the schemes, gives an insight into deeper thinking about the role of scholarships in development and diplomacy within the Menzies Government.

By the mid-1950s, conversations within the Department of External Affairs had begun about the possibility of granting scholarships to other countries and territories – especially in the Pacific and the Pacific Rim. This was in part due to the belief that the Colombo Plan was a successful program, and the 'tool' of scholarships could be utilised more broadly.[26] A briefing note written by David Dexter notes 'there is a gap in our training aid programs as far as Oceania, Korea and Formosa are concerned'.[27] Debate continued within the Department of External Affairs, with multiple briefing notes being prepared proposing Pacific Scholarship Schemes, or the extension of the South-East Asian Scholarship Scheme. In 1955 it was advertised in the *Pacific Islands Monthly* that 'the Australian Government had decided to make a scholarship available to a Fiji student under the South-East Asian Scholarship Scheme'.[28] The short extract also notes that the scholarship will be allocated by the Fiji Government and 'as far as Australia is concerned the successful applicant could be any Fiji-born person, regardless of race'.[29] As will be shown later, this perception of a 'race-blind' selection policy was not entirely true, and went on to cause issues for the Australian scholarship administrators. Nevertheless, the next edition of the *Pacific Islands Monthly* in February 1955 notes that the 'first award under the recently established Australian Government Scholarship for Fiji has gone to Oscar Emberson'.[30] Emberson was a 19-year-old from Suva who planned to study dentistry.

---

26   The Colombo Plan was sometimes referred to as the Marshall Plan for South-East Asia – in reference to the plan for the reconstruction of Europe after the end of the Second World War.
27   'Briefing Note – Training for Pacific Territories, Korea and Formosa, 25 May 1956 (DEA)', A1838, 2047/1, NAA.
28   'Australian Scholarships for Fiji', *Pacific Islands Monthly*, 1 January 1955, 59.
29   'Australian Scholarships for Fiji', *Pacific Islands Monthly*, 1 January 1955, 59.
30   'Fiji's Outsanding Students Win Scholarships', *Pacific Islands Monthly*, 1 February 1955, 67.

A Cabinet submission in October 1957 proposed an expansion of the scheme, with the Director of the Commonwealth Office of Education, William Weeden, seeking new awards in addition to the ongoing South-East Asian Scholarship Scheme.[31] William (Jock) Weeden was an experienced administrator in the tertiary sector, having been involved in the development of the Commonwealth Scholarship program, the same scheme that supported Cyril Chan's study in Sydney.[32] The Cabinet approved the additional funding request, despite the protestations of Treasury, which was concerned that the funding request was coming from the Office of Education, with the Assistant Secretary, Bruce Hamilton, writing:

> If the purpose is the fostering of good relations with other countries then this appears to be a responsibility of the Department of External Affairs rather than the Office of Education.[33]

In July 1958 the South-East Asian Scholarship Scheme was officially renamed the Australian International Award Scheme. In September 1958 the number of awards under the scheme increased from six to twelve.[34] Records from the Fijian colonial administration showed that in 1957 there were three Fijian students studying in Australia under the South-East Asian Scholarship Scheme – one Fijian male studying commerce, one Indian male studying medicine and one European male studying dentistry,[35] most likely the aforementioned Oscar Emberson.

Students in Australia from Pacific territories were not only sponsored by the Australian Government, but also by churches, their home governments and their families. In March 1956 there were 175 students from Pacific territories in Australia,[36] and some in the Department of External Affairs felt that while a government scholarship program would allow for only a small increase in that number, the political benefits would be worthwhile. There was an understanding with the department that the concept of a Pacific

---

31 William Weeden, 'Australian International Scholarships | Cabinet Submission | August 1957', A4926, 886, 1957, NAA.

32 William J Weeden, interview by Tony Ryan, 'Jock Weeden Interviewed by Tony Ryan in the Conversations with Australian Educators Oral History Project' [sound recording], 22 March 1995, National Library of Australia (NLA), nla.gov.au/nla.obj-217270737.

33 'Cabinet Submission No 886 | Australian International Scholarships | Treasury', A4926, 886, 1957, NAA.

34 'Cablegram to Australian Mission at the Commonwealth Montreal Conference, 18 September 1958', A1838, 2047/1, NAA.

35 These ethnic/race designations were common under the Fijian colonial administration. 'Scholarships and Bursaries – 1957', F28/451/1, 1957, Fiji National Archives (FNA).

36 'Draft Ministerial Briefing , 30 July 1956', A1838, 2047/1, NAA.

scholarship program was politically and diplomatically advantageous, the minister himself noted it was 'logical enough',[37] but funding and support from Cabinet proved elusive. Difficulty arose from a number of sources; the Department of External Affairs wanted control over where the scholarships would be allocated (and were determined for Korea and Formosa to be included) and conversations were taking place with the Prime Minister's Department and the Commonwealth Office for Education about alternative scholarship programs. Emerging nations in Africa were also a focus for the Department of External Affairs – Ghana was identified as a newly independent, new member of the Commonwealth, that Australia would do well to support in some way.[38]

The Colombo Plan for Cooperative Economic Development in South and South-East Asia, as the Colombo Plan was more formally known, was a comprehensive aid agreement that included a capital aid program and a technical assistance program. The scholarship program that the Colombo Plan is well known for was a part of the technical assistance program, which also included sending technical experts in agriculture, engineering and other fields to regional member countries. The Colombo Plan was formalised by a meeting of Commonwealth foreign ministers in 1950.[39] The program was significantly larger than any previous scholarship programs – by mid-1958 nearly 2,300 individuals had completed or were in the course of training.[40] In comparison, the South-East Asian Award scheme granted at most 10 scholarships per year, and by 1957 had only offered 18 awards.[41]

---

37 'Briefing Note by D Dexter – Proposed Pacific Training Scheme – 19 February 1957', A1838, 2047/1, NAA.
38 'Briefing Note to Dexter – Prime Minister's Department's Proposals, 6 March 1957', A1838, 2047/1, NAA.
39 There is a growing body of literature about the Colombo Plan, including: David Lowe, 'The Colombo Plan and "Soft" Regionalism in the Asia-Pacific: Australian and New Zealand Cultural Diplomacy in the 1950s and 1960s' (Alfred Deakin Research Institute Working Paper Series 1, 2010); David Lowe, 'The Colombo Plan: Modernisation, Memory and Cultural Engagement in Australia and New Zealand', *Journal of Australian Studies* 28 (2015): 142–53, doi.org/10.20764/asaj.28.0_142; Daniel Oakman, *Facing Asia: A History of the Colombo Plan* (Canberra: Pandanus Books, 2004); Daniel Oakman, '"Young Asians in Our Homes": Colombo Plan Students and White Australia', *Journal of Australian Studies* 26, no. 72 (2002): 89–98, doi.org/10.1080/14443050209387741; Daniel Oakman, 'The Seed of Freedom: Regional Security and the Colombo Plan', *Australian Journal of Politics & History* 46, no. 1 (2000): 67–85, doi.org/10.1111/1467-8497.00086; Auletta, 'A Retrospective View of the Colombo Plan'; Lyndon Megarrity, 'Regional Goodwill, Sensibly Priced: Commonwealth Policies Towards Colombo Plan Scholars and Private Overseas Students, 1945–72', *Australian Historical Studies* 38, no. 129 (2007): 88–105, doi.org/10.1080/10314610708601233.
40 'Commonwealth Conference, Montreal – Extension of Intra-Commonwealth Training Awards | Letter from CT Moodie (DEA), 5 Sept 1958', A1838, 2047/1, NAA.
41 'Draft Submission for Cabinet Approval – Proposals for an Australian Overseas Scholarship Scheme', A1838, 2047/1, 1957, NAA.

The Colombo Plan had a much firmer rationale to build on than the less obvious South-East Asia Scholarships Scheme. The plan was largely designed by ministers at the Commonwealth Conference, including Ceylon's Junius Richard Jayewardene and Australia's new Minister for External Affairs, Percy Spender,[42] as an attempt to stem the perceived flow of communism from Russia and China through South-East Asia. At the time, the Department of External Affairs believed that the scheme would promote development and encourage students to adopt Western liberal-democratic ideals and values.[43] Historians have, over subsequent years, debated the true motivations of Australia's participation and championing of the scheme. Historian Daniel Oakman contends that the Colombo was a 'major vehicle for extending Western influence'.[44] On the other hand, while accepting that some of the motivations for the Colombo Plan and other aid were strategically aligned, Nicholas Ferns argues that Australian policymaking in the postwar period was significantly influenced by theoretical debates about development and humanitarianism.[45] The Colombo Plan also served as an encouragement for the United States to become more closely involved as a foreign aid donor in Asia. David Lowe argues that Spender was using the Colombo Plan 'very much as a vehicle for his pursuit of sweeping measures, including an American alliance'.[46] While the USA did participate in both the technical assistance and capital aid components of the Colombo Plan, its involvement in the region was more focused on the Korean War.

In addition to the strong and 'urgent' rationale for the scheme, the Colombo Plan had significant political support. Minister for External Affairs Percy Spender led the Australian delegation to the meeting of Commonwealth foreign ministers in Ceylon, which included representatives from the United Kingdom, South Africa, Canada, New Zealand, Southern Rhodesia, India, Pakistan and Ceylon.[47] The Australian delegation was large and included representatives from across divisions within the Department of External Affairs, the Department of Defence and Treasury, and a number of high

---

42 Oakman, *Facing Asia*.
43 Oakman, '"Young Asians in Our Homes"', 90.
44 Daniel Oakman, 'The Politics of Foreign Aid: Counter-Subversion and the Colombo Plan, 1950–1970', *Pacifica Review: Peace, Security & Global Change* 13, no. 3 (2001): 257, doi.org/10.1080/13239 100120082710.
45 Nicholas Ferns, 'Beyond Colombo: Australian Colonial and Foreign Policy in the Age of International Development, 1945–1975', PhD thesis, Monash University, 2017.
46 David Lowe, 'Percy Spender and the Colombo Plan 1950', *Australian Journal of Politics & History* 40, no. 2 (1994): 162, doi.org/10.1111/j.1467-8497.1994.tb00098.x.
47 Auletta, 'A Retrospective View of the Colombo Plan'.

commissioners.[48] This afforded a level of bureaucratic interest not seen in the scholarship schemes coming solely through the Department of External Affairs. Spender's successor, Richard Casey, also 'championed the scheme throughout his career, extolling the virtues of cultural exchange facilitated by the scholarship program'.[49]

As will be seen in further chapters, the Colombo Plan offered politicians a useful framing for aid, but also a concrete program to argue against. In the mid-1950s, the Labor Opposition Leader, Arthur Calwell, advocated for funding to be allocated to PNG instead of the Colombo Plan – stating 'The benefits for ourselves and those we are helping will be far greater than we will ever get from our Colombo Plan pay-outs'.[50] He was not alone in this feeling, with Treasurer Arthur Fadden expressing a similar view.[51]

The scheme was also, by the very limited metrics of number of students, a success. The profile of Australia's educational institutions in Asia was boosted by the Colombo Plan. Opportunities for scholarships were promoted, and while demand outstripped supply, those who were unable to gain a scholarship were in some cases able to study in Australia by other means. Australia's diplomats also reported that the positive reports of returning students were essential to the successful outcomes of the scheme. Universities, social and service organisations (such as Rotary and Apex) and Coordinating Committees for the Welfare of Overseas Students were convened across the country in the 1950s to support these overseas students while they were in Australia. These organisations were focused on supporting Colombo Plan students, but their activities and actions, such as the construction of International Houses across various universities, also benefited non–Colombo Plan students.

The size of the Colombo Plan program, the prominence of its sponsors, and the ability for Australia to stake its claim as a generous nation within the Commonwealth, all served to reinforce its status as the most influential scholarship program Australia has been party to. But as officials from the

---

48   Auletta, 'A Retrospective View of the Colombo Plan'.
49   Oakman, '"Young Asians in Our Homes"', 89.
50   Arthur Calwell, 'Statement for ABC and Radio Australia by Deputy Leader of the Opposition | 30 July', Papers of Sir Donald Cleland, circa 1960–circa 1990, General letters 1951–57, 1956, MS9600/11/1, NLA.
51   'Notes Taken by 9PA Reporter at Interview with Sir Arthur Fadden', Papers of Sir Donald Cleland, circa 1960–circa 1990, General letters 1951–57, 1957, MS9600/11/1, NLA.

Department of External Affairs noted at the time, the program excluded the territories of the Pacific, an area where Australia wished to expand its influence.[52]

There were other scholarships offered to students from the Pacific during the 1950s. Many of these scholarships allowed for students to study in Australia should they choose. These included scholarships offered by the United Kingdom – the Colonial Development and Welfare Scholarships (CD&W) and the Fiji Scholarships offered by the colonial administration in Fiji. The CD&W scheme was in place from the mid-1940s, and offered scholarships to many British colonial territories across the world. It was, according to a Fijian colonial administration report, in place to 'encourage Colonial people to qualify for the staffing of the Government Service as the necessary corollary of the wider objective of self-Government in Colonial territories'.[53] In its communications with the Secretary of State of the Colonial Office in the United Kingdom, the colonial administration in Suva estimated that between 30 and 33 scholarships would be necessary over a 10-year period to fill roles such as engineers, veterinary officers and dietitians for the administration. These scholarships were to be divided between the three ethnic groups that made up the population of Fiji – European, Fijian and Indian. By 1957, 58 students were studying overseas with scholarships and bursaries. The largest groups were sponsored by what are termed 'Government Bursaries' (19 students) and Government of India Scholarships (15 students).[54]

Aside from scholarships provided by other nation states and donors, 1950 also saw the establishment of the United Nations Technical Advice Administration (TAA), which as part of its remit provided scholarships. The TAA offered 800 fellowships in 1951 to individuals from over 60 nations[55] including Pacific territories.

The archival documentation across countries and scholarship programs indicates that scholarship recipients were largely selected by the recipient administration or nation. For example, a scholarship was offered by the Australian Government to the Fijian Administration under the South-East

---

52   More members joined the Colombo Plan across the 1950s.
53   'Final Report of the Interdepartmental Committee to Consider the Award of Scholarships, 4th October', 25/296/7, 1947, FNA.
54   'Scholarships and Bursaries – 1957', F28/451/1, 1957, FNA.
55   Hugh L Keenleyside, 'U. N. Technical Assistance Programme', *Pakistan Horizon* 5, no. 1 (1952): 33–38.

Asian Scholarship (Australian International Award). The awarding of this scholarship was made under the process established by the Fijian colonial administration to allocate the variety of scholarships offered to (and by) the colony, which did not have a university at the time. These decisions involved an Education Advisory Council that assessed applications and awarded scholarships for Suva Grammar School, the Fiji Scholarships and others. For many Fijian students the only option was to find a scholarship for post-secondary studies, so the decisions of the Education Advisory Council were consequential. From the minutes of a number of meetings of the council, it is clear that students were sometimes interviewed, but the reports of nominees, teachers and workmates were very influential on the decisions made. In 1957 when deciding on the allocation of the Fiji Scholarship, the council agreed the scholarship should be allocated to Bramah Nand Singh, with three alternative candidates.[56] The second of these students was Mark Johnson, who was soon after offered the Australian International Award scholarship, demonstrating the rigour of the process of awarding scholarships by the Fijian colonial administration.[57]

What these minutes demonstrate is the manner in which the Fijian Administration was addressing the issues of race, or more precisely attempting to balance the needs of three main racial groupings in the colony. The Australian Government was also making decisions based on assumptions and policies centred around race – both its role in the territories and immigration policy. For example, the White Australia Policy may have influenced colonial administrators in Fiji who decided, when offered a scholarship by the Department of External Affairs, to send a 'European' for study, a man referenced in the Australian archives as Mr Johnson, who was the Mark Johnson who had been runner-up for the Fiji Scholarship.[58] Department of External Affairs officials reacted to this decision with derision, but it is clear that Fijian administrators were genuinely confused about the 'type' of student the Australian Government was looking to attract, given their careful processes to allocate scholarships to each of the three racial groupings. And as was reported in the *Pacific Islands Monthly*, the scholarship was to be awarded regardless of race. Documents from

---

56 'Minutes of the Meeting of the Education Advisory Council Held on Friday 1st March 1957 18/57 – Award of Fiji Scholarship', F28/451/1, FNA.
57 'Australian International Scholarship Awards 1958/59, DEA Note, 28 May 1958', A1838, 2047/1, 1958, NAA.
58 'Australian International Scholarship Awards 1958/59, DEA Note, 28 May 1958', A1838, 2047/1, 1958, NAA.

the time indicate, however, that Department of External Affairs officials were keen to counteract the impact of the White Australia Policy, and the reputation it was garnering for Australia around Asia and the Pacific. Thus, the attempts by the Australian Government to support the development of Fiji were made without consideration of the policies or processes of the Fijian Administration.

Other Pacific Island territories were also offered awards under the Australian International Awards Scheme – with allocations made in the 1958/59 round to New Hebrides and New Caledonia (with one scholarship each).[59] The allocation to the New Hebrides offers another insight into the forces and institutions that controlled access to scholarships in Australia. The Resident British Commissioner in Port Vila noted that he sought the input of both the Presbyterian Mission and the Melanesian Mission for suggestions as to potential candidates.[60] The Commonwealth Office of Education in Sydney attempted to place a framework around the selection of students, which is discussed in more detail in the next chapter. However, finding qualified candidates who were deemed capable of undertaking tertiary study in Australia was difficult. The Resident British Commissioner in Port Vila wrote that his preferred candidate as awardee from New Hebrides may not 'be able to cope with the academic work straight away'.[61]

The story of Australian Government scholarships started in 1948, with the South-East Asian Scholarship Scheme. This was a scheme being used as both a tool for developing a footprint of influence in its geographic region and attempting to spread Australian political and social ideals. The multifaceted purposes of this first scheme lived on through those that followed over the decades, which following chapters will illuminate.

In 1950s, through the Colombo Plan, this development and influence was focused on nations and regions considered 'at-risk' from communism, and the Australian International Award Scheme covered other areas of the world that the Australian Government considered worthy of 'development' or wished to seek influence in. The Department of External Affairs worked to influence the nations and territories to which scholarships were provided, but in relation to the Australian International Award Scheme they were

---

59   A1838, 2047/1, NAA.
60   'Letter from DEA to Commonwealth Office of Education, Australian International Awards Scheme, 18 September 1958', A1838, 2047/1, NAA.
61   'Letter from DEA to Commonwealth Office of Education, Australian International Awards Scheme, 18 September 1958', A1838, 2047/1, NAA.

often competing with the Commonwealth Office for Education and the Department of Prime Minister for allocations, and arguing with Treasury for the provision of funding and resources.

Rivalries between departments and the influence they could wield with scholarships would only increase during the 1960s. And while Australian officials from various departments fought for scholarship allocations to be provided to specific nations, officials had little to no say about the students who were awarded the scholarships. Offers were made to nations, or more specifically administrations, who then allocated the scholarships according to their own practices or customs. Race and class played a significant role in the selection and awarding of scholarships, often because race and class played a role in access to secondary schooling. But these factors were not deeply considered by the Australian Government when they communicated with recipient governments and administrations. In the Pacific, these missteps highlighted how little the Australian Government understood about the administration of territories such as Fiji.

The context in which scholarships were implemented was one of change at the international level. It was apparent that the Department of External Affairs well understood from its effort to allocate scholarships to Ghana that the British Empire was in terminal decline. But such actions did not mean that the Australian Government was universally supportive of independence for former colonies, as its moves to stymie such momentum in the Pacific show. These internal conflicts continued to play out over the next decades, as the rationale for scholarships became more complex and multifaceted.

In 1958, the Australian International Award Scheme and Colombo Plan award numbers were increased. These moves were made, and promoted, in order to demonstrate Australia's position as a substantial contributor to scholarships in the context of the Commonwealth Heads of Government meeting held in Montreal in 1958. The conference in Montreal led to what is known as the Oxford Conference, a gathering of Commonwealth nations focused on education. This conference led to the formalisation of the Commonwealth Scholarships Scheme, which is discussed in later in this book.

2
Administrative labyrinths

As the story of Cyril Chan has demonstrated, access to higher education for non-Europeans from the Territory of Papua and New Guinea (TPNG) was complicated and required navigation of a variety of intersecting and often contradictory policies. The policy and administrative situation by the late 1940s and into the 1950s was influenced by a number of factors, including postwar obligations, conservative government and a patronising and colonial approach fixed in the minds of politicians and bureaucrats. Even within the Australian bureaucracy, more power was held in Canberra than in the TPNG Administration in the territory. This situation was puzzling and frustrating for the bureaucrats involved, but was far more damaging and affecting for the students and potential students, as the stories at the beginning of Part One have illustrated.

In the 1940s and 1950s, Australia had pressing and present responsibilities within the Pacific. These arrangements began when British New Guinea (geographically, largely the south-eastern quarter of the island of New Guinea) became the Territory of Papua in 1906, administered by the newly formed Commonwealth of Australia. The Commonwealth had convinced Britain to entrust the newly formed nation with colonial responsibilities, and as Patricia O'Brien has written: 'Australian politicians hoped for a new era of colonisation'.[1]

---

1 Patricia O'Brien, 'Remaking Australia's Colonial Culture?: White Australia and Its Papuan Frontier 1901–1940', *Australian Historical Studies* 40, no. 1 (2009): 98, doi.org/10.1080/10314610802663043.

With the outbreak of the First World War, German New Guinea was forcibly occupied by Australia (geographically the north-eastern half of the island and the large islands to the north of the mainland). Following the war, this became a League of Nations mandated territory under Australian rule (from 1921). In fact, O'Brien argues that,

> Prime Minister Billy Hughes argued vociferously at the Paris Peace Conference that New Guinea should be annexed to Australia on the grounds of security and as compensation for the immense loss of blood and treasure in the war.[2]

In 1949 the administration of Papua and New Guinea was merged, after which they became the Territory of Papua and New Guinea (TPNG). Those who lived in TPNG, particularly those deemed non-European, were treated differently for purposes of citizenship, rights and, importantly in the context of this book, access to education.

The Australian TPNG became a key site of conflict during the Second World War. In this period, thousands of subjects of the territories supported – or were forced into supporting – the war effort, with many dying in the process.[3] The environment and lives of those who lived in Papua and New Guinea were significantly impacted by the conflict, as the land was occupied by Japanese forces, and Australian forces saw the islands and their inhabitants as providing a buffer, preventing an advance of Japanese forces to Australia. These physical and psychological sacrifices were made in support and defence of Australia, often without consent. Nevertheless, Scott MacWilliam, who argues 'victories made possible reconstitution of the ties',[4] pointed to a stronger bond between Australia and Papua and New Guinea after the Second World War than had existed previously, when there had been a more hands-off approach to governing and supporting the territories. Brian Jinks has argued that before the Second World War, 'Australian governments believed that their main colonial

---

2   O'Brien, 'Remaking Australia's Colonial Culture?', 107.
3   Kokoda Initiative, *Voices from the War: Papua New Guinean Stories of the Kokoda Campaign, World War Two* (Canberra: Government of Papua New Guinea and Government of Australia, 2015).
4   Scott MacWilliam, 'Papua New Guinea in the 1940s: Empire and Legend', in *Australia and the End of Empires: The Impact of Decolonisation in Australia's Near North*, ed. David Lowe, 25–42 (Geelong: Deakin University Press, 1996), 26.

charges ... should be self-supporting'.[5] This benign neglect of the prewar period was replaced after the war with a more active approach to governing and 'development'.[6]

The manner in which Australia administered the territories on the island of New Guinea changed after the Second World War. This responsibility was formalised by the Papua – New Guinea Provisional Act of 1945, which led to the two territories being administered by one civil administration.[7] Outside the internal legislative and logistical machinations within the parliament and bureaucracy of Australia, the manner of administration was also affected by broader United Nations activities. Obligations under the UN Trusteeship System included a requirement for the trustee territory to be moved towards self-government or independence, and involved reporting to the United Nations on a regular basis.[8] Tracy Banivanua-Mar argues that Australia worked towards convenient, self-serving, outcomes as the trustee and – along with the United Kingdom, USA and New Zealand – worked to manage the process and agenda in the United Nations, which led to 'the imposition of independent national statehood, bound by administratively expedient colonial borders wedding the procedure of decolonisation to colonialism itself'.[9]

Managing this situation in Papua and New Guinea from 1949 was the Minister for Territories, Paul Hasluck. Hasluck plays an influential role in Australia's colonial administration of the territories, spending 12 years as Minister for Territories before assuming the role of Minister for External Affairs. This followed a distinguished career in the Department of External Affairs before he entered parliament. Hasluck assumed the territories of Papua and New Guinea would 'ultimately attain self-government, either through independence or through some constitutional association

---

5   Brian Jinks, 'Australia's Post-War Policy for New Guinea and Papua', *The Journal of Pacific History* 17, no. 2 (1982): 86, doi.org/10.1080/00223348208572438.
6   Nicholas Ferns argues that this is in part a result of a broader shift in attitudes within the international community, with Australian policymakers being influenced by changes in thinking around aid and development. Nicholas Ferns, 'Beyond Colombo: Australian Colonial and Foreign Policy in the Age of International Development, 1945–1975', PhD thesis, Monash University, 2017.
7   Lyndon Megarrity, 'Indigenous Education in Colonial Papua New Guinea: Australian Government Policy 1945–1975', *History of Education Review* 34, no. 2 (2005): 3, doi.org/10.1108/08198691200500009.
8   Stuart Robert Doran, ed., *Australia and Papua New Guinea, 1966–1969*, Documents on Australian Foreign Policy (Canberra: Department of Foreign Affairs and Trade, 2006).
9   Tracey Banivanua-Mar, *Decolonisation and the Pacific: Indigenous Globalisation and the Ends of Empire*, Critical Perspectives on Empire (Cambrdige: Cambridge University Press, 2014), 218.

with the Commonwealth, such as statehood'.[10] However, Hasluck and his colleagues in government were more concerned by the broader implications of the Cold War, and saw the decolonisation agenda in the Pacific as being outside that prism. Given Hasluck assumed that TPNG's moment of self-determination was many decades in the future, he sought its gradual development. In a speech to parliament in 1960 he noted that 'political advances could follow only after social and economic improvements'.[11]

Cyril Chan's experience, navigating the labyrinthine administrative processes as he did to access education in Australia, was not isolated. While TPNG was, in fact, a territory of Australia, its (albeit limited) geographic distance from the mainland engendered an isolation from policymaking when it came to scholarship eligibility. In the case of the Australian International Awards Scheme (formerly known as the South-East Asian Scholarship Scheme), bureaucratic changes and announcements made their way to Port Moresby via a number of routes.

The Australian Administration in TPNG discovered the existence of the Australian International Scholarship Scheme largely via circulars and letters sent by the Department of External Affairs (DEA). In February 1958 a letter sent by DEA to the Department of the Territories noted that the South-East Asian Scholarship Scheme had been 'absorbed' into the Australian International Scholarship Scheme which would provide up to six awards to 'persons from outside the Colombo Plan area'.[12] The letter noted that Fiji was being offered one award in the current financial year. A few months later, in April, the South Pacific Commission sent a circular to commissioners and territorial administrations about the Australian International Scholarship Scheme, noting that the scholarships would be awarded to 'students from countries in which Australia has a special interest'.[13] A note from Geoffrey Roscoe in the Department of Education in Port Moresby noted that he had never heard of the scholarship scheme, but he thought it might be of

---

10   Megarrity, 'Indigenous Education in Colonial Papua New Guinea', 5.
11   Paul Hasluck, *Australian Policy in Papua and New Guinea: Statement in the House of Representatives* (Canberra: Government Printer, 1960), 7–11. Hasluck was to agree to a faster move to self-government in the year after this statement, recognising that he could not fight the accelerating push for decolonisation around the world.
12   'Scholarship for Fiji | 4th February', Box 340, File 6-2, Australian International Scholarship Scheme 1958, PNG National Archives.
13   'Australian International Scholarship Scheme | Savingram from the South Pacific Commission | 16th April', Box 340, File 6-2, Australian International Scholarship Scheme 1958, PNG National Archives.

interest to students from Papua and New Guinea.[14] Donald Cleland, the administrator at the time, decided to seek more information from the Department of Territories, asking the secretary for 'further particulars' as the 'scheme may be of interest to students from this Territory'.[15] This request was passed on to DEA, which clarified that students of the TPNG were not eligible for the scheme because it was designed for students from outside Australia and its territories.[16]

This exchange of letters and memoranda across the Pacific to clarify that the TPNG was, in fact, a part of Australia and thus ineligible for an 'international' scholarship scheme is instructive. The distance in thinking and the lack of communication between DEA and the Department of Territories is striking. Perhaps it also indicates the isolation from Canberra, and official decision-making, felt by the administration in TPNG – they were receiving information about Australian programs (for which they were ineligible) from the South Pacific Commission, rather than from their own colleagues in Canberra.[17]

It was clear that the educational needs in TPNG were significant, and Australia was obligated under the conditions of its trustee status to support TPNG on a path to self-government. In the interwar period, the two administrations responsible for these territories, according to Lyndon Megarrity, 'left educational matters largely to the Christian missions'.[18] This was, as a rule, restricted to the primary school level, what is now known as basic education. Megarrity argues that in addition to outsourcing educational matters, the administrators did not put sufficient funding towards education, and the reality that '95 per cent of Papua New Guineans remained illiterate by the end of World War II' supports this argument.[19]

---

14 'Australian International Scholarship Scheme | Letter from GT Roscoe to the Assistant Administrator | 22nd May', Box 340, File 6-2, Australian International Scholarship Scheme 1958, 1958, PNG National Archives.
15 'SPC – Australian International Scholarship Scheme | Letter to DOT from DM Cleland | 28th May', Box 340, File 6-2, Australian International Scholarship Scheme 1958, 1958, PNG National Archives.
16 'Letter from Cr Lambert to Cleland Re SPC Australian International Scholarship Scheme | 29 July', Box 340, File 6-2, Australian International Scholarship Scheme 1958, 1958, PNG National Archives.
17 As the exchanges note, however, the DEA had clearly informed the administration regarding the change of name of the scholarship to the Australian International Scholarship Scheme, and its purpose, in circulars sent earlier in 1958.
18 Megarrity, 'Indigenous Education in Colonial Papua New Guinea', 2.
19 Megarrity, 'Indigenous Education in Colonial Papua New Guinea', 2.

As discussed earlier, the Minister for Territories, Paul Hasluck, played a formative role in policy decisions regarding education in TPNG. Hasluck wished to avoid the development of an elite of highly educated Papua New Guineans and was more concerned with developing the education system from the ground (or primary school) up. Hasluck was concerned that 'an Indigenous educated elite would gain too much influence and power in an era when the standard of education of most Papua New Guineans was profoundly limited'.[20] Nevertheless, from 1954, scholarships were provided to a small group of indigenous and mixed-race young people for study at secondary school on the mainland of Australia.[21] This created a two-tier system, where some students were given the opportunity to study in Australia and others were unable to access adequate secondary schooling. With lack of political will in Australia, a minister who believed that slow progress was sufficient, and very little funding, the prospects for the growth of an education system in Papua and New Guinea were dim. Despite his misgivings, three key objectives for the scholarship scheme had been outlined by the minister in 1956 – a superior education, better fluency in the English language and a sympathy with and understanding of the efforts being made by Australia and Australian objectives in the territory.[22] The *Pacific Islands Monthly* reported on the arrival of '19 Native Scholars' from TPNG in Australia in February 1954 – noting that the scheme had been criticised because 'these young natives should be training in their own Territories and not subjected to the innumerable social influences which must affect their training in Australia'.[23] The same article highlighted criticism of Australia's education programs in Papua and New Guinea; 'sporadic, piecemeal attempts at native education may be excellent in themselves, but they only emphasise the Territory's lack of an overall plan of native education'.[24]

The number of students coming to mainland Australia for secondary schooling was not large, with only small numbers each year qualifying for a scholarship under the territory's scheme. Only 16 students qualified in 1954,[25] but owing to what the territory's Senior Guidance Officer called 'the extension and progressive improvement and consolidation of the school organisation in the Territory', 92 students passed the qualification exam

---

20   Megarrity, 'Indigenous Education in Colonial Papua New Guinea', 1.
21   Megarrity, 'Indigenous Education in Colonial Papua New Guinea', 6.
22   'TPNG Native Secondary Scholarship Scheme, Memorandum, 12 June 1957', A452, 1961/2382, National Archives of Australia (NAA).
23   '19 Native Scholars Arrive in Australia', *Pacific Islands Monthly*, 1 February 1954, 18.
24   '19 Native Scholars Arrive in Australia', *Pacific Islands Monthly*, 1 February 1954, 18.
25   Although 19 students were listed as travelling to Australia in reporting in the *Pacific Islands Monthly*.

in 1958.[26] Reviews of the scholarships program over the late 1950s led to changes and improvements, but as the provision of secondary education within TPNG increased, questions were asked of the logic behind the scheme. As the standard of schools in the territory improved, the first objective outlined at the beginning of the scheme, a superior education, was less easily achieved. However, territory administrators were concerned that the mixing of non-native and native students would cause problems – an issue highlighted in the 1954 article by the *Pacific Islands Monthly* and in the experiences of the students sent home from Charters Towers, as discussed earlier.

Despite these reservations about 'racial' mixing, among the students who travelled to Australia from Papua and New Guinea to undertake university study were some who were not of 'European' descent. These students accessed a program called Commonwealth Scholarships, the scheme that Cyril Chan was ultimately able to access. This scheme, designed to increase the number of Australian students attending university, was established by the Menzies Government in 1951. Each state was allocated a quota of scholarships that were awarded on the basis of academic merit, with fees paid for all awardees, and a means test deciding the payment of a living allowance.[27] In 1952 the Universities Commission decided there was no justification to provide a special quota of scholarships for the TPNG, despite the fact that these students could be considered eligible for the scholarship as subjects of Australia's colonial administration. Instead, it was the 'policy of the Commission to afford children of residents of New Guinea the opportunity of competing for Commonwealth scholarships in the state in which they complete the examination qualifying for matriculation'.[28] Thus, the scholarships formed an opportunity for students from TPNG to study in Australia, provided they could in the first instance come to Australia for their secondary schooling. If a student was not able to access the TPNG secondary school scholarships, this added financial burden proved an additional hurdle to access. In addition, the stipend provided via the Commonwealth Scholarship was designed as a supplement – with stipend amounts reducing according to the income of an awardee's parents. In 1957 this was equivalent to approximately A£240 per year. This was in

---

26   JA Lee, 'Review of the Native Secondary Scholarship Scheme, 14 March 1958', A452, 1961/2382, 1958, NAA.
27   Dale Daniels, 'Student Income Support: A Chronology' (Research Paper Series, 2017–18, Parliamentary Library, Canberra, 2017).
28   'Acting PM Fadden to Minister Hasluck Letter, 1952', A452, 1958/743, NAA.

stark contrast to the A£561 per year provided for Colombo Plan students.[29] Thus, even with a scholarship, the opportunity for tertiary education in Australia was out of reach for most 'native' students from the territories.

All of this evidence, along with the stories of Cyril Chan and the young men sent to Charters Towers, serves to reinforce several aspects of Australian colonial administration in TPNG. The isolation of policymaking from on-the-ground implementation created myriad problems for those seeking access to higher education opportunities. Hasluck pursued his slow approach to development because of his own beliefs and agenda and could only be forced to change tack when it became clear that TPNG and the broader global community would not tolerate it any longer. The situation in TPNG, with hundreds of different language groupings and no national identity, was difficult for white Australians to comprehend. Trying to implement education policies across the varied and often difficult-to-traverse terrain (both literally and metaphorically) was complex. It was clear that neither the Department of Territories nor the TPNG Administration was able to do so competently, ensuring what was described by an Australian academic who taught in TPNG as a 'trickle of scholarships' was available for students over the 1950s.[30]

Australia's obligations in the territories it administered created confusion and misunderstanding. The Department of Territories was unaware of the entitlements of the citizens under its administration, who often sought access to 'International' scholarships despite their status as part of Australia. The award of scholarships, and the control of mobility that they represented, demonstrates the layers of policies and bureaucracy that were created and enforced by Australia as the trust power. Students from TPNG could only access Commonwealth scholarships for university education on mainland Australia if they had completed their matriculation in one of the states (rather than territories). This highlighted the tiered nature of Australian citizenship, with full benefits only available to a limited few and benefits closely linked to race. It also highlighted Australia's slow approach to developing the education system in Papua and New Guinea – with a functioning secondary system not yet in place by the end of the 1950s. The assumptions in this approach to development would continue to have impacts for decades after.

---

29 JA Lee, 'Mr JA Lee – Tour of Duty in Australia – April 25th – June 13th', A452, 1961/2382, 1957, NAA.
30 Ian Maddocks with Seumas Spark, '"Taim Bilong Uni": Ken Inglis at the University of Papua New Guinea', *History Australia* 14, no. 5 (2017): 547, doi.org/10.1080/14490854.2017.1389233.

PART 2: 1958–1970

The periodisation for this part of the book is again driven by the beginnings of a scholarship. This scheme, the Commonwealth Scholarship and Fellowship Scheme (CSFP), differs from others investigated in detail throughout this book in that it was offered across the Commonwealth of Nations. The scholarship was designed by a collection of nations that made up the new Commonwealth of Nations, a body made up of former (and current) British colonies. The scheme was confirmed and agreed to at a Commonwealth education conference held in Oxford in 1958.

The second chapter of Part 2 is largely focused on the 1960s, a period of rapid change in attitudes to development and higher education in the Territory of Papua and New Guinea (TPNG). External and internal pressures forced the hand of the Australian Government, and the University of Papua New Guinea was established in 1965. Preparations for self-government continued, with a recognition in Canberra that access to secondary and tertiary education for a larger proportion of the TPNG population was required.

The end of this part marks the beginning of a new and more radical approach to policies in TPNG and foreign affairs from the new government of Gough Whitlam, to be discussed in Part 3.

Judy Annemarie Wong and other 'Commonwealth' scholars

As with the 1950s, there was not a huge number of students coming to Australia from the Pacific in the 1960s. One of the small number of students was Judy Annemarie Wong, who was awarded a Commonwealth Scholarship in the early 1960s to study a Master of Arts in Urban Planning at the University of Sydney.[1] Wong was born in China and had moved to Fiji with her parents as a child. Like all her contemporaries in Fiji, Wong had to leave Fiji in order to study past secondary school, and completed her undergraduate degree in New Zealand. She returned to Fiji to work at the National Archives for a year before leaving for Australia.

Wong's story does not follow the normal or ideal trajectory of a development scholarship recipient, but in many ways highlights the power of the connections that the Commonwealth offered. Following her graduation in 1964, Wong married Wayne Lo, and lived for two years in the British colony of Hong Kong before moving to Canada. Judy Lo (as she was then known) made a significant contribution to civic society in Canada, with positions in human rights and immigration organisations including the Calgary Canadian Citizenship Council. In 1994 she received the Haider Dhanani award for her contribution to the rights of immigrants in Canada.[2]

The story of Judy Lo (Wong) provides a counter-narrative to the rigid expectations of scholarship students, that they should return to their 'home' country and contribute to development there and only there. There is no questioning that Judy Lo contributed to society and development in the broader Commonwealth, it was just that that contribution was not made in Fiji.

Other Commonwealth scholars travelling to Australia included Uttaman Gopal, a Fisheries Assistant with the Fijian Agriculture Department, who was awarded a scholarship to study a Bachelor of Science in Marine Biology in Queensland in 1966.[3] Gopal was one of a number of students nominated by their government department for the scholarships, which were allocated by the colonial administration. Despite the intimate

---

1 'Letter from Weeden to the Director of Education (Fiji) – Commonwealth Scholarship and Fellowship Plan', A1361, 53/20/2 PART 1, 1960, National Archives of Australia (NAA).
2 'Judy Lo Fonds', Glenbow Museum Archive, Calgary, Canada.
3 'Fisheries Assistant's Scholarship', *Fiji Times*, 6 January 1966, 5.

involvement of departments in the selection of students, disquiet remained about the training of students overseas, and the issues they faced when they returned. Newspaper reports in 1966 noted that students who had been sent away for study 'came back to work in the Colony, but many complained they were not given good jobs'.[4]

Even those alumni who had studied teaching were not guaranteed an easy time. A Fijian Indian student who had completed her teaching qualification in Australia tried to travel to New Guinea to teach, in order 'to overcome the reputed teacher shortage there and to pass on to the natives some of her knowledge'.[5] The woman was a British subject, but was denied permission because she was not eligible for Australian citizenship (due to her ethnicity). This made the front page of the *Fiji Times* in 1966, perhaps undoing much of the positive work that scholarships were intended to perform in countering the negative impacts of the White Australia Policy.

In 1967 a young Papua New Guinean man returned to Port Moresby as the territory's first ever indigenous Queen's Counsel. Joseph Stanislaus Aoae completed his law degree at the University of Queensland, under an 'Administration Scholarship'. Aoae had undertaken his secondary schooling in Australia, also with a scholarship, waiting for a year after his return to Papua New Guinea to get a scholarship for his tertiary studies. In an article in the *Fiji Times*, Aoae said, 'Now I will be able to help my people in a way I think they have needed for a long time'.[6] Aoae's patience, like Cyril Chan's persistence, allowed him to navigate a system not designed to send 'native' students to Australia for tertiary study. These students were always the exception rather than the rule, ensuring that their experiences were often difficult and success far from guaranteed. In this way, the administration in Fiji was far more organised and had put systems in place to manage the needs of sending students away for higher education, with Education Advisory groups meeting to allocate the numerous scholarships available to students from Fiji from the UK, New Zealand, Australia, India, Pakistan and the USA.

---

4   'Long-Range Planning Urged in Development', *Fiji Times*, 26 July 1966.
5   'Fiji Teacher Refused Permission to Enter New Guinea', *Fiji Times*, 17 January 1966, 1.
6   'Dream Has Come True for Papuan', *Fiji Times*, 1 August 1967, 2.

3

Uncertain decolonisation

The 1950s marked the beginning of what is arguably the most significant, influential international Australian Government scholarship program – the Colombo Plan. Decisions made by the Department of Immigration in 1951 had led to rapid growth in the number of students coming to Australia for study from Asia and the Pacific. However, by the late 1950s and into the 1960s, colonial administrations in the Pacific and Australian representatives who worked in the Pacific were keen for the Menzies Government to expand its scholarships to Pacific Island territories, including Fiji, which was being prepared for independence by the British colonial administration. These agitators were attempting to draw attention to the Pacific as they saw policy focus, and scholarships, being directed towards South and South-East Asia. For these actors a new opportunity came about with the introduction of the Commonwealth Scholarship and Fellowship Plan. This chapter will discuss the emergence of this plan, and the way in which different government departments worked to influence the outcome of discussions at a meeting of Commonwealth nations in the United Kingdom in 1959. Even with this new scholarship, opportunities for students from the Pacific to study in Australia were limited and the focus of policy and decision-makers was not directed towards the Pacific in any sustained manner.

The scholarships that had begun in 1948 as South-East Asian Scholarship Scheme was by then known as the Australian International Awards Scheme. It continued over the decade, bringing students from 'outside' the Colombo Plan area into Australian universities. By this time the various uses of scholarships were becoming clear: development, diplomacy, influence and the protection of Australia's national interests. Each of the scholarships the Australian Government funded served many masters, interpreted differently by each actor. The success of the Colombo Plan gave politicians and bureaucrats an easy shorthand for the type of program, and success, they wished to see in various areas of Australian engagement, including the Territory of Papua and New Guinea (TPNG). It also provided, as shown in the previous chapter, a program to rail against.

Decolonisation within the British Empire reshaped the relationships between the colonies, former colonies and the metropolitan power of the UK. The Commonwealth of Nations officially came into being in 1949, and the nations that considered themselves part of the Commonwealth declared themselves free and equal members of the organisation. This included Australia, New Zealand, Pakistan, Ceylon (later Sri Lanka), India, Canada, South Africa and, of course, the UK. Education was discussed in various forums of the Commonwealth, but at a conference in Montreal in 1958 it was noted that discussions concerning trade and politics prevented a more comprehensive examination of education across the Commonwealth states. An Australian Government report from the Montreal Conference noted that:

> The conference agreed that the expansion of education and training within the Commonwealth is an essential condition of economic development. It was agreed in principle that a new scheme additional to existing programmes of Commonwealth scholarships and fellowships should be established … [1]

The report went on to explain that the details of the scholarships were to be worked out at a special conference to be held in the UK the following year. Prime Minister Menzies was not entirely comfortable with the way the Commonwealth was evolving.[2] Nevertheless, his department supported this mooted Commonwealth Scholarship Scheme. The Department of External Affairs (DEA) was less convinced. The dispute about where the geographic and political focus of any scholarship program should lie troubled the DEA, which believed that responsibility for allocation of scholarships should lie with the department. It was also aware of the negative connotations that could be implied by a scholarship program centred around the Commonwealth and an older concept of empire including colonies and dependencies yet to be independent. A DEA briefing note included the statement

---

1 'Cablegram from Montreal Conference Delegation', A1838, 2047/1, 1958, National Archives of Australia (NAA).
2 Chris Waters, 'Macmillan, Menzies, History and Empire', *Australian Historical Studies* 33, no. 119 (2002): 93–107, doi.org/10.1080/10314610208596203.

> I think that we should explain to the Prime Minister's [Department] that although we do not want a purely 'Empire' or 'Commonwealth' Scheme, we have been considering granting scholarships to certain underdeveloped British territories that are outside our 'sphere of influence' – such as the British Territories in Africa. And, in order to bring Prime Minister's Department around to our way of thinking, I think we should be prepared to offer scholarships to certain other British territories and countries.[3]

The detail that these reports from the Montreal Conference and its aftermath outline show that the motivations for scholarships to developing countries around the world were not consistent across the Australian Government. Menzies was not happy about the way in which the Commonwealth was evolving, away from the 'Crown Commonwealth' that he was comfortable with and towards what David Goldsworthy describes as a 'nest of republics'.[4] Given, however, the number of British colonies in the Pacific Islands, any Commonwealth scholarship scheme would play some role in the region. The Department of External Affairs was concerned that the involvement of other Commonwealth nations, such as Canada and the UK, offering scholarships to students from the Pacific could dilute Australia's status in its own region. This showed concern, but was not matched by a willingness on the part of the department to dedicate sufficient resources and energy towards relationships with Pacific countries.

It is worth noting at this point that while there is some scholarship about the Commonwealth Scholarship and Fellowship Plan (CSFP), including a history of the plan by Hilary Perraton, much of the investigation of the program is from the perspective of the UK.[5] This is not surprising given the evolution of the scholarship, with the secretariat eventually being established in the UK. However, this does highlight one of the problems raised by Australian and other bureaucrats, about the plan, that is the dominance of the UK in what was intended to be a pan-Commonwealth education cooperation plan.

---

3 'Briefing Note to Dexter – Prime Minister's Department's Proposals, 6 March 1957', A1838, 2047/1, NAA.
4 David Goldsworthy, 'Australian External Policy and the End of Britain's Empire', *Australian Journal of Politics and History* 51, no. 1 (2005): 17–29, doi.org/10.1111/j.1467-8497.2005.00357.x.
5 Hilary Perraton, *Learning Abroad: A History of the Commonwealth Scholarship and Fellowship Plan*, rev. ed. (Cambridge: Cambridge Scholars Publishing, 2009).

The CSFP was not only a project of the UK, and the negotiations before and at the Oxford Conference give an insight into the motivations of the various delegations. Delegates from around the Commonwealth were involved in the conferences that decided on the form and purposes of these scholarships. They all brought their own understandings of the purposes and priorities of scholarships to these conferences, their own biases and ideas about regions of focus. It is possible these conferences also provided for a cross-pollination of ideas, where the purposes, priorities and designs of scholarships could be shared.

Australia had its own scholarships to demonstrate expertise in the field: the Australian International Award Scholarships and the Colombo Plan. Many of the developed nations involved had their own programs – for example, the Colonial Development and Welfare Scholarship Scheme was a huge program established by the UK, and all scholarship administrators were watching the progress of the Fulbright Scheme in the United States. It is likely that the sharing of knowledge at these events led to what was to become a 'standard' scholarship design that has persisted both in Australia, but also around the world, since this period. As was shown in a previous chapter, the Rhodes Scholarship influenced the Fulbright Scholarships and was almost certainly the basis for the Morris Hedstrom Scholarship in Fiji; forums like the Oxford Conference allowed for further dissemination of ideas and methods.

At the Commonwealth Trade and Economic Conference, held in Montreal in 1958, the Canadian delegation proposed a Commonwealth Scholarship and Fellowship Scheme that would strengthen Commonwealth cooperation, and offer educational development to new and old Commonwealth nations. The proposal was a result of discussions leading up to the Montreal Conference. Australia did not commit to the scholarship program in Montreal, but did agree to attend the planned conference in Oxford the following year.[6] Australia also announced, just prior to the Montreal Conference, an increase in the Australian International Awards, in part to highlight Australia's efforts in the area of scholarships and education aid.[7] Nevertheless, in the context of the numbers of scholarships that were being discussed at the time, in both the Colombo Plan and the proposed Commonwealth Scholarships, an increase to 12 awards per year

---

6   'Oxford Conference on Education | Cabinet Submission – 3 June 1959', A463, 1958/4459 Attachment, 1959, NAA.
7   'Oxford Conference on Education, Briefing Document', A463, 1958/4459 Part 2, 1959, NAA.

was but a drop in the ocean. In a draft Cabinet submission on Australia's participation in the Oxford Conference, the author was dismissive of the outcomes of the conference, noting that 'frankly, we thought that the whole thing was put on in an attempt to rescue the Montreal Conference from failure'.[8] Nevertheless, not wishing to be seen as a pariah within the Commonwealth, the Menzies Government committed itself to the concept of education cooperation across the Commonwealth, and the proposed scholarship scheme.[9]

In the lead-up to the conference in Oxford, officials from Australia House in London met regularly with the Commonwealth Relations Office and other Commonwealth nations' representatives to gauge interest, the extent of planning and the membership of delegations to the conference. News of the preparations were reported in the papers, with a small excerpt in Sydney's *Daily Telegraph* in May 1959 listing the leaders of the British Delegation.[10] The subheading of the article, 'Empire Education', likely frustrated the staff at the DEA, who were, as noted earlier, working to distance the Commonwealth Scholarship Scheme from the concept of empire.

Not everyone was excited by the prospect of the Commonwealth Scholarship Scheme. In a candid letter to Prime Minister Menzies, the Treasurer, Harold Holt, wrote that he felt the proposed scheme was not based on any review of the needs across the Commonwealth, and the announcements and discussions in Montreal were 'aimed primarily at making newspaper headlines'.[11] Holt outlined the many ways he felt the Australian Government was already contributing to educational opportunities across the Commonwealth. He was concerned that universities in Australia were already under stress, noting that the University of Melbourne Annual Report had reported a 'critical situation' and the introduction of quotas for university places. His letter provided Menzies with a less than enthusiastic position on the scholarship scheme, but did not call for it to be boycotted all together.

---

8   'Draft Cabinet Submission – Oxford Conference (1959)', A463, 1958/4459 Part 2, NAA.
9   Perraton has published a more in-depth account of the circumstances leading up to the Montreal Conference and the establishment of the Commonwealth Scholarship and Fellowship Plan. Perraton, *Learning Abroad*.
10 '150 Delegates for Oxford | Empire Education', *Daily Telegraph*, 22 May 1959. The article does not mention Australia's participation in the event.
11 'Letter from Holt to Menzies Re Commonwealth Education Cooperation | 8 April', A463, 1958/4459 Attatchment 1959, NAA.

Dr Ronald Mendelsohn, in the Prime Minister's Department, an experienced bureaucrat who wrote extensively on social security and social housing, prepared a brief for the Australian delegation to the conference. He sought advice from others, including the Commonwealth Scientific and Industrial Research Organisation (CSIRO), which supplied Mendelsohn with a detailed account of the organisation's studentship system.[12] Advice was also provided to Mendelsohn from across the government on existing teacher exchange programs, the Colombo Plan and other educational programs that may help to inform and support the delegation in their discussions.[13]

Australian representatives from High Commissions across the Commonwealth wrote with thoughts and news about the participation of Commonwealth nations. These reports, letters and memoranda suggest that Commonwealth nations were speaking across each other, each nation with a different view of what the scholarship scheme was intended to achieve, each with a different view of the size, scope and structure. For example, a memorandum from Canada was titled *Oxford Conference on Commonwealth Education Co-operation* whereas from India a letter is titled *Oxford Conference on Commonwealth Technical Co-operation*.[14] These subtle but important differences highlight the differing expectations of participating nations. It is also possible to see the influence of the Colombo Plan on discourse around scholarships, with India – a donor and recipient in the Colombo Plan – viewing the potential of the Commonwealth plan in a similar frame.

A significant paper prepared for Canadian university representatives was obtained by the Department of External Affairs and forwarded to the Prime Minister's Department. The document went into great detail about the origins of the concept at the Commonwealth Trade and Economic Conference in Montreal in 1958. The Canadian Government had broad ambitions for the scheme, proposing scholarship committees operating in all independent Commonwealth countries, with awards to be split across

---

12   Guy B Gresford, 'Notes on CSIRO Studentships | 17/06/1959', A463, 1958/4459 Part 2, 1959, NAA.
13   'Oxford Conference on Education', A463, 1958/4459 Part 2, 1959, NAA.
14   'Oxford Conference on Commonwealth Educational Co-Operation | Memorandum from HC Ottowa | 21 April 1959', A463, 1958/4459 Part 2, 1959, NAA; and D Dexter, 'Oxford Conference on Commonwealth Technical Co-Operation | Letter from HC New Dehli to DEA | 25 April 1959', A463, 1958/4459 Part 2, 1959, NAA.

the 'Old Commonwealth' (one quarter), 'New Commonwealth' including Nigeria and the West Indies (one half) and the final quarter to colonial and trust territories.[15]

The New Zealand Government was aware of the Canadian position, as well as those of the UK and Australian delegations. Like Australia, the New Zealand Government was concerned about the way the proposed scheme would interact with the Colombo Plan. The Department of External Affairs (NZ) wrote in its submission to the prime minister that it remained concerned about the capacity of the education system to cope with the influx of Colombo Plan students, let alone with additional sponsored students. The department was concerned that 'the influx of overseas students, particularly those at the undergraduate level, has accentuated existing shortages of classrooms, living accommodation and qualified teaching staff'.[16] It was equally worried about the focus on university education that was implicit in the UK proposals being discussed. Like the Australian Department of External Affairs, its New Zealand counterpart was concerned that the new scheme worked to encourage engagement across the Commonwealth (new and old), and noted that the UK proposal 'would simply re-emphasise traditional dependence on the UK for higher educational opportunities rather than foster an interchange of skills and experience amongst the Commonwealth countries as a whole'.[17] This distancing by New Zealand from traditional conceptions of empire – the hub and spoke model that had persisted since European settlement – is notable. The New Zealand submission instead advocated a broader conception of the scheme, including professional exchanges, 'with the objective of securing the widest possible sharing of Commonwealth knowledge and techniques on a reciprocal and cooperative basis'.[18]

The UK Government took a leadership role from the outset. By June 1959 it had prepared a proposal that envisaged a £10 million fund over five years to support educational assistance across the Commonwealth. This proposal included a £6 million contribution from the UK, with

---

15 'Commonwealth Scholarship Scheme | Confidential Briefing | Canada | 8 April', A463, 1958/4459 Part 2, 1959, NAA.
16 'Commonwealth Education Conference | New Zealand Submission | June 1959', A463, 1958/4459 Part 2, 1959, NAA.
17 'Commonwealth Education Conference | New Zealand Submission | June 1959', A463, 1958/4459 Part 2, 1959, NAA.
18 'Commonwealth Education Conference | New Zealand Submission | June 1959', A463, 1958/4459 Part 2, 1959, NAA.

the remaining £4 million to come from 'appropriate contributions' from other Commonwealth countries.[19] The UK was also providing the bulk of scholarships (500 awards at any one time), and also offering to make 500 additional teacher training places available at UK teacher training institutions for Commonwealth students.[20] Proposals such as these contributed to the reticence of New Zealand to accept the dominance of the UK in the program – encouraging more Commonwealth students to study in the UK rather than flows of students across the Commonwealth.

The UK Government tightly controlled the agenda of the conference. Australia's delegation head, Sir Allen Brown (the Deputy Australian High Commissioner who had served as the Secretary of the Prime Minister's Department before being appointed to London), noted in a letter to the Prime Minister's Department that he suspected the UK were 'specifically avoiding' general discussions about the broad principles of Commonwealth education.[21] This allowed for focus to remain on tertiary-level scholarships, rather than other complicated issues that were being by experienced by education departments around the Commonwealth.

Brown also noted concerns that the Australian delegation couldn't speak about teacher supply issues, given this was a responsibility of state governments. This was an even more significant issue for the Canadian delegation, because higher education was funded and managed through the provinces, meaning the Canadian federal government was allocating funds for the scholarship program within a system they otherwise did not fund directly.

The Colombo Plan remained front of mind as the Australian Government discussed its participation in the proposed new scheme: 'it can be thought of as an extension of the Colombo Plan to the whole Commonwealth'[22] noted one draft Cabinet submission. A briefing report prepared in May 1959 by the Commonwealth Office of Education (COE) noted Australia's contribution to the Colombo Plan: 'Australia's contribution to training under the Colombo Plan has been considerable. In absolute terms it has

---

19 'Commonwealth Education Conference – United Kingdom Proposals | Commonwealth Relations Office | 11 June 1959', A463, 1958/4459 Part 3, 1959, NAA.
20 'Commonwealth Education Conference – United Kingdom Proposals | Commonwealth Relations Office | 11 June 1959', A463, 1958/4459 Part 3, 1959, NAA.
21 Allen Brown, 'Letter Regarding Oxford Conference Preparations | 24 June', A463 1958/4459 Part 3, 1959, NAA.
22 'Draft Cabinet Submission – Oxford Conference (1959)', A463, 1958/4459 Part 2, NAA.

been greater than that of the UK and far greater than that of Canada'.[23] This was part of a broader goal of highlighting Australia's contribution to the Commonwealth at the Oxford Conference.

Discussions and briefings in the Department of External Affairs and the COE addressed the perception that the Commonwealth Scholarship program had the potential to open up a scholarship program to the humanities and social sciences, areas of study that were not available in the Colombo Plan. A briefing note highlighted that the scheme will 'supplement the Colombo Plan in the countries concerned and would be wider in range, since it includes provision for scholarships not directly concerned with economic development'.[24] The possibility of opening up Australian scholarships to non-technical fields was not just about diversifying the overseas student body:

> Students in non-technical fields may often have greater potential political influence than technical trainees and there could be definite advantages in giving members of the new Commonwealth countries whether in Asia or Africa, whose background is in fields such as law, political science and the humanities, some direct experience of the working of Australian institutions and of Australian democratic practices.[25]

The same briefing noted that half the Colombo Plan awards had been provided to Commonwealth countries in South and South-East Asia. This demonstrated a concern that a balance had to be found between the Colombo Plan and the Commonwealth Scholarships. Thoughts of reducing the number of Colombo Awards to Commonwealth countries, in line with the number of Commonwealth Scholarships, was considered, but rejected as the government felt that it would 'leave us open to criticism within the Colombo Plan region and also within countries of the Commonwealth'.[26]

---

23 'Oxford Conference on Education | Commonwealth Office of Education | 25 May 1959', A463, 1958/4459 Part 2, 1959, NAA. That Australia has contributed significantly to the development of the Commonwealth via the Colombo Plan is noted in many of the documents prepared in advance of the Oxford Conference. There is a sense that the authors of these reports feel that Australia's contribution has not been sufficiently recognised by Canada and the UK.
24 'Oxford Conference on Education, Briefing Document', A463, 1958/4459 Part 2, 1959, NAA.
25 'Oxford Conference on Education, Briefing Document', A463, 1958/4459 Part 2, 1959, NAA.
26 'Oxford Conference on Education, Briefing Document', A463, 1958/4459 Part 2, 1959, NAA.

The Menzies Government's desire to clearly demarcate between the new Commonwealth scheme and the existing Colombo Plan scheme was not unique. The Indian Government was also concerned about the distinction between the two, not only because of administrative arrangements but also because of funding. David Dexter, who was at the time Counsellor at the Australian High Commission in New Delhi and who was soon to be appointed secretary of the Australian Universities Commission, noted in late April 1959 that India was:

> seeking clarification from the UK about the demarcation between the Colombo Plan and the proposed new Commonwealth scheme .... The Indians are ... trying to ascertain whether the United Kingdom intend to finance the new scheme from their promised lift in technical assistance under the Colombo Plan.[27]

In the final briefing for the Australian delegation, delegates were asked to 'ensure that adequate recognition is given to our Colombo Plan activities'.[28] The Australian Government was determined that Australia's position in the Commonwealth as part of the 'old' Commonwealth was to be recognised.

There is an undertone in much of the preparatory documentation for the conference, both the Australian and some of those prepared by other Commonwealth nations, that the scholarship program was not going to live up to the overseas development potential that had been envisaged at Montreal. This is in part because of the role already being played by the Colombo Plan. UK Secretary of State for Commonwealth Relations, Lord Home, noted in a letter to Menzies that the scholarship scheme 'will tend to help the older Commonwealth countries proportionately more than the others'.[29] Lord Home goes on to explain that the proposed teacher training support would be of greater benefit to the newer Commonwealth countries and colonial territories, and this was more 'in line with the Montreal philosophy'.[30]

---

27 D Dexter, 'Oxford Conference on Commonwealth Technical Co-Operation | Letter from HC New Dehli to DEA | 25 April 1959', A463, 1958/4459 Part 2, 1959, NAA.
28 'Australian Participation in the Scheme of Commonwealth Co-Operation in Education | Delegation Brief', A463, 1958/4459 Part 3, 1959, NAA.
29 'Letter to Robert Menzies Re Commonwealth Education Conference | 10 July', A463, 1958/4459 Part 3, 1959, NAA.
30 'Letter to Robert Menzies Re Commonwealth Education Conference | 10 July', A463, 1958/4459 Part 3, 1959, NAA.

3. UNCERTAIN DECOLONISATION

Preparations for the conference were made largely without the input of Menzies, who was overseas at the time of the lead-up to the conference. A Cabinet submission signed by John McEwen as acting prime minister in June 1959, prior to the conference, provides insight into the thinking of the government. He noted that the decision not to commit in Montreal in 1958 was based on a wariness to participate in a scheme – given Australia was already substantially financially invested in the Colombo Plan – and there was a risk that it 'might strain both our financial resources and our capacity to train more people'.[31] However, McEwen noted that by 1959 the situation was different. Once again, the Colombo Plan loomed large in the thoughts of policymakers. McEwen wrote that the new program could be thought of as 'an extension of the Colombo Plan to the whole Commonwealth'.[32] This realigning of the scholarship within the parameters of the familiar Colombo Plan was also paired with an understanding that the scheme had been developed by the UK and Canada, and not participating 'could have bad effects on our own prestige'.[33] McEwen framed the potential of the new Commonwealth Scholarship as an opportunity to connect with old 'friends' Canada, New Zealand and South Africa, while limiting aid to developing countries through the Colombo Plan. McEwen was savvy enough to know that this approach should not be publicised, lest it be poorly received in the developing world, in particular what he termed 'new Commonwealth members'.[34] But McEwen's thoughts provided an insight into the way in which the Colombo Plan was part of the structure of Australian aid. Rather than, in McEwen's mind, an opportunity to expand Australia's aid, the Colombo Plan gave the government a frame within which they could limit Australia's aid. If the government could point to the Colombo Plan, which was popular, they had less of an obligation to do anything more.

The briefing prepared for the delegation prior to the conference provided a more settled guide to the thinking of the Australian Government, with instructions for delegates to speak to other delegations to determine where Australia's contribution could best be made. The government had created

---

31 'Oxford Conference on Education | Cabinet Submission – 3 June 1959', A463, 1958/4459 Attachment, 1959, NAA.
32 'Oxford Conference on Education | Cabinet Submission – 3 June 1959', A463, 1958/4459 Attachment, 1959, NAA.
33 'Oxford Conference on Education | Cabinet Submission – 3 June 1959', A463, 1958/4459 Attachment, 1959, NAA.
34 McEwan also notes that the scholarship scheme is likely to entitle Australia to up to 20 awards from what he terms 'Old Commonwealth countries'. 'Oxford Conference on Education | Cabinet Submission – 3 June 1959', A463, 1958/4459 Attachment, 1959, NAA.

for its delegation the difficult task of supporting the scholarship plan, but trying to avoid the sole focus being newer Commonwealth members, while not allowing countries to get 'the impression that Australia's contribution to the scheme of awards discriminates against the undeveloped countries of the Commonwealth'.[35] This impression would be difficult to avoid, given the proposed allocation of 50 scholarships, provided as an illustration in the delegation briefing. This allocated 12 awards to the UK, 10 to Canada, seven to South Africa and four to New Zealand. Five awards were to be allocated to Colombo Plan countries, and only 12 awards were 'allocated' to be shared between 'Commonwealth countries and dependencies in Africa, the West Indies and the Pacific'.[36] The geographic focus put into the briefing by the Prime Minister's Department was not necessarily supported by the Department of External Affairs, which suggested the briefing be changed given the lack of 'political interest' in the West Indies. The Department of External Affairs was also concerned that Colombo Plan nations were not disadvantaged in the new scheme, suggesting a more nuanced wording allowing scholarships to be provided to Colombo Plan nations.[37]

The Prime Minister's Department briefing envisaged the scheme operating in a similar manner to the Colombo Plan – a series of bilateral arrangements under the umbrella of one scheme. The briefing for delegates noted that the administration of the scheme at the Australian end could be facilitated with little additional staffing – a benefit of the infrastructure put in place for the placement and support of Colombo Plan students over the preceding decade.

The Australian delegation represented a variety of interested parties. A portion of the delegation was made up of representatives from Australia House, Australia's High Commission in London. Mendelsohn represented the Prime Minister's Department and JJ Pratt was the COE representative. The vice-chancellors of the Universities of New England and Adelaide represented the university sector, with directors of education from New South Wales and Tasmania rounding out the 'educationalist' portion of the

---

35 'Australian Participation in the Scheme of Commonwealth Co-Operation in Education | Delegation Brief', A463, 1958/4459 Part 3, 1959, NAA.
36 'Australian Participation in the Scheme of Commonwealth Co-Operation in Education | Delegation Brief', A463, 1958/4459 Part 3, 1959, NAA.
37 'Oxford Conference on Education | Letter from DEA to PMD | 24 June 1959', A463, 1958/4459 Part 3, 1959, NAA. Despite this request, the final briefing provided to the delegation included reference to the West Indies.

delegation.[38] Sir Allen Brown, the Deputy High Commissioner for Australia in the UK, led the delegation, which by mid-June was still being arranged. There was a desire to have a departmental representative from Treasury take part in the delegation,[39] reflecting the understanding that any financial commitment for the scholarship program was going to require Treasury approval, and including them in the decision-making process would make these approvals more likely.

Every member country of the Commonwealth attended the Oxford Conference in 1959, with colonial territories being represented by what was described by H Lionel Elvin as a 'wing of the United Kingdom delegation'.[40] In Elvin's contemporaneous account of the conference, the number of attendees was framed positively; *all* independent nations attended. However, in an article from 2009 by Malcolm Skilbeck and Helen Connell this is described as *only* 10 nations attending,[41] perhaps failing to note the greater context of decolonisation in which the conference was taking place. The *Commonwealth Survey* report of the conference noted the attendees as being:

> the United Kingdom, Canada, Australia, New Zealand, South Africa, India, Pakistan, Ceylon, Ghana, the Federation of Malaya, and the Federation of Rhodesia and Nyasaland. The following United Kingdom dependencies were represented in an advisory capacity to the United Kingdom delegation – Aden, British Guiana, British Honduras, Fiji and the West Pacific, Hong Kong, Kenya, Malta, Mauritius, Nigeria, North Borneo and Sarawak, Sierra Leone and the Gambia, Somaliland Protectorate, Tanganyika, Uganda, The West Indies and Zanzibar.[42]

While some of the nations represented at the Oxford Conference were the same as those who had been at the table at the beginning of the Colombo Plan 10 years earlier, the group was now much larger and included both newly

---

38   While the Vice-Chancellor of the University of New England was to participate as part of the delegation, government representatives were keen to 'steer him away from any real work', suspecting he may prove a problem. 'Australian Delegation List | Letter to Australian High Commission', A463, 1958, 4459 Part 3, 1959, NAA.
39   'Australian Delegation List | Letter to Australian High Commission', A463, 1958, 4459 Part 3, 1959, NAA.
40   H Lionel Elvin, 'First Commonwealth Education Conference Oxford, July, 1959', *International Review of Education* 6, no. 1 (1960): 79, doi.org/10.1007/BF01416669.
41   Malcolm Skilbeck and Helen Connell, 'Commonwealth Education in its Changing International Setting', *The Round Table* 98, no. 405 (2009): 690, doi.org/10.1080/00358530903371395.
42   'Commonwealth Survey, Volume 5, No. 17 (Central Office of Information)', A463, 1958/4459 Part 4, 1959, NAA. In 1959 members of the Commonwealth were Canada, Ghana, India, Malaysia, New Zealand, Pakistan, Sri Lanka, the UK and Australia.

independent nations, such as Ghana, and dependencies from across the globe. Conflicts and confrontations formed the backdrop of the conference, as the Commonwealth Relations Office took on the mantle being handed to it by the Colonial Office, and the UK attempted to negotiate where it might fit in this new Commonwealth of Nations, while remaining a colonial power in areas of the world such as the Pacific and much of Africa. In his history of the CSFP, *Learning Abroad,* Hilary Perraton describes the period as the 'afterglow of empire and at the dawn of the new Commonwealth'.[43]

In John Lee's analysis of the papers of the chair of the conference, Vice-Chancellor of the University of Bristol Sir Philip Morris, he noted that 'there were strong hints about the Commonwealth as an expression of the civilisation that could counter the influence of Soviet communism'.[44] The effort to develop a sense of the Commonwealth as a group was also encouraged through inspirational speeches. A speech given by the conference president and Chancellor of Oxford, the Earl of Halifax, was theatrical (and somewhat ahistorical) with his characterisation of the Commonwealth organisation as:

> The co-operative spirit of this association, forged in the search for freedom, and burnished in its defence, that gives a special sense of dedication and inspiration to Commonwealth Conferences such as this.[45]

He was equally effusive in his description of the problems to be addressed by education: 'Freedom itself will depend on the education we are providing now for our young people'.[46] Lord Home, Secretary of State for Commonwealth Relations, was also keen to stress the commonalities of the Commonwealth, noting that the members shared 'literary traditions together with habits of thought and outlook which are remarkably similar'.[47] This determination to create a positive sense of common history, while not mentioning the empire that had created it, was reminiscent of the DEA efforts to keep the concept of empire out of conversations about scholarships.

---

43 Perraton, *Learning Abroad*, 1.
44 John Michael Lee, 'On Reading the Morris Papers: 1959 Revisited', *Round Table* 98, no. 405 (2009): 775, doi.org/10.1080/00358530903371445.
45 'News from Britain – Commonwealth Education Conference | UK Information Service (UK High Commission in Australia) | 16 July', A463, 1958/4459 Part 3, 1959, NAA.
46 'News from Britain – Commonwealth Education Conference | UK Information Service (UK High Commission in Australia) | 16 July', A463, 1958/4459 Part 3, 1959, NAA.
47 'News from Britain – Commonwealth Education Conference | UK Information Service (UK High Commission in Australia) | 17 July', A463, 1958/4459 Part 3, 1959, NAA.

There was recognition, however, that despite their shared history, the nations of the Commonwealth were not the same. H Lionel Elvin's report of the conference noted that the event highlighted the differences across the nations of the Commonwealth, especially 'the difficulties of low-income countries anxious to extend and improve their systems of education'.[48] The inequity was also noted by Philip Morris, who:

> went into the Oxford Conference with a strong sense of the inequalities to be found across the Commonwealth ... with ... an awareness of the vulnerability of new states emerging from decolonisation.[49]

This awareness of the uneven nature of the nations of the Commonwealth aligned with discussions that had been occurring within the DEA, particularly in relation to support for Ghana, and other British colonies expecting to be declaring independence within the coming years.

While delegates were met with a firm framework in relation to the proposed scholarship scheme, there was room for negotiation about what the final scheme would look like. Australia, as discussed, had gone in burnishing its own scholarship credentials, as had other nations such as the UK. The Colonial Development and Welfare Scheme put in place prior to the Second World War was winding down, after a massive investment over the previous decade. Given this, Allen Brown, the Australian delegation head, wrote in a briefing to DEA that:

> the Committee was firmly convinced of the need to establish clearly that the Commonwealth Scholarship was additional to, and distinct from, all existing schemes in the field of training and assistance.[50]

In short, this scheme could not be rolled into or double counted along with other schemes being offered by participant nations.

Just prior to the completion of the conference, Brown wrote to the Prime Minister's Department that Australia had offered 100 scholarships. A press remark noted that the scheme was to be 'a most significant experiment in Commonwealth partnership'.[51] In the end, the commitment of numbers

---

48   Elvin, 'First Commonwealth Education Conference', 79.
49   Lee, 'On Reading the Morris Papers', 773.
50   Allen Brown, 'Report from Commonwealth Education Conference | Cablegram | 24 July', A463, 1958/4459 Part 3, 1959, NAA.
51   'Report from Commonwealth Education Conference | Cablegram | 29 July', A463, 1958/4459 Part 3, 1959, NAA.

was as expected prior to the conference, with the UK contributing 500 scholarships, Canada 250, India 100 (the same as Australia), New Zealand 50 and other nations contributing a small number of scholarships, among them newly independent nation Ghana.[52] Brown's message to the press expounded the success of the conference and noted the potential that education offered for Commonwealth cooperation. This message of the momentous role that education could play for the nations of the Commonwealth was encouraged during the conference.

Elvin's report provided a positive view of the conference and the outcomes to emerge from it, and indicated a feeling at the time that mobility across the Commonwealth might create possibilities for training and education for all members. Other evidence suggested tension was ever present. Morris's papers noted that 'Ghana, for instance, wanted to create Commonwealth scholarships for only its own students in its own colleges',[53] while others preferred a regional approach. In the briefings that Philip Morris received from British civil servants, the future of education collaboration was seen along:

> radial terms – lines reaching out from the mother country to the self-governing dominions – even if they did not have the details to hand, without a proper knowledge of some of the principle cross-cutting links.[54]

The imperial mindset, as feared by New Zealand, persisted in the minds of some of these civil servants.

The Australian delegation's reports from the conference judged the event a success, with Australia making the expected commitment of scholarships, and not being overly drawn on other points of cooperation, such as teacher training.[55] One early briefing prepared by the COE concluded with a qualification-filled sentence highlighting Australia's confused position:

> I believe our strong delegation may have enabled us and the Canadians to have ... indicated, without unduly committing us, that we are able and willing to make a definite, if limited, contribution to Commonwealth development.[56]

---

52 Elvin, 'First Commonwealth Education Conference', 80.
53 Lee, 'On Reading the Morris Papers', 774.
54 Lee, 'On Reading the Morris Papers', 771–72.
55 'Report from Commonwealth Education Conference | Cablegram | 29 July', A463, 1958/4459 Part 3, 1959, NAA.
56 'Brief Note on Oxford Conference | W.J. Weeden | 29 July', A463, 1958/4459 Part 3, 1959, NAA.

What these records reveal is the confused nature of the inception of the Commonwealth Scholarship and Fellowship Plan. The plan was a development scholarship for some nations, a scholarship to promote exchange across the 'old' Commonwealth for others and an opportunity for technical training for yet others. The failure to settle on this point at the conference allowed for these different understandings to persist once the scholarship scheme was in action. Harold Holt identified this in his letter to Prime Minister Menzies, noting that the scheme had been created without an understanding of what the needs were across the Commonwealth. In many nations, Holt observed, the need for postgraduate scholarships was low, but the need for primary education was significant.[57] A survey of participating states was an attempt to understand the needs, but it did not necessarily translate into appropriate scholarships. In a note provided to the Australian National University professor of history, Keith Hancock, William Weeden wrote that it was expected that Australia would offer 50 scholarships in the first year (50 less than the 100 announced), and it had been invited by a number of states, including the UK, Canada, Malaya and East Africa, to submit applications. Unsurprisingly, nominations were only submitted for the UK and Canada,[58] highlighting the radial terms expected by more cynical bureaucrats. The Australian position was also confused by the Colombo Plan, which had emerged from a largely Commonwealth arrangement, and was very much focused on economic and technical development in the developing nations of South and South-East Asia. To have a significant new scholarship scheme enter into the region had the potential to confuse students and administrators.

In the colonial outposts, news of the outcomes of the Oxford Conference travelled fast. Sir John Gutch, the High Commissioner of the Western Pacific, wrote to the UK's High Commissioner in Australia to note that Australia had committed to 100 scholarships under the Commonwealth scheme. He wrote:

> The three Western Pacific High Commission territories – the Gilbert and Ellice Islands Colony, the British Solomon Islands Protectorate and the New Hebrides – will, in the years ahead, be in increasing need of assistance of this kind.[59]

---

57 Harold Holt, 'Letter to the Prime Minister | 8 April 1959', A463, 1958/4459 Attachment, NAA.
58 William Weeden, 'Notes from Commonwealth Oxford Conference', A3211, 1960/2725 1960, NAA.
59 'Commonwealth Education Conference, Sir J Gutch Letter', A463, 1965/2353, 1960, NAA.

This assumption that Australia would have scholarships to scatter across the Pacific was something the Director of the Office of Education in Sydney was well aware of. William Weeden noted in a conversation with officials from the Pacific (representing colonial administrations) that while Australia had 50 scholarships to award under the Commonwealth scheme, there 'would clearly be a very limited number for the Pacific'.[60] Weeden was at pains to downplay expectations about what Australia could offer and highlight the level of difficulty that managing a scholarship program could represent. He noted the difficulty in managing 'school boys', especially during the school holidays, and was of the belief that there would be few eligible candidates for university studies in the Pacific territories: 'most of their needs would be for training in Technical Colleges and Teachers' Colleges'.[61] The message regarding the scarcity of scholarships for the Pacific was received by the Governor of Fiji at least; the Governor's deputy wrote in a letter to the Australian Department of External Affairs that: 'I am glad to note that two of the fifty scholarships to be awarded this year will be in respect of the Pacific area'.[62] His letter also noted the continuation of the Australian International Awards Scheme, which, while a very small program with 12 awards in 1958/59,[63] remained fixed in the minds of Pacific Administrators. In this way, Weeden, as a scholarship administrator faced a similar problem to that of his contemporaries managing the embryonic Fulbright Scholarship program: balancing the political and educational elements of the scholarships.[64]

These concurrently developing and expanding scholarship programs, the Australian International Awards Scheme, the Commonwealth Scholarships and Fellowships Program and the Colombo Plan, highlighted overlaps and confusion within the Australian bureaucracy. The Department of External Affairs was disappointed to be left out of conversations about the emerging

---

60 'Commonwealth Office of Education Minute (12 May 1960)', A1361, 53/20/1 Part 1, 1960, NAA.
61 'Commonwealth Office of Education Minute (12 May 1960)', A1361, 53/20/1 Part 1, 1960, NAA.
62 'Commonwealth Scholarship Scheme (Letter from Fiji Deputy Gov. To Dea)', A1361, 53/20/1 Part 1, 1960, NAA.
63 'Letter from Prime Minister's Department to Department of External Affairs, 12 Sept 1958', A1838, 2047/1, NAA.
64 Alice Garner and Diane Kirkby note in their history of the Australian Fulbright Program that 'managing the tension between adherence to government-imposed policy and funding, and avoidance of becoming simply an instrument of government, was a constant challenge for program administrators'. Alice Garner and Diane Kirkby, *Academic Ambassadors, Pacific Allies: Australia, America and the Fulbright Program* (Manchester: Manchester University Press, 2019), 88, doi.org/10.7228/manchester/9781526128973.001.0001.

3. UNCERTAIN DECOLONISATION

Commonwealth plans, which took place within the Prime Minister's Department and the COE. The COE was exasperated with scholarships being requested outside normal nomination processes.

Following the Oxford Conference, the Commonwealth Scholarship and Fellowship Scheme (CSFP) became a feature of Australia's scholarship suite, although as with the Australian International Awards Scheme, it did not involve large numbers of students coming from the Pacific to study in Australia. In 1961 the COE reported that four CSFP awardees from the Pacific were in Australia – two from Fiji, one from Western Samoa and one from the British Solomon Islands.[65] In the 1966 annual report the numbers showed a slight increase, with nine Pacific awardees, four from the Western Pacific, and three from Tonga.[66] Nearly all of these students were undergraduates, while most other CSFP awardees in Australia were postgraduates. The awards provided the DEA and the COE an opportunity to allocate scholarships to nations that were outside the Colombo Plan area, and offer scholarships for areas of study not supported through the Colombo Plan, although each department and office maintained its position regarding the countries to which scholarships should be offered, the ideal type of candidates and how the programs should be administered.

Given the influence of the Colombo Plan concept on policymakers, politicians and the general public during this period, it was not surprising that consideration was given to using the format in other regions. In 1961 the Minister for Territories, Paul Hasluck, received a letter from Dr Harold Wood,[67] the Acting President-General of the Methodist Church of Australia. Wood suggested that the Australian Government should put in place a Pacific Islands Plan, similar to the Colombo Plan.[68] Hasluck forwarded this letter to the prime minister, suggesting that the Department of Territories and the DEA work together to develop a paper to propose a Colombo Plan in the Pacific. The proposal suggested that the South Pacific Commission could be reoriented to manage aid in a manner similar to the Colombo Plan Consultative Committee. The rationale for the proposal was simple:

---

65   *Commonwealth Office of Education Annual Report for 1961* (Canberra: Government of the Commonwealth of Australia, 1962).
66   *Commonwealth Office of Education Annual Report for 1966* (Canberra: Government of the Commonwealth of Australia, 1967).
67   Dr Wood noted in his letter that he had also been a missionary in Tonga.
68   'Correspondence Relating to Pacific Islands Plan', A452 1960/5670, 1961, NAA.

> As the territories in the region develop – and to assist in that development – there will be an increasing need for the training of men and women from the region in technical and professional skills and an increasing demand for technical assistance.[69]

The proposal was considered by the secretaries of the DEA and the Department of Territories, but in August 1961 the Assistant Secretary of the DEA, David McNicol, wrote to his counterpart at the Department of Territories, Dudley McCarthy, to temper expectations around the plan. He articulated a number of points to explain why the proposal was problematic, not least that it 'would have a rough passage in Cabinet'.[70] McNicol pointed out that Australia's own colonial obligations in TPNG required significant investments, and offering aid to other colonies was not politically advisable. This situation provides a useful example of an occasion where the Australian Government's obligations in Papua and New Guinea took focus and potential funding away from other Pacific territories.

McNicol also noted that Cabinet was likely to ask if this would, in effect, lead to other nations offering aid to New Guinea (Australia's territory). This is a crucial question, and one that began to occupy the minds of those within the Australian bureaucracy as the obligations of trusteeship to prepare Papua and New Guinea for self-government became more pressing. So, despite encouragement from Hasluck to consider the plan, the Pacific version of the Colombo Plan never got past the proposal stage.

Nevertheless, that the concept was put forward demonstrated, once again, that the Colombo Plan provided a frame through which those interested in aid and development could suggest aid expansion. Conversely, it was also a way in which politicians, such as McEwan, could limit aid to the boundaries provided by the Colombo Plan.

By 1967 the limitations that Australia was placing on its support for the Pacific, notwithstanding the scholarships on offer through the CSFP and the Australian International Awards Scheme, were angering some in the region. An editorial in the *Fiji Times* in July 1967 was scathing of the 'apparent indifference of official Australia to the Colony's condition'.[71] The editors noted that Britain was at the other end of the world, and dealing

---

69 'Draft Pacific Islands Plan Paper', A452 1960/5670, 1961, NAA.
70 'Letter from McNicol (DEA) to Mccarthy (DOT) Re Pacific Plan | 10 August', A452 1960/5670, 1961, NAA.
71 'Official Australia and Fiji', *The Fiji Times*, 17 July 1967, 2.

with requests for assistance from all corners of the former British Empire, whereas Australia was but four hours away by plane. The editorial ended with a threat that further indifference could ensure that 'steps may be taken, or contemplated, which will hurt Australian interests in the fields of commerce and finance'.[72] The editors of the *Fiji Times* were clearly dissatisfied with the Australian Government, especially given the perception that Australian businesses were very happy to invest in the colony. In some quarters Australia was perceived to be only taking from the Pacific, exploiting financial and business opportunities without commensurate support for the development of Fiji, or as the *Fiji Times* noted: 'Australia's responsibilities and obligations in the South Pacific.'[73]

This chapter, covering the end of the 1950s and into the 1960s, has considered the role of the Commonwealth of Nations, internal disputes within the Australian Government and bureaucracy about the purpose and role of scholarships, and the development of a university in Papua New Guinea (PNG). The creation of the University of Papua New Guinea went against all previous activities of the Australian Administration in the territory, which had stymied and made difficult access to higher education for most. The decade was also one in which many nations of the South Pacific moved towards independence, with Nauru's independence in 1968 marking the first new Pacific nation. The Australian Government was concerned with developments towards decolonisation in the Pacific in the 1960s. Historian Chris Waters explained the desire of the Australian Government (along with the governments of New Zealand and the USA) to mould decolonisation in a way that allowed for continued influence.[74]

The period also highlighted division within the Australian bureaucracy, particularly between DEA, which saw decolonisation as an important issue Australia needed to be addressing as part of its diplomatic and policy approaches, and the Prime Minister's Department. DEA staff were keen for Australia to support newly independent states such as Ghana, while the Prime Minister's Department and COE were wedded to the idea of keeping a scholarship bound within the loosening ribbons of empire. The compromise achieved, an increase in the numbers of Australian International

---

72   'Official Australia and Fiji', *The Fiji Times*, 17 July 1967, 2.
73   'Official Australia and Fiji', *The Fiji Times*, 17 July 1967, 2.
74   Chris Waters, 'Official Influence in the Making of Foreign Policy: The Washington Study Group on the South Pacific, 1962', in *Australia Goes to Washington: 75 Years of Australian Representation in the United States, 1940–2015*, ed. David Lowe, David Lee and Carl Bridge, 105–22 (Canberra: ANU Press, 2016), 109, doi.org/10.22459/AGTW.12.2016.06.

Awards Scheme, allowed the Prime Minister's Department to trumpet the generosity of Australia at the Montreal Commonwealth Conference in 1958. Australia's participation in the Oxford Commonwealth Education conference of 1959 then led to its inclusion in the CSFP, a program that not only allowed students from developing nations to study in Australia, but also supported Australian students to study across the Commonwealth (usually in the UK). This approach is analogous to many debates about aid and development assistance at the time – with Australian politicians still believing Australia to be a 'developing country', while simultaneously wanting to support the development of other developing countries in the region (not always for purely altruistic reasons). These events also highlighted, once again, the lack of focus of policymakers and policy negotiators (in the case of the Oxford Conference Delegation) on the Pacific. The Colombo Plan loomed large as a focus, and a frame for Australian scholarships and aid. It was not only a model to emulate (as the proposed Pacific Colombo Plan highlights), but it was also a way to limit aid, which was demonstrated by discussions around the CSFP.

The CSFP is an example of the fact that scholarship programs were interpreted differently by different actors. Each participant nation had a different view of what purpose the scholarships would serve, and the decentralised nature of the scheme allowed that differentiation to flourish. The scheme, and the negotiations that led to it, offer a glimpse into the thinking of newly independent Commonwealth countries and British and Australian colonies as decolonisation approached. Politicians struggled with the new power structures, and it is perhaps unsurprising that the Australian version of the scheme was used to strengthen existing connections (or by the description provided by the New Zealand delegation – spokes) to the metropole hub (the UK) and other developed Commonwealth nations such as Canada. There were awards for students from the Pacific, but only a small proportion of the overall total. Power was not equal; the dynamic of empire was still very much in play. The Oxford Conference also provides an interesting view into a moment of policy sharing: each nation brought its own plans to the table. The sharing of knowledge around scholarships is clear in the adaptation of policies around the world, but the unbalanced nature of the exchange was clear. Understanding how these negotiations took place is important because, as historian Charlotte Riley has noted: 'More closely interrogating the history of these processes, then, enables both historians and practitioners to more fully understand the ongoing legacies of imperial rule around the globe'.[75] The CSFP is both a legacy of imperial rule, and a signifier of the end of that rule.

While the CSFP was a part of the government's suite of scholarships until the 2000s, it never became a feature of the aid program and was more readily used to send Australian students to the UK for study – in the radial, hub-and-spokes model predicted by British civil servants and feared by bureaucrats from New Zealand at the time of the Oxford Conference. For some students, such as Judy Wong, it served as part of a story of a life that took her far from Fiji. The opportunity to study in Australia under other scholarships was also life changing for others, such as Joseph Aoae, who went on to become a lawyer and a member of parliament in PNG. And while Joseph Aoae was able to achieve this success, this was despite significant problems in the approach of the Australian Government in relation to widening access to higher education in the colony of TPNG. These are addressed in further detail in the following chapter.

---

75 Charlotte Lydia Riley, '"Tropical Allsorts": The Transnational Flavor of British Development Policies in Africa', *Journal of World History* 26, no. 4 (2015): 864, doi.org/10.1353/jwh.2016.0065.

4

Gradual development

The Australian Government's approach to higher education in the Territory of Papua and New Guinea (TPNG) changed over the 1960s. The establishment of the University of Papua New Guinea (UPNG) in the middle of the decade altered the dynamics around university education, opening access to students who could not obtain a scholarship to study in mainland Australia. However, a lack of universal secondary schooling ensured that access to university study was still difficult, given the requirements for entry. In addition, concerns within the Australian Administration about the revolutionary ferment that could be created by a university was ever present. This chapter also addresses the emergence of UPNG, and the way in which the Australian Administration fought to control a rapidly changing environment in TPNG.

As the Commonwealth Scholarship and Fellowship Plan took shape, and administrators across the Pacific rushed to avail themselves of the opportunities, Australia's colonial and trust power responsibilities in TPNG continued. Australian Government efforts to develop higher education and education more generally in TPNG had been based on the expectation that self-government for the territory was many decades in the future. A notice was issued in 1961 to inform education officers around TPNG that there would be 20 scholarships available for students to study in high school in Australia. Demonstrating the confused understanding of the place of the territories within Australian bureaucracy, the awards were termed 'overseas scholarships'.[1] Considering the lack of secondary schooling

---

1 'Circular Memorandum No 17 of 1961 – Scholarships to Enable Natives to Attend Secondary Schools in Australia', A452 1961/2382, 1961, National Archives of Australia (NAA).

available in TPNG, the provision of 20 scholarships would not have had any significant impact on the number of students as a proportion of the population. However, as is demonstrated shortly, those that were given these opportunities often had a disproportionately high impact on the future of an independent PNG.

The 1960s did lead to a greater international focus on decolonisation and the independence of former colonies. Australia could see the international focus not just through events in the United Nations, but also through interactions at the Commonwealth level, where former colonies were now peers at conferences of prime ministers and heads of government. A UN mission to the Trust Territory of New Guinea in 1962 was led by British representative on the UN Trusteeship Council Sir Hugh Foot. The mission 'was highly critical of the Australian Government's attitude towards PNG education'.[2] Despite Hasluck's desire that development in TPNG be gradual, building from primary education upwards, the Foot Report called for a 'comprehensive education framework encompassing primary, secondary and tertiary training … because highly trained local public servants, politicians and lawyers were needed to make early self-government a workable reality'.[3] The Foot Report was realistic in recognising the social, economic and geographical impediments to development in TPNG, but the Visiting Mission found that the number of educated New Guineans (and by extension Papuans who were in the other, related, territory) would multiply and 'they must be given every opportunity to play their full part'.[4] In short, an educated elite was required to ensure self-government, and that elite needed to have access to, and be created by, educational institutions.

It can be argued that the Foot Report was the catalyst for a change in policy. However, historian Stuart Doran contended that there is little sign in documents that the UN was influencing officials in the Department of Territories. Rather, he argued: 'Hasluck thought a degree of movement at the top would deflect some of the Afro-Asian aggression at the United Nations and satisfy the related anxieties of Australia's allies'.[5] Hasluck himself

---

2 Lyndon Megarrity, 'Indigenous Education in Colonial Papua New Guinea: Australian Government Policy (1945–1975)', *History of Education Review* 34, no. 2 (2005): 12, doi.org/10.1108/08198691200500009.
3 Megarrity, 'Indigenous Education in Colonial Papua New Guinea', 12.
4 *United Nations Visiting Mission to the Trust Territories of Nauru and New Guinea, 1962 – Report on New Guinea* (New York: United Nations Trusteeship Council, 1962).
5 Stuart Robert Doran (ed.), *Australia and Papua New Guinea, 1966–1969*, Documents on Australian Foreign Policy (Canberra: Department of Foreign Affairs and Trade, 2006), xxii.

believed that his gradualist approach to the social and political development of Papua and New Guinea was shared by the people of Papua and New Guinea, and they would tell the Australian Government when they were ready for self-government: 'It is our firm intention to defend the freedom of choice and respect of the wishes of those dependent on us'.[6]

Nevertheless, following the Foot Report, in 1963 Hasluck took a concrete step towards advancing tertiary education in PNG, appointing a Commission on Higher Education.[7] The commission, led by Sir George Currie, was established to report on:

> the means for further developing tertiary education to meet present and prospective needs of the Territory of Papua and New Guinea and to serve the best interests of its people and enable them to take an active part in the social, economic and political advancement of their country.[8]

Currie's report recommended the establishment of a university and an Institute of Higher Technical Education.[9] This led to the creation of UPNG in 1965.[10] The mid-1960s were an important time in the development of TPNG. Not only was the university opened, but a Papuan member of the House of Assembly (to that point a body with little influence in the administration of the territories), John Guise, began work on a draft constitution.[11] These two concurrent events are important, and can be seen as linked, because educational institutions, according to Evangelia Papoutsaki and Dick Rooney, have acted as a point of contact for the hundreds of cultural and language groups in PNG – in a sense playing a nation-building role.[12] The university and other educational infrastructure built by the Commonwealth of Australia became locations where the people of TPNG could gather, find things in common, and work towards a shared future.

---

6   Commonwealth, *Parliamentary Debates*, House of Representatives, 7 May 1963, 1071 (Hasluck).
7   Doran, *Australia and Papua New Guinea*, xxi.
8   CE Barnes, 'Report of the Commission on Higher Education for Papua and New Guinea', news release, 30 July 1964.
9   Barnes, 'Report of the Commission on Higher Education for Papua and New Guinea', news release.
10 Jemma Purdey, 'Scholarships and Connections: Australia, Indonesia and Papua New Guinea' (Alfred Deakin Research Institute Working Paper Series Number 46, 2014).
11 Doran, *Australia and Papua New Guinea*, xxiii.
12 Evangelia Papoutsaki and Dick Rooney, 'Colonial Legacies and Neo-Colonial Practices in Papua New Guinean Higher Education', *Higher Education Research and Development* 25, no. 4 (2006): 421–33, doi.org/10.1080/07294360600947434.

After more than 12 years in the position, in December 1963 Hasluck passed the baton of the Minister for Territories to Charles Barnes (who himself held the position for over eight years). Barnes's administrative style followed Hasluck's gradualist development approach. Stuart Doran wrote that 'under Barnes, the Australian Government was not a rapacious coloniser'.[13] However, what coloured the style of administration was undoubtedly a sense of paternalistic responsibility, as Doran notes 'Charles Barnes was attracted to explicitly familial language – and his actions show that he lived by it'.[14] The government and administration faced separatist movements in both Bougainville and Gazelle Peninsula, drawing attention to expressed fears that opening up the territories to education when the population was not 'ready' would lead to unwanted outcomes.

A comprehensive review of Australian external aid in 1965 highlighted the need to prioritise TPNG as recipients of Australian aid. This is a significant outcome, considering that Australia's obligations in TPNG were as the coloniser, not as a provider of external aid. Department of External Affairs officer CE McDonald highlighted this fact in a comprehensive paper he wrote in February 1968, titled *Transition Arrangements for Papua and New Guinea*. McDonald noted that PNG would continue to be reliant on Australian aid, and lessons could be learned from experiences across the world when a state financially dependent on its colonial power becomes independent. McDonald suggested that one option for Australia, rather than continuing to support PNG through providing grants to its budget, would be to structure aid to PNG like the Colombo Plan, with technical assistance, capital aid and scholarships. McDonald argued that 'this would fit into the pattern of worldwide programmes of a similar nature, and in political terms would gain more for Australia than a direct grant to the budget'.[15]

The Australian Government was not open to all offers of outside assistance, however. At the 19th Session of the United Nations General Assembly, the Australian delegation included members of the PNG House of Assembly,

---

13 Doran, *Australia and Papua New Guinea*, lv.
14 Doran, *Australia and Papua New Guinea*, liv.
15 'Paper by CE McDonald (Transition Arrangements for Papua and New Guinea)' A1838, 936/1/10 Part 1, NAA, in Doran, *Australia and Papua New Guinea*, 706.

4. GRADUAL DEVELOPMENT

and Hammer DeRoburt, at the time the Head Chief of Nauru.[16] An urgent note was sent to the Prime Minister's Department in Canberra during the session noting that the delegates from PNG, and a number of 'Australian Aboriginals' had spoken with the Minister for External Affairs from Kenya, Mr Joseph Murumbi. The record of conversation noted that the delegation had asked Murumbi about education and he had responded that:

> if they did not receive sufficient assistance from the Australian Government they should let their needs be known to other governments; and he drew attention to the number of scholarships which, among other countries, the Iron Curtain bloc were offering to students of developing countries.[17]

Murumbi also offered to put the delegation in touch with any potential donors. The record of conversation is concerned that the 'blandishments' of these and other politicians 'may result in these relatively unsophisticated men believing some of the advice given to them'.[18] The Prime Minister's Department was anxious about the interaction, and the Acting Assistant Secretary of the Department, AT Griffith, noted:

> the practice of building a leadership on Communist lines in Commonwealth and African countries by offering training scholarships behind the Iron and Bamboo Curtains has been practised with great success in East Africa. There can be no doubt that these scholarships represent a very considerable security threat.[19]

Griffith also wrote that ASIO (the Australian Security Intelligence Organisation) was to be informed of the threat that these connections, and potential scholarships, represented. This interaction illustrates the dilemma faced by the Australian Administration, which was being forced to encourage indigenous leadership at the same time as wishing to keep a tight control on political influence in the territories.

---

16 Hammer DeRoburt was to go on to be 'problematic' for the Australian and British governments. His negotiations with Australia (and the United Kingdom and New Zealand) in the process of Nauru's push for independence (and separately the rights of Banabans) proved to be powerful – with the United Kingdom threatening 'the Banabans with prosecution under the British Official Secrets Act if they talked to him during the course of their … negotiations for increased phosphate royalties': 'Australian Problems with Nauru (Airgram from US Embassy, Canberra)', RG59, Box 1840 – Central Foreign Policy Files 1964–66, 1966, National Archives and Records Administration (USA) (NARA).
17 'Record of Conversation at UN General Assembly | February 1965', A1209, 1965/6088, 1965, NAA.
18 'Record of Conversation at UN General Assembly | February 1965', A1209, 1965/6088, 1965, NAA.
19 AT Griffith, 'Note on Mr Murumbi', A1209, 1965/60881965, NAA.

Tension in the relationship between the growing 'elites' and the Australian Government was brewing, perhaps pointing to Hasluck's own prediction towards creating a group of elite, university-educated Papua New Guineans. The stress was clear in a meeting between ministers, officials and members of a Select Committee from the House of Assembly in Papua and New Guinea held in 1966. Discussions with the Minister for Immigration included questions about the travel of citizens born in Papua and New Guinea. Although they travelled with Australian passports, these citizens were prevented from freely entering Australia. Discussion also centred around what was to happen to students who had been sent to Australia for training or education. The Select Committee sought clarity on what Papuans or New Guineans might be able to do following their training in Australia: could they stay in Australia? This, the Minister for Immigration, Hubert Opperman, made clear, was not desirable:

> [I] Can understand why [there are] some cases where people who come here and like it desire to remain. But any one with the interests of their country at heart and [who] can contribute to their country, should submerge those ideas and go back and help their own country.[20]

Opperman's comments were, on face value, altruistic. The return of Territorians to their home was for the benefit of their territory. In the same discussions, however, Opperman also made clear that one of the impediments to PNG Territorians staying on mainland Australia was the risk of them failing to integrate, which, in the context of the White Australia Policy, was related to the colour of their skin.[21] There was a clear shift in the relationships between those able to access educational and other opportunities in Papua and New Guinea and the administration. A 1966 intelligence briefing noted the administrator had 'lost the trust and respect of the younger educated section of the urban native community'. However, 'because of their education the influence of members of this section on other members of the native community is out of proportion to their numbers'.[22]

---

20 'Notes of Discussions between Ministers, Officials and Select Committee', MS 8254, Box 8, Folder 1, National Library of Australia (NLA), in Doran, *Australia and Papua New Guinea*, 138.
21 'Notes of Discussions between Ministers, Officials and Select Committee', in Doran, *Australia and Papua New Guinea*, 136.
22 'Minute, Davis to Plimsoll', A1838, 936/3/15 Part 2, NAA, in Doran, *Australia and Papua New Guinea*, 11.

In addition, student protests occurred throughout the late 1960s, including a student march and petition in protest against the 'Act of Free Choice' that had taken place in Irian Jaya (West Papua).[23]

While UPNG was established in 1965, rising concern is obvious in the writings of administrators and public servants tasked with the move towards self-determination, particularly in relation to the lack of a sufficiently educated workforce to fill the roles essential to the creation and maintenance of a nation-state. Pressure was coming from all sides – growing unrest in TPNG, the missions and questions from multilateral organisations like the UN and a sense that the Australian Government could no longer be fully in control of the future in TPNG. McDonald conveyed this sense of disquiet in a briefing paper on transitional arrangements:

> In terms of world respect and influence, Australia gains little, if anything, from continuation of our colonial role, irrespective of the extent of our financial generosity and the considerations which make our administration wanted in Papua and New Guinea. A prolonged refusal to give effect to self-determination is even likely to weaken our standing in the eyes of our Western and Asian friends who now accept our bona fides towards the Territory.[24]

By 1968 there was concern from within the Australian Government that more needed to be done to educate Papua New Guineans for specific bureaucratic, technical and educational roles to manage a state. Warwick Smith from the Department of Territories sent a terse telex to David Hay, the administrator, expressing his concern that:

> no, repeat no, indigenes are currently being trained to full professional levels in key areas such as agricultural science, forestry and veterinary science as [I] believe it important (a) intrinsically (b) for political reasons that some indigenes be qualified to take senior and top Administration posts in these fields as a matter of urgency.[25]

Smith's suggested solution involved specific and targeted scholarships, noting that with a lack of qualified candidates in the matriculating class of 1969, those already in Australia, or teachers or other already trained staff, may be required for further training. This training or educating for a specific, and

---

23 Doran, *Australia and Papua New Guinea*, xliv.
24 'Paper by CE McDonald (Transition Arrangements for Papua and New Guinea)', in Doran, *Australia and Papua New Guinea*, 695.
25 'Telex, Warwick Smith to Hay', A452, 1968/5647, NAA, in Doran, *Australia and Papua New Guinea*, 627.

often limited, purpose was evident in the government and administration's approach to education more broadly, but specifically in relation to tertiary education and scholarships.

With independence coming into view, the concerns that Hasluck had expressed in the previous decade about the development of a TPNG elite was highlighted. The physical and social realities of TPNG were stark. Megarrity described the situation by noting the 'urban-orientated elite were ... very removed from the predominately rural nature of the electorates they were later to represent in the PNG House of Assembly'.[26] This disparity included the gulf in educational attainment between the elites and the general population, in part because there had not been sufficient investment in primary and secondary education during the colonial era.[27] But independence was not necessarily the goal of all of these 'elites'. Two members of the Assembly who travelled to the USA to speak at the UN Trusteeship Council stopped in Fiji on their return journey, where they were interviewed by the *Fiji Times*. The report noted that 'the people of New Guinea did not want early independence'.[28] The two MPs, Mr Edric Eupu and Mr Zure Zurecnuoc were complimentary of the capacities of the Fijian 'locals' to 'run their own affairs', but they expressed that they did not seek early independence:

> We told the Trusteeship Council that we didn't want independence forced on us by people outside. We want it at our own speed and in our own time. The Australian Government has not denied us the right to be independent and they will give us independence when we want it and not when anyone else wants it for us.[29]

Eupu and Zurecnuoc and those who shared their view could not hold off the push towards self-government and independence for TPNG. The opening of a university in TPNG did allow for more access to higher education for the people of TPNG. Access to high school remained a problem for some. As can be seen in the stories of Cyril Chan and Joseph Aoae, the first non-European university graduates from TPNG undertook their secondary

---

26 Megarrity, 'Indigenous Education in Colonial Papua New Guinea', 14.
27 Megarrity, 'Indigenous Education in Colonial Papua New Guinea', 14.
28 '"Right Calibre Men" – Fiji Politically Ahead of New Guinea Say MPs', *The Fiji Times*, 21 July 1967, 3.
29 '"Right Calibre Men" – Fiji Politically Ahead of New Guinea Say MPs', *The Fiji Times*, 21 July 1967, 3.

education in Australia. Despite scepticism from Minister Hasluck, sending students to Australia had ensured that about 200 students had completed secondary schooling by the late 1960s.[30]

As TPNG moved rapidly towards self-government and independence by 1975, the demand for educated Papua New Guineans to fill the roles formerly occupied by colonial administrators was high. And PNG was not the only nation on a path to independence, with many Pacific states on a similar trajectory in the 1970s. These dramatic changes in the Pacific complemented dramatic changes in the Australian domestic political landscape, which affected policy towards international students and scholarships. This is discussed in the next part of this book.

---

30   Ian Howie-Willis, *A Thousand Graduates: Conflict in University Development in Papua New Guinea 1961–1976*, ed. EK Fisk (Canberra: Pacific Research Monograph, ANU, 1980), 28.

PART 3: 1971–1983

This part of the book begins at a time of radical political change in Australia after decades of conservative rule. These radical policies were not limited to the domestic sphere, and included fundamental changes to the aid and international education sectors. For the Territory of Papua and New Guinea (TPNG), changes included a rapid progression towards independence, a step further than self-government.

The introduction of a subsidy scheme for international students, and the abolition of fees for domestic students, opened up Australian universities to a broader range of students. The equity of access for middle-class students from Australia's region, including the South Pacific, was interpreted as an acknowledgement of the obligation Australia had to the region. The concept of soft power was not in use at the time, but the outcomes of the decision to subsidise higher education for all students were a powerful symbol of Australia's soft power.

Both the subsidy program and the independence of Papua New Guinea were part of Whitlam's radical policy changes. In conjunction, however, the policies clashed and bureaucrats and departments were required to negotiate through the difficulties. This part offers a clear overview of the complex and intersecting nature of international education policy. These intersections between foreign policy, bilateral relationships and international education continue to cause difficulties for politicians and bureaucrats in the next part of this book.

MANDATES AND MISSTEPS

William Kaputin and Jaking Marimyas

Scholarships are never free from politics, whether through selection (or non-selection), conditions, areas of study or any of the myriad other elements of a scholarship program. In pre-independence Papua New Guinea (PNG) even the perception of intervention in scholarships was enough to stir controversy. A young man, William Kaputin, had a scholarship from the Territory Administration to study at the University of Papua New Guinea (UPNG). In 1970 Kaputin found his scholarship cancelled by authorities. Kaputin was not, however, just any unfortunate student. His brother, John Kaputin was a well-known anticolonialist, had strong connections to Australia and had spent time in Australia in 1970.[1] Australian activist Graeme Dunstan saw the cancellation of William's scholarship as part of a broader program of intimidation of the Kaputin brothers, and wrote to *The Australian* newspaper to complain of 'the destruction of the influence of political leaders such as John Kaputin'.[2] The accusation that William Kaputin's scholarship had been cancelled for political reasons sparked furious responses within the Department of External Territories. Cables were sent refuting the accusation, stating that Kaputin's scholarship had been cancelled because he had failed subjects,[3] and James Griffin, an Australian lecturer in history who would go on to become Professor of History at UPNG, responded to the Dunstan accusations with his own letters to the editor of *The Australian*. The second of these notes that Kaputin's scholarship had been reinstated after he passed his examinations.[4]

This event is consequential, not because a scholarship was cancelled for political reasons – a claim that is plausible but for which there is insufficient evidence – but because the accusation of such was so potentially damaging to the colonial administration. The administration was furious that such an accusation was made.

---

1   John Kaputin completed his Junior Certificate in Australia, and had also spent two years at the East–West Center in Hawai'i on a scholarship – the first Papua New Guinean to do so. His feelings about Australia and Australian colonial rule were well known – in an interview published in the *Pacific Islands Monthly* in February 1970 he was explicit: 'New Guinea must eventually be for the New Guineans'. John Kaputin, 'In New Guinea, as Elsewhere "Violence Is a Reality Which You Have to Face"', *Pacific Islands Monthly*, 1970.
2   Graeme Dunstan, 'Letter to the Editor: Kaputins Victimised', *The Australian*, 12 June 1970.
3   'Kaputin | Cablegram | 30 June', A452, 1970/2871, 1970, National Archives of Australia (NAA).
4   JT Griffin, 'Letter to the Editor: Reinstated', *The Australian*, 1970.

Taking a less controversial path, Jaking Marimyas was a TPNG student who came to Australia in 1974 to upgrade her teaching qualification in Canberra.[5] Marimyas was educated in a mission environment; her father was a pastor in the Evangelical Lutheran Church of Papua New Guinea. In order to further her education, she had to travel to a boarding school two hours by boat from her house – and then a second school in Lae. All her teachers in this school were expatriates. Her older brother had been given a church scholarship to study in Australia when he was 12, so the idea of travel for education was clearly accepted within her family. In an interview, however, Marimyas notes that her younger sister was only able to study until Year 2 because the church had a limited number of places and these were to be rationed out between families. Marimyas did not continue past Year 9, as she did not achieve the required grades, but instead went on to Teachers College. After a few years teaching she returned to Teachers College for a 'localisation program'. The college itself was run by the Lutheran Church, but the Australian Government and the PNG Administration funded a program to send students to Australia to upgrade their Certificate qualifications to Diplomas. Marimyas's partner, also a teacher, was also selected to travel to Canberra.

Marimyas returned to PNG and continued to teach and was married in the same year that PNG gained its independence. She continued to teach after the birth of her children, and to teach along with her husband. In the 1990s Marimyas and her husband were both selected for another Australian Government scholarship, and studied in Brisbane. Their initial scholarships, in 1974, no doubt put them in a good position when it came to accessing further opportunities. It also provided Jaking with a level of independence and autonomy that was rare for women in PNG in the 1970s.

As Marimyas's story and stories from previous decades have shown – the path to education from TPNG in Australia was incredibly difficult and relied on a whole series of events and decisions being made in support of the students. The story of William Kaputin highlights the contingent nature of Australian support. Despite these factors, there were few other options for the pursuit of higher education for aspiring Papua New Guineans.

These student stories also allow us to see the different roles that scholarships played, particularly in the 1970s. They also highlight the political overlay when it came to scholarship awarding, and rescinding.

---

5   Jaking Marimyas, interview by Jemma Purdey, 17 December 2014, in David Lowe, Jemma Purdey, and Jonathan Richie, 'Scholarships and Connections: Australia, Indonesia and Papua New Guinea, 1960–2010', oral history data set, Deakin University, 2015.

5
Radical subsidies

The election of the Whitlam Government in 1972 had a significant impact on the Australian foreign and domestic policy landscape. His approach in relation to higher education was radical. The removal of university fees was a historically significant decision that opened up access to Australian higher education to many previously excluded, bringing thousands of students into the country. These sweeping changes also impacted overseas students already in the country, such as 'private' students and those sponsored under various scholarship programs. Changes were also made to the aid and development sector, with the introduction of an agency focused on the delivery of aid: the Australian Development Assistance Agency (ADAA). The ADAA sharpened the Australian Government approach to aid and while the agency did not survive a change of government in 1975, it marked an important milestone in Australia's aid program and the development of policies related to aid and development.

As part of these profound changes to Australia's policy settings, Prime Minister Gough Whitlam did not, however, move the focus of Australia or Australia's foreign policy towards the Pacific. His active 'middle power' foreign policy was more focused on Asia and relationships with Indonesia and China.[1] The Whitlam Government's most comprehensive Pacific policy was related to the acceleration of independence in Papua New Guinea (PNG). For Whitlam, and Fraser after him, the broader Pacific was not an area of foreign policy focus. This is despite the 1970s marking a period of significant political and social change in the Pacific, with Fiji gaining independence in

---

1   Derek McDougall, 'Edward Gough Whitlam, 1916–2014: An Assessment of his Political Significance', *Round Table* 104, no. 1 (2015): 31–40, doi.org/10.1080/00358533.2015.1005360.

1970, and decolonisation being a part of Pacific political deliberations for the whole decade. Scholarships and the subsidies mentioned above did have an impact for many students in Pacific Island countries and territories, but while they were offered there, they were administered without a focus on the Pacific.

This chapter investigates the radical policy of overseas student subsidies introduced by the Whitlam Government and kept in place by the Fraser Government. Because of its size and scale, this subsidy scheme had a far greater reach and impact in Australia's geographic region than any previous or concurrent scholarship program. The chapter addresses the more formal scholarship programs that continued during this period, collectively known as Development Training Scholarships. It also addresses the development of a significant South Pacific regional institution, the University of the South Pacific (USP), and how USP both supported and conflicted with Australia's scholarship programs in the South Pacific over the 1970s and into the 1980s.

Until 1973, private overseas students in Australia (who were by far the majority of overseas students) paid the same tertiary fees as Australian students. Whitlam's policy of abolishing fees for tertiary study also applied to those overseas students. However, a quota of 10,000 overseas students was put in place.[2] This decision turned Australia's entire overseas students' cohort into an aid program overnight, with the government effectively underwriting the tertiary education of any student who could gain entry to an Australian institution (and also get a visa). Whitlam embraced this facet of the policy change, noting in a speech at the University of Adelaide in 1974 that while the previous system of fee-paying students had been an adjunct to the aid program, the abolishment of fees would 'considerably increase indirect assistance to private students of this kind', while he emphasised that most private students were coming from developing countries.[3] Whitlam also used this speech to outline what he saw as the benefits of sponsored and private overseas students in Australia, both to the developing countries that they came from and returned to, and to Australia, where he saw the program as achieving the 'growth of bonds between Australia and the developing countries, a heightened level of understanding between us, and … a withering away of xenophobia, isolationism and racism in Australia'.[4]

---

2 David Lim, 'Jackson and the Overseas Students', *Australian Journal of Education* 33, no. 1 (1989): 3, doi.org/10.1177/000494418903300101.
3 Gough Whitlam, 'Australia and Asia: The Challenge of Education (Speech at the University of Adelaide, 5 March 1974)', A1209, 1974/6740, 1974, National Archives of Australia (NAA).
4 Gough Whitlam, 'Australia and Asia: The Challenge of Education (Speech at the University of Adelaide, 5 March 1974)', A1209, 1974/6740, 1974, NAA.

The Whitlam Government was in power for less than two years after this speech. However, during that short period the ADAA was constituted, which had an impact on the way the overseas student policies, sponsored and private, were implemented and managed. These new administrative arrangements continued to influence the management of students, both positively and negatively, until a subsequent review in 1977.

The period over the 1970s and into the 1980s was marked by a number of changes in the way the Australian aid program was managed. The short-lived nature of the ADAA, and then the creation of the Australian Development Aid Bureau (ADAB) within the Department of Foreign Affairs, led to focus being placed on the administration (rather that the implementation) of aid. Nevertheless, scholarships were still being provided under the Colombo Plan, and the aforementioned Development Training Scholarships. The administration of those programs was shared across the Department of Education and the Department of Foreign Affairs, leading to confusion. This led to a review of the services provided to sponsored overseas students in 1977, which is discussed later in this chapter.

In 1979 the Fraser Government made an attempt to rein in what was an incredibly popular subsidy program with the introduction of an Overseas Student Charge (OSC), which was set at approximately 25 per cent of the full costs of tertiary education. This was part of a suite of policy changes also requiring overseas students to return to their home country for at least two years after completion of their studies before being eligible to apply for migrant entry to Australia.[5]

The 1970s were monumental in the politics and status of Pacific Island territories, colonies and nations. The year 1970 marked the independence of Fiji, after 10 years of constitutional negotiations between the United Kingdom, iTaukei leaders and Fijian Indian leaders. In this process, however, there was little community consultation or parliamentary debate, and independence was not universally supported by the indigenous iTaukei community in Fiji. As Tracey Banivanua-Mar noted, this process was 'not about Indigenous nationalist movements making it impossible for colonial administrations to stay',[6] but more about the United Kingdom no longer having the funds or electoral mandate required to maintain an empire on the other side of the world. The process of independence also failed to resolve

---

5   John Goldring, *Mutual Advantage* (Canberra: Australian Government Publishing Service, 1984), 33.
6   Tracey Banivanua-Mar, *Decolonisation and the Pacific: Indigenous Globalisation and the Ends of Empire*, Critical Perspectives on Empire (Cambridge: Cambridge University Press, 2014), 159.

many of the lingering issues of race and representation, a stratification in Fijian society that had been encouraged by the colonial administration. Historian Brij Lal has written that the constitution did not resolve issues of race and representation:

> the 'consensus' constitution of independent Fiji did not mark any radical departure from the colonial past; on the contrary, it entrenched the very same principles that had governed Fiji's colonial politics.[7]

The situation across the Pacific was changing for many island territories and colonies; a process of decolonisation was forced as the British divested itself and the international community became less tolerant of wealthy nations maintaining colonies or trustee territories.[8] This wave of change created unique problems for the small island states of the Pacific. Although Tuvalu's independence came at the end of the 1970s, at independence 'Tuvalu had just two university graduates, and in one ministry only the minister and his secretary had more than primary education'.[9] Those that were educated, across the Pacific, were often the beneficiaries of tertiary education in the 'metropole', the universities of the imperial powers. Rosewarne noted that this ensured that 'so many of the personnel who made up the independent states, including the incumbent political leaders, were products of the colonial systems'.[10] This was not unique for decolonising nations across the world, but the nature of formal decolonisation and the small populations which characterised the Pacific made this reliance more complicated.

The growth of regionalism, not only the type forced by colonial powers, was also a feature of the 1970s. As territories became self-governing they were entitled to entry into the South Pacific Forum. PNG became a member in 1974, with Michael Somare, PNG's Chief Minister, noting that their 'ethnic and cultural ties were with the island nations of the South Pacific',[11] a clear signal that PNG saw their political future tied firmly to the Pacific, not only Australia.

---

7   Brij V Lal, 'Politics since Independence: Continuity and Change, 1970–1982', in *Politics in Fiji: Studies in Contemporary History*, ed. Brij V Lal, 74–106 (Sydney: Allen & Unwin, 1986), 75.
8   Despite this shift in mood, both the USA and France have maintained territories in the Pacific.
9   Jack Corbett and John Connell, 'All the World is a Stage: Global Governance, Human Resources, and the "Problem" of Smallness', *Pacific Review* 28, no. 3 (2015): 445, doi.org/10.1080/09512748.2015.1011214.
10 Stuart Rosewarne, 'Australia's Changing Role in the South Pacific: Global Restructuring and the Assertion of Metropolitan State Authority', *Journal of Australian Political Economy*, no. 40 (1997): 85.
11 'PNG Hails its New Ties with Islands', *The Fiji Times*, 25 March 1974, 4.

Overseas student subsidies were introduced after higher education fees for domestic students were abolished by the Whitlam Government in 1974. The subsidies were not targeted or directed towards a particular nation or area of study. Students from any country in the world, but largely from the Asia-Pacific region, were able to come to Australia for school and tertiary education without incurring fees. This opened up access to many in the region who could not have previously afforded study in Australia. The funding for international students by the government quickly became part of university funding structures, and overseas students became a larger proportion of students on campus. In 1974, just prior to the introduction of subsidies, overseas students made up over 6 per cent of the university student population.[12] Some students were still sponsored via aid scholarship programs, but most students were privately funded. Some of these scholarships are discussed later in this chapter. The government was later able to claim the subsidy amount as a proportion of Australia's Official Development Assistance (ODA) when reporting to the Organisation for Economic Co-operation and Development's Development Assistance Committee (known as OECD DAC), marking it as an aid program. The subsidy scheme became a significant investment; by 1983 the Commonwealth was spending $85.4 million on private overseas students through the subsidy arrangement.[13]

The subsidy program appealed primarily to nations with a strong or growing middle class, such as Malaysia and Singapore. The subsidy system allowed for private students to study in Australia, but it also allowed governments from around the region to sponsor their students to study in Australia without having to pay significant fees, allowing them to pay the stipends for a greater number of students. The subsidy program grew in popularity across the years after its introduction. In 1979 the subsidy scheme was amended by the Fraser Government to include an Overseas Student Charge (OSC). This was equal, at the time of introduction, to about 25 per cent of the potential 'full cost' fee. The revenue from the fee was not provided to the institution, but was considered part of the government's consolidated revenue. David Lim argued that:

---

12   This figure of 5,899 students was a reduction from a high of 6,300 students in 1972; Australian Universities Commission, *Report of the Australian Universities Commission* (Canberra: Australian Government Publishing Service, 1957), nla.gov.au/nla.obj-1363949525, accessed 29 July 2020.
13   Howard Conkey, 'Australia Benefits from Taking Foreign Students', *The Canberra Times*, 7 June 1984, 7.

> [the] OSC was introduced because it was felt that Australia's policy on overseas students was not meeting the country's foreign aid and foreign policy objectives, and that the existing policy was abused as a means for back-door immigration.[14]

Importantly, the OSC was waived for students from PNG and the South Pacific, and paid by the government as a form of aid. The OSC did not overly damage the demand for Australian education, and the numbers of students continued to increase into the 1980s, even with the OSC in place.

By the 1980s the number of Pacific students taking advantage of the subsidies was only one fifth of the number coming from Asia, but between 1980 and 1982 there was an increase of nearly 71 per cent of students from Fiji, and a nearly 90 per cent increase in students from PNG.[15] In 1980 only three students from Tonga were studying in Australia, but by 1982 the figure was 53.[16] Despite these increases, the subsidy program was a minor component of the number of overseas students from the Pacific; for example, in 1983, 205 students from Tonga were sponsored and only 45 were subsidised. In PNG (after independence), 760 students were sponsored, and only 31 were subsidised. Reflecting its higher per capita income, Fiji had 244 sponsored students with 420 students subsidised.[17] In 1982, students from the Pacific represented less than 5 per cent of all private overseas students in tertiary and post-secondary study in Australia.[18]

As the Table 5.1 shows, for countries with a larger or growing middle class, the subsidy program was popular. For smaller, poorer nations such as an independent PNG and Tonga, the number of students who could afford to access the scheme was much smaller. For large, developing nations such as Indonesia, the split between sponsored and subsidised students was almost even.

---

14 Lim, 'Jackson and the Overseas Students', 3.
15 According to the World Bank, Gross National Income increased in Papua New Guinea from (per person) USD220 in 1970 to USD640 in 1979, and in Fiji from USD400 in 1970 to USD1,660 in 1979. These increases reflect a growing income base in these nations, allowing for a greater number of citizens being able to access educational opportunities in Australia. 'The World Bank Data – Fiji', The World Bank Group, data.worldbank.org/country/fiji; 'The World Bank Data – PNG', The World Bank Group, data.worldbank.org/country/PG, accessed 19 April 2023.
16 Stewart E Fraser, 'Australia and International Education: The Goldring and Jackson Reports – Mutual Aid or Uncommon Advantage?', *Vestes* 27, no. 2 (1984): 29.
17 Lim, 'Jackson and the Overseas Students', 15.
18 Fraser, 'Australia and International Education', 28.

5. RADICAL SUBSIDIES

Table 5.1: Sponsored and subsidised overseas students

Country of origin	Sponsored	Subsidised
Fiji	244	420
Tonga	205	45
PNG	760	31
Malaysia	274	6,016
Hong Kong	0	1,388
Indonesia	524	593

Source: David Lim, 'Jackson and the Overseas Students', *Australian Journal of Education* 33, no. 1 (1989): 15.

One of the key elements of the subsidy scheme was that it was a 'catch-all' program. Students were not means tested, meaning that those from wealthy nations, or wealthy individuals from poorer nations, were able to access the scheme without differentiation. While the scheme was open to all, it was more extensively utilised by individuals from particular nations, Malaysian students in particular. There were arguments about the extensive use of the scheme by these students, and the reason for those debates can be seen in the breakdown of Malaysian student numbers in 1983. Two hundred and seventy-four Malaysian students were sponsored by the Australian Government in 1983, but 6,016 students from Malaysia were subsidised.[19] The number of students from Malaysia utilising the scheme became a significant issue for the government in later years when the subsidy program was discontinued. This is discussed in a later chapter. For the time being, however, it is important to note that the subsidy scheme covered the majority of overseas students in Australia. There was a sponsorship program in place, but it was a much smaller program; by 1983 4,270 students were sponsored compared to 10,656 subsidised students.[20]

This scheme opened up the Australian education system, and in particular, Australian universities, to a large number of overseas students who had previously faced multiple barriers to entry. As well as abolishing fees, the changes brought in by the Whitlam Government included changes to the immigration system, and the formal end of the White Australia Policy. These policy shifts made it much easier for students to gain entry into Australian educational institutions. Because the subsidy scheme was not restricted to particular areas of study, the scheme also opened up opportunities to

---

19 Fraser, 'Australia and International Education', 15.
20 Fraser, 'Australia and International Education', 15.

students in areas that were not necessarily considered important for their nation's 'development'. Students were able to choose their institution, and their course, without the influence of their government. This was a marked change to the way in which overseas students were able to access education in Australia.

While the Colombo Plan, the Australian International Award Scheme and the Commonwealth Scholarship and Fellowship Scheme continued into the 1970s, a new scheme with a development focus was also put in place. These Development Training Scholarships were run by the International Training Section of the Department of Foreign Affairs, who worked in collaboration with various other departments including Education and External Territories.[21] These scholarships were 'aimed at promoting goodwill',[22] which again highlights the amorphous nature of scholarships: a 'development' scholarship where the aim is goodwill rather than development. The scholarships, by the name they were given, were able to serve multiple goals and be interpreted by stakeholders in the way they preferred.

Because of the engagement of so many departments and divisions, these scholarships were difficult and time-consuming to administer. In 1972 a Parliamentary Joint Committee on Foreign Affairs reported on the training policies within the aid program. The committee noted that the 'basic principle guiding sponsored training arrangements has remained that it is for the recipient governments to determine their own needs and priorities and to select candidates for training abroad'.[23] This highlighted the lack of control exercised by the Australian Government and its representatives in selection of candidates, and control over the areas of study that students could enrol in. The programs were, by the nature of their administration, divorced from the country-specific bilateral aid programs that were operating at the time. In 1971 there were 3,020 overseas students in Australia sponsored by the Australian Government, and 24 students in third country arrangements, sponsored by the Australian Government to study in regional countries (usually in the South Pacific).[24]

---

21   'Development of Australia's Overseas Training Aid Program | Background Paper', A4250, 1984/1428, 1984, NAA.
22   'Development of Australia's Overseas Training Aid Program | Background Paper', A4250, 1984/1428, 1984, NAA.
23   'Parliamentary Joint Committee on Foreign Affairs 1972', A1838, 561/6/18/3 Part 1, NAA.
24   'Parliamentary Joint Committee on Foreign Affairs 1972', A1838, 561/6/18/3 Part 1, NAA.

The decision of the Whitlam Government to create a specialised aid agency allowed for the policy and administration elements of these scholarships to be concentrated in one place. This consolidation occurred in December 1973. Despite this merging of scholarship management and administration, the scholarships continued to be largely disconnected from the bilateral aid programs that were in place. The types of awards available included secondary school scholarships, undergraduate awards (the bulk of the scholarships), ad hoc attachments (such as with research institutes) and International Training Courses (ITCs). These ITCs were often focused on training civil servants.

In 1977 the Fraser Cabinet made a decision to integrate the training program into the broader aid program, making more explicit the 'development' element of these scholarships. A decision was also made to concentrate on in-Australia training, and scholarships for secondary school study to be avoided where possible.[25] The Development Training Scholarships remained a very small element of the overall student intake, with the majority of overseas students benefiting from the subsidy scheme. Nevertheless, all students, sponsored and subsidised, were being supported by the government in some way, either through the process of application and placement, or through welfare support that was coordinated through the Department of Foreign Affairs aid bureau, with support from state offices of the Department of Foreign Affairs.

A review of services provided for overseas sponsored students was conducted from 1977 to 1978. Bureaucrats preparing for the review found 'there has been no formal definition of both needs and the range and level of servicing'[26] of these students.[27] In 1977/78, according to the Department of Prime Minister and Cabinet, there were 4,293 sponsored students in Australia.[28] A variety of advice was circulated at the time of the review, including one paper that advised that 'ADAB should maintain control over the nature and allocation of placement. (In other words, self or home

---

25 'Development of Australia's Overseas Training Aid Program | Background Paper', A4250, 1984/1428, 1984, NAA.
26 'Report on a Review of the Range and Level of Services for Sponsored Overseas Trainees under the Australian International Training Aid Program | B. Bray, Principal Executive Officer, International Training and Education Branch, Department of Foreign Affairs | 2 February', A4250 1977/1724 1978, NAA.
27 In the context of this review and investigation, the sponsored students were considered to be those funded by both the Australian Government and those sponsored by other governments.
28 'Overseas Students | JT O'Connor, First Assistant Secretary Welfare Division, Department of Prime Minister and Cabinet | 30 March', A1209 1977/609 Part 2, 1979, NAA.

government placement is not a practicable proposition)'.[29] The review represented a fairly comprehensive stocktake of both the services provided to students, and the options for what could and should be provided.

This review of services provided for overseas students had been triggered by a number of factors, including staffing levels within the Department of Foreign Affairs, and the way in which sponsored students had been supported after the consolidation of the scholarship functions into that department. Support had previously been spread between the Department of Education and the Department of Foreign Affairs. So, a change that had been designed to make the administration of sponsored and overseas students more efficient and easier to manage had, in practice, increased the workload for Australian aid administrators to an unmanageable level.

One outcome of the review was a list of principles to apply to the range and quality of services to sponsored overseas students. This list was intended to be a guide for policy development and implementation:

1. The student should be made to feel at home and increasingly at ease in our country without being allowed to become alienated from his own. We should be particularly sensitive to the trainee's cultural differences and see that his needs are handled with professional competence.
2. We should not lose sight of the basic objective of the student's presence in Australia – not primarily his personal interest but the development of his home country; both are more likely to be promoted if the student is at ease and free of serious worries.
3. Special attention should be paid to personal welfare problems of students, or to signs that such problems may be arising. 'Welfare' in this sense means personal and emotional difficulties and not problems arising from routine day-to-day obligations.
4. A high degree of self-reliance should be fostered in the trainee – he should be guided to stand on his own feet and handle his own routine requirements himself or through non-ADAB channels. Outright 'cosseting' is to be avoided.
5. Increasing use should be made of existing student facilities in institutions, national students groups and community groups, with a modest measure of financial support from the Bureau in appropriate instances for this purpose.

---

29 'Report on a Review of the Range and Level of Services for Sponsored Overseas Trainees under the Australian International Training Aid Program | B. Bray, Principal Executive Officer, International Training and Education Branch, Department of Foreign Affairs | 2 February', A4250 1977/1724 1978, NAA.

6. The difficulty of differentiating between sponsored and private overseas students should be accepted as a fact of life. There should, however, be a distinct shade of difference in the Bureau's handling of the private group which should be directed even more firmly to attend to their own routine needs and rely on their student/national organisations or diplomatic missions …[30]

The issues highlighted by this list of principles, in particular that students should not be overly supported and that differentiating between sponsored and private students was futile, were concerns that have reappeared over the decades of policymaking on international students. The advice that students should be made to feel at home and free of worries had also featured in efforts to bolster student support since the establishment of the Overseas Student Coordinating Committees in the 1950s.[31] The government appeared keen, through these principles, to support the development of national groupings of students, perhaps to facilitate student support with minimal government intervention. In this approach, and even within the principles themselves, a key tension in overseas sponsored student support was highlighted. Successive governments saw great value in the overseas student cohort for development potential and the potential for influence in developing countries in the region, identified as goodwill, and they acknowledged that supporting students during their studies was required to achieve this goal. However, they were also concerned that students should not be 'cosseted', and the Fraser Government was not prepared to fund extensive student support infrastructure. Thus, they sought to have these services provided by peers and community volunteers. In a final twist in the policy conundrum, it appeared that government then became concerned about the political activities of students, with a desire to direct the 'agency' that students had developed during their period of study.[32] This ended in the government coopting or directing the services that were being offered to students. There was a conflict between the desire to be 'hands off' and the desire to control student development to ensure that it supported the outcomes the

---

30   'Principles to Apply to Range and Quality of Services to Sponsored Overseas Students in Australia Following Approval by the Minister for Foreign Affairs (File 77/1724) | 24 February', A1209 1977/609 Part 2, 1978, NAA.
31   Anna Kent, 'Overseas Students Coordinating Committees: The Origins of Student Support in Australia?', *Transitions: Journal of Transient Migration* 4, no. 1 (2020): 99–114, doi.org/10.1386/tjtm_00015_1.
32   'The Sinister Role of ADAB in Overseas Students' Affairs', *Tharunka*, 24 September 1979, 6.

government sought. The review of services to overseas students in 1977/78 is an excellent example of how this conflict between ambitions and actions played out, but was never fully resolved.

Public servants also wished to disentangle the way in which sponsored and private students were supported, with ADAB very keen only to support private students in welfare cases when absolutely necessary.[33] ADAB was able to outsource some of the work they undertook to Coordinating Committees for Overseas Students, organisations that had been sidelined over the 1970s as the number of overseas students in Australia increased through the subsidy scheme. This move was controversial for some: an article in the University of New South Wales student newspaper *Tharunka* was scathing of the role of ADAB and the Coordinating Committees, describing the committees as being cultivated as 'some "yes" men on some country campuses acting on their behalf'.[34] Some students and others were suspicious of the motivations of these groups and their government sponsors.

While the 1977 review of services made some changes, the overall support for sponsored students in the broader overseas student program remained a consistent, although small, element of the overall international student program. By 1982, the largest number of sponsored students was from Indonesia, with 404 students. Reflecting its position as both a key aid recipient, and a very low-income country (and thus with a smaller population able to make use of the subsidy scheme), an independent PNG was the second largest sponsorship recipient, with 175 students. No other Pacific nations were in the top recipients of scholarships. However, including students who were part of third country programs (for example, students sponsored by Australia to study at the University of South Pacific or the University of Papua New Guinea), there were 313 Pacific sponsored students in undergraduate programs. A review of education in the South Pacific commissioned by ADAB in the early 1980s noted that the 'students are drawn from all main South Pacific regions, but the greater numbers are from Fiji, Western Samoa, Solomon Is., Vanuatu and Tonga'.[35]

---

33   'Report on a Review of the Range and Level of Services for Sponsored Overseas Trainees under the Australian International Training Aid Program | B Bray, Principal Executive Officer, International Training and Education Branch, Department of Foreign Affairs | 2 February', A4250 1977/1724 1978, NAA.
34   'Development of Australia's Overseas Training Aid Program | Background Paper', A4250, 1984/1428, 1984, NAA.
35   TN Lockyer, 'Undergraduate and Postgraduate Training for Students from South Pacific Countries', ed. Bureau Australian Development Assistance, A8950, 5270, 1983, NAA.

Reflecting an issue that would become more important over the 1980s, between 1979 and 1982 the majority of sponsored students (from all nations) were male, with the proportion hovering around 80 per cent of the total number.[36] This was a particular issue as legislation mandating equal opportunities for both men and women was passed in parliaments across a number of jurisdictions in Australia.

The subsidy program was put in place by Whitlam for a variety of reasons, and it was a very popular policy within the region. In concert with the full removal of the White Australia Policy, the subsidy scheme was a demonstration that the Australian Government was acting in the best interests of most of its regional partners, not only itself. In this instance, the subsidy scheme achieved the outcomes that the Chifley Government had expected that the South-East Asian Scholarship Scheme would when it was introduced in 1948. The subsidy scheme was of a scale not imagined in 1948, and had a far greater impact on Australia's relationships in the Asian and Pacific regions.

The subsidy scheme also led to a huge increase in overseas student numbers in Australia. The numbers decreased slightly after the Fraser Government introduced an Overseas Student Charge, but soon recovered. The management of students in Australia was constantly under review, whether as part of the Australian aid program (1972) or as a standalone review (1977). This was driven in part by the expansion of the number of students, which increased the workload for those tasked with welfare and social support for the students. The Coordinating Committees that had been established to deal with the first large influx of overseas students in the 1950s were reinvigorated by Australian aid funding. The reviews were also driven by change and uncertainty in the administration of the Australian aid program. With the establishment of the Australian Development Assistance Agency (ADAA) as a standalone agency by the Whitlam Government, aid policy was given a more dominant position within the government and foreign policy conversations. The Aid Policy Section still had to work hard to gain a seat at the table for important discussions, such as those surrounding the future of an independent PNG. Even though the ADAA was very short lived, a specialised section dealing with aid funding lasted through the

---

36 Stewart E Fraser, 'Overseas Students in Australia: Governmental Policies and Institutional Programs', *Comparative Education Review* 28, no. 2 (1984): 282, doi.org/10.1086/446435.

changes. The independent nation of PNG became the centre of Australian aid funding, once again preventing serious policy deliberation or focus on the broader Pacific, which itself was shifting politically and socially.

By the early 1980s there was a feeling that the subsidy scheme could not be sustained in the long term. This situation, and uncertainty about the place of overseas students within the aid program, led to the commissioning of two reviews that addressed overseas students: the Goldring Report and the Jackson Report, which are discussed in detail in the next part of this book.

The introduction of Overseas Student Subsidies by the Whitlam Government had a profound and long-lasting impact on the Australian tertiary education system. In this period the focus of bureaucrats and stakeholders was largely on this broad-based scheme, not on the Development Training Scheme. In previous decades, schemes such as the Colombo Plan and the Commonwealth Scholarships had overwhelmed discussions of overseas students, in many cases giving an unrealistic picture of the overseas student cohort. While the subsidy scheme did not dominate discourse or frame discussions of aid as the Colombo Plan did, it did open up the Australian education sector to a demographic that had previously been unable to afford overseas education, in particular the growing middle classes in South-East Asia and in some parts of the South Pacific. It also allowed for students to study across a range of subject areas, rather than those deemed important for the development of recipient countries.

Nevertheless, for the vast majority of the population of the South Pacific, the opportunity for access to the Australian tertiary education system came with scholarships, not subsidies. And access to those scholarships was largely controlled by the colonial administrations, and then after independence, new governments. The Australian Government had, until the mid-1970s, been relatively comfortable with this situation, perceiving that it allowed for governments 'on the ground' to make the best decisions in relation to candidates and areas of study that were most relevant to the development of these fledgling states. One consequence of this mode of selection was that about 80 per cent of awardees were men, which became a difficult issue for the Whitlam Government in particular. Women had gained the right to equal pay for equal work in Australia in 1972, and various changes to legislation to mandate equal opportunities were introduced federally, and in various states over the 1970s. In addition, the passing of the Racial Discrimination Act of 1975 raised concerns over how racially discriminatory selection policies in countries such as Fiji and Malaysia would reflect on the scholarship programs. The issue of selection policies was also raised in the review of overseas students commenced in 1977. It was almost a decade later that these issues of gender and race were comprehensively addressed within a scholarship program design, but it is worth noting that the status quo of male-dominated cohorts was not entirely satisfactory to the Whitlam, and then Fraser, governments.

The political situation across the Pacific changed at a rapid rate during the 1970s, with a wave of decolonisation sweeping across Fiji, PNG, Tuvalu, Kiribati and later Vanuatu. But as discussed in this chapter, in many of these nations that independence came not at the insistence or resistance of the indigenous population, but rather as a result of British and Australian domestic pressures, financial and social.

This process of decolonisation was also part of the Australian story, with self-government and then independence for the Territory of Papua and New Guinea. This is discussed in the next chapter.

6

Independence for Papua New Guinea

The 1970s again featured the confused manner in which the Territory of Papua and New Guinea (TPNG) was viewed by bureaucrats in both TPNG and Canberra. Adding to the confusion, however, was the move towards self-government, and by 1975, independence. Funding of education in the territories was very limited in the 1960s, as has been discussed in previous chapters. The move to independence, accelerated by the Whitlam Government, highlighted the previous lack of investment and created a demand for more active intervention by the Australian Government to support secondary and tertiary education.[1]

The nature of Australia's colonial rule and slow progress towards facilitating Papua New Guinea (PNG) independence did not prove to be robust building blocks for PNG as a nation-state. Stephen Henningham wrote for the Parliamentary Library in 1995, 'nothing had ever been done by the Australian colonial administration to create a national spirit amongst the 500 or so ethnic groups in Papua New Guinea'.[2] The Australian Government had established a Legislative Assembly and there was a flag and national anthem;

---

1   Derek McDougall argues that the foundations for this accelerated timeline were laid by Andrew Peacock as Minister for External Affairs in the previous coalition government: Derek McDougall, 'Edward Gough Whitlam, 1916–2014: An Assessment of his Political Significance', *Round Table* 104, no. 1 (2015): 31–40, doi.org/10.1080/00358533.2015.1005360. A report in the *Pacific Island Monthly* in 1970 noted that when Gough Whitlam toured PNG as opposition leader he ended the 'gentleman's agreement' keeping Papua New Guinea out of Australian domestic politics. See: 'New Guinea Becomes Battlefield for Australian Party Politics', *Pacific Islands Monthly*, 1 Febuary 1970.
2   Stephen Henningham, 'No Easy Answers: Australia and the Pacific Islands Region', ed. Parliamentary Research Service (Canberra: Department of the Parliamentary Library, 1995), 360.

however, there was also an ongoing separatist conflict, which escalated in Bougainville. The Australian Government understood the reality and the possibility of divisions in PNG following independence. Briefing notes written in 1970 for a visit to PNG by Prime Minister Gorton mentioned that one of the fragmenting factors in the country was 'regionalism pressure in Bougainville and Gazelle Peninsula'.[3] More positively, these same briefing notes observed that education and the creation of an indigenous police force was 'helping to remove tribal rivalry and suspicion between different groups'.[4] The election of the Whitlam Government in 1971 accelerated the push for independence, and the government made a commitment to grant PNG independence by 1975.

Scholarships, both the domestic Commonwealth Scholarships and the territory scholarships, continued to be offered in TPNG in the early 1970s much as they had in the 1960s, with scholarships offered to students for secondary schooling and some awards given for tertiary-level study. There were also many scholarships awarded for students to study in tertiary institutions in TPNG, such as the University of Papua New Guinea (UPNG). However, with self-government and independence far more likely at the beginning of the 1970s than they were only a few years earlier, the pressure on the Australian Government to lift educational attainment in TPNG was acute.

A note written by the Department of External Territories in April 1970, in response to a parliamentary question, discussed the status of tertiary scholarships in TPNG. The note explained the status at the time as being '370 indigenous scholarship holders and 17 expatriate scholarship holders'.[5] The use of the word 'expatriate' represented an evolution in terminology from previous government documents (from the 1960s) that referred to these students as 'European'. This is a formal acknowledgement of what had been implied by previous scholarships: that race was fundamental to the understanding of who was an Australian citizen. Expatriates is a term that represents foreign nationals, despite TPNG being a territory of Australia at the time. In addition to the changing language in 1970, officials in the Department of External Affairs in Canberra were concerned that non-indigenous students were not mandated to return to TPNG to work in

---

3   'Briefing Notes for PM Trip to PNG July 1970', A452 1970/3068, 1970, National Archives of Australia (NAA).
4   'Briefing Notes for PM Trip to PNG July 1970', A452 1970/3068, 1970, NAA.
5   'Tertiary Scholarship PNG, Minute | 8 April', A452, 1970/4026, NAA.

the administration, which was considered by George Warwick Smith, the Secretary of the Department, as an 'unsatisfactory feature' of the PNG tertiary scholarship scheme.[6]

However, the Department of External Territories wished to have a 'non-discriminatory scheme', so recommendations were made that some level of means testing should be supported. Another Department of External Territories minute also recommended that students should be bonded to the administration, given the advantages that a qualification would grant them on return to TPNG, such as opening a private medical practice.[7] This minute, written by the Acting Assistant Secretary and seen by the Secretary of the Department, reflects a concern that the administration should not be exploited for personal gain through the scholarship program. This desire to bond students to the TPNG Administration on return reflects a fundamental contradiction in the policy settings. These students were consistently understood as being 'non-Australians', but to seek for them to be bonded indicated a level of control only possible within a scholarship for citizens. These contradictions and concerns were again raised only months after this minute was written, when indigenous graduates in TPNG were expressing their concerns that their pay rates were being determined by their skin colour, rather than their qualifications. An article in the *Post-Courier* in June 1970 noted that 'Australian' doctors were paid A$170 a fortnight while 'coloured' doctors were paid A$45 for the same period.[8] This issue was raised by a delegation of medical students from TPNG, who were concerned that the pay they were to receive following their training would have little to do with their qualifications.

The early 1970s also marked a widening view of the options for development assistance to TPNG, with moves to open up the territory to outside aid and development agencies such as the World Bank and Japan, among others. Max Loveday, a senior Department of Foreign Affairs official, suggested Australia should seek to sponsor TPNG's entry into the Colombo Plan arrangement, allowing it to access further bilateral donors, and perhaps the scholarships that had to that point been reserved for foreign nationals.[9] In 1972 the Minister for External Territories in the Coalition Government, Andrew Peacock, made a speech at the Australian Institute of International

---

6   George Warwick Smith, 'Tertiary Scholarships – Eligibility of Expatriate Residents | 18 May', A452, 1970/4026, 1970, NAA.
7   'Tertiary Scholarship PNG, Minute | 8 April', A452, 1970/4026, NAA.
8   'Salary Policy "Based on Skin Color"', *Post Courier (Port Morsby)*, 11 June 1970, 8.
9   'Salary Policy "Based on Skin Color"', *Post Courier (Port Morsby)*, 11 June 1970, 8.

Affairs advising the TPNG Administration to seek financial help from countries other than Australia. A newspaper article about his speech reports that he said 'Papua New Guinea would have an important place in its foreign relations for Indonesia, Singapore, Malaysia, the Philippines, Japan and the island nations of the South Pacific'.[10] Discussions were also held in early 1973 about the potential for Japan to become a donor to TPNG, with Department of Foreign Affairs officials suggesting that Australia could act as a facilitator for discussions.[11] With senior government officials making speeches and bureaucrats seeking alternative donors and funding sources, it is not surprising that bureaucrats in Australia, and leaders in TPNG, were not entirely clear on Australia's position regarding ongoing aid funding to an independent PNG.

The path towards independence was accelerated by the Whitlam Government, following its election in 1972. The federal government was grappling with the changes necessary to reflect the change of TPNG from colony to nation. Finding itself in a potentially vulnerable position as preparations for independence took shape, the Aid Policy Section of the Department of Foreign Affairs (DFA) prepared a comprehensive paper: 'External Aid and the Future Development of Papua New Guinea'. The Aid Policy Section was concerned that it needed a seat at the table of the interdepartmental discussions about the future status of PNG. The report outlined the perceived and known positions of other government departments, including Treasury: 'Treasury may seek to preserve present arrangements for as long as possible through tight budgetary control over official capital flows to PNG'; Trade: 'we may expect difficulties in persuading Trade to give sufficient attention and sympathy to the trading needs of PNG'; Defence: 'the most attractive type of defence aid to PNG will ... be that associated with the maintenance of internal security and order'; and other areas of government.[12] This briefing paper reflected the concerns of the DFA, who understood that as soon as PNG became independent it would be responsible for the diplomatic and aid relationships. This in itself was not necessarily a problem, but the DFA expected resistance from the Department of External Territories, who was the lead agency on all things related to TPNG at the time. However, Department of External Territories

---

10   'Welcome New Aid Peacock Tells PNG', *Post Courier*, 9 June 1972, 1.
11   Max Loveday, 'Foreign Aid to Papua New Guinea | 2 February', A1838, 3080/10/4/3 Part 1, 1973, NAA.
12   'External Aid and the Future Development of Papua New Guinea | Aid Policy Section | April', A1838, 3080/10/4/3 Part 1, 1972, NAA.

was a department that was 'running down'[13] as its main colonial responsibility gained independence. The worries, both large and small, expressed in this document reflected tensions within the bureaucracy at the time. The DFA wanted to be able to shape the responsibilities and relationships it required in TPNG prior to independence, and felt that interdepartmental disputes would overwhelm a measured and deliberate process.

Despite his department preparing for its own inevitable closure, the Minister for External Territories was endeavouring to ensure that the transition of aid administration was smooth. In 1973 Bill Morrison wrote to Prime Minister Gough Whitlam to 'seek an early government decision on future aid administration'.[14] Morrison suggested that the prime minister establish a PNG Aid Unit within a new aid administrative body (the Australian Development Assistance Agency, or ADAA). He wrote '[W]hichever way the decision runs on this issue I am convinced that the unique character of Papua New Guinea aid has to be a dominant factor in future aid administration'.[15] There was a clear recognition and acceptance that aid to PNG was going to be a dominant, if not overwhelming, component of Australia's aid program in the future, and designing the administration around the requirements of PNG would be prudent.

Papua New Guinean leaders were also concerned about the allocation and administration of aid. In a January 1973 letter to Prime Minister Whitlam, PNG Chief Minister Michael Somare wrote that he was deeply concerned about aid administration after independence, and the impact it could have on national cohesion. His letter highlighted the gravity of the situation:

> Perhaps one of the greatest fears of independence in my country stems from the belief by a very substantial number of my people, particularly the Highlanders, that Australia will make severe reductions in aid as soon as we become independent … Unless we have some firm assurances that this will not be the case, I believe the country could be seriously divided because of this additional strain on a very difficult existing situation.[16]

---

13 'External Aid and the Future Development of Papua New Guinea | Aid Policy Section | April', A1838, 3080/10/4/3 Part 1, 1972, NAA.
14 'Letter to PM Whitlam Re Aid Administration | 8 March', A1838, 3080/10/4/3 Part 1, 1973, NAA.
15 'Letter to PM Whitlam Re Aid Administration | 8 March', A1838, 3080/10/4/3 Part 1, 1973, NAA.
16 Michael Somare, 'Letter – Chief Minister Somare to PM Whitlam | 25 January', A1838, 3080/10/4/3 Part 1, 1973, NAA.

With policy decisions coming from a number of different departments and ministers, and an understanding of the previous failures of Australian efforts to 'develop' TPNG, the concern from PNG leaders that Australia's aid and support could be suddenly reduced was understandable. There were also many areas with a potential for important policy or practical considerations to fall through the cracks – not through malice, or even incompetence, but because of the unforeseen impacts.

The overseas student subsidy scheme was one example of policies having changing implications across the independence period. The planned introduction of the overseas student subsidy program, as discussed in the previous chapter, included the removal of a requirement that the course of study of overseas students had to be of relevance to their homeland. This was a policy that had been put in place by the Department of Immigration, and was perceived to have limited the influx of 'Asian' students into the country to those studying in a priority area. The DFA was troubled with this proposal as it applied to an independent PNG. A briefing written by the Director of the International Training Section, Ric Throssell, noted that:

> [the] policy proposed by the Department of Immigration appears to be quite inconsistent with the special needs of Papua New Guinea in the transitional period and in the period immediately following independence.[17]

Throssell believed that private PNG students should be directed towards courses that 'will be of direct and immediate value in the social and economic development of Papua New Guinea as an independent country'.[18] Throssell also used this briefing note to raise questions around a future training policy for an independent PNG, and how PNG students were to be supported as 'overseas students' in the future. In response to Throssell's brief, the Pacific Branch within DFA responded with its own submission on the changing student policy. Importantly, while they agreed with Throssell in the main, the response from the Pacific Branch noted that they 'would hope Papua New Guinean students can be treated on exactly the same basis as other foreign students, or very close to it'.[19] The note goes on to explain that:

---

17   'Private Students from Papua New Guinea | 5 March', A1838, 3080/10/4/3 Part 1, 1973, NAA.
18   'Private Students from Papua New Guinea | 5 March', A1838, 3080/10/4/3 Part 1, 1973, NAA.
19   'Private Students from Papua New Guinea | Pacific Branch | 8 March', A1838, 3080/10/4/3 Part 1, 1973, NAA.

Papua New Guinea (for good cause) is extremely sensitive to paternalism and could be expected to react sharply to any special arrangements made in their case, irrespective of the purity of our motives.[20]

These events demonstrate that the transition from TPNG as colony to PNG as independent created challenges for Australian policymakers across the federal government. But with an existing (small) cohort of students not subject to the same structures and strictures that were imposed on other overseas students, this was just one more policy question that needed to be answered in the period before PNG became independent.

Meeting agendas and notes from 1974 detail the discussions between Australian DFA officials and PNG Officials, who had travelled to Canberra for talks. These talks included discussions about specific educational aid programs; for example, additional support to UPNG in an effort to support the 'education of more Papua New Guineans at a tertiary level' by increasing the enrolments and decreasing the dropout rate.[21] The Chief Minister, Michael Somare, used a letter from Prime Minister Whitlam to assure members of the PNG Assembly that the Australian Government was committed to giving aid to PNG after independence, noting that he had a 'guarantee' from Whitlam that aid would continue.[22]

Right up to (and past) formal independence on 16 September 1975, the Australian Government was working with the PNG Assembly on the education policies of the newly formed nation, and how the policies of PNG and Australia would intersect. An area of considerable discussion was the prospect of students being sent by their parents to study in Australia. Senior leaders in PNG were eager to send their children to Australia, while the official position of the PNG Government was that PNG students should be educated in PNG, particularly for secondary school. Australian diplomats reported back to Canberra that the Director of Education had determined:

---

20 'Private Students from Papua New Guinea | Pacific Branch | 8 March', A1838, 3080/10/4/3 Part 1, 1973, NAA.
21 'Draft Agenda for Discussions with PNG Officials Canberra | February', A1838, 3080/10/4/3 ANNEX, 1974, NAA. At the time there was also a number of Australian academics working at UPNG including Ken Inglis and James Griffiths .
22 'PNG Promised Conditional Aid', *The Fiji Times*, 5 March 1974, 4.

that educational needs of Papua New Guinea children [are] best served by PNG oriented curriculum, and cited [a] decision by his department to withdraw PNG Government scholarships previously provided for secondary schooling of selected Papua New Guineans in Australia.[23]

Despite this stated policy, a senior official (the Minister for Commerce, Mr NE Olewale) requested permission for his nephews to study their final years of secondary school in Australia.[24] PNG students still had to seek permission to be allowed to enter mainland Australia. Australian diplomats were confused by the situation, agreeing that accepting the students was necessary to maintaining good relations with PNG, while noting the officially stated policy. In this case the students were given permission to enter Australia – but the case did highlight significant conflicts between the policy goals of Australia and PNG when it came to support for the secondary and tertiary education of PNG citizens.

Following on from independence, the relationship between Australia and PNG continued to evolve. However, while these were now two nations working as 'equals', the power dynamics remained firmly colonist–colony. PNG also developed its own bilateral relationships with other nations in the South Pacific, which were more equal.

Australia's aid to PNG continued to support the fledging nation, funding more than 40 per cent of the central government expenditure in 1975.[25] Eligible students seeking tertiary study were able to attend universities in PNG, but those wishing to study in Australia were, finally, able to access the international scholarships available, or make use of the subsidy scheme. As noted earlier, the Development Training Scholarships were selected by the recipient government, and only a very small number of PNG students were able to utilise the subsidy scheme (in 1983 there were 760 sponsored students, and only 31 subsidised students in Australia).

---

23   'Cablegram from Port Moresby to Canberra | 24 January | Peter Aitsi – Ministerial Representations', A1209, 1974/6740, 1975, NAA.
24   'Cablegram from Port Moresby to Canberra | 24 January | Peter Aitsi – Ministerial Representations', A1209, 1974/6740, 1975, NAA.
25   This represented 60 per cent of Australia's aid budget at the time. See *The Contribution of Australian Aid to Papua New Guinea's Development 1975–2000*, Evaluation and Review Series No. 34 (Canberra: AusAID, 2003), 24.

While the future of TPNG had been a point of debate and discussion for the 70 years since Federation, Whitlam revitalised the discussion about the future of Papua New Guinean independence into domestic political debates with a visit to TPNG as Opposition Leader in 1970. In doing so, he placed pressure on those tasked with transition arrangements to hasten policy development, which were further complicated when the subsidy scheme for overseas students was introduced. Bureaucrats, such as Ric Throssell, were attempting to implement policies that were designed without TPNG at front of mind in the design. The Australian colony of TPNG, and then the independent nation of PNG, provided a unique problem for scholarship administrators. Independence in 1975 did allow for PNG to be considered another Pacific nation with which the government had a bilateral relationship. However, the long colonial relationship between Australia and PNG marked all interactions, even though they were now technically equal in the community of nations. For the students of PNG, this now allowed them access to the subsidy scheme and other international development schemes. But these schemes did not address the disadvantage that had been created by decades of insufficient investment in education.

PART 4: 1984–1996

While the 1970s were marked by radical subsidy schemes and independence for Papua New Guinea (PNG), by the 1980s the subsidy scheme was under review. The period covered in this part of the book starts with the handing down of two reports that were intended to guide policy in relation to aid and international students. The intersection of these two reports at the point of international development scholarships is discussed in depth in the first chapter of this part.

The second chapter returns to the more radical theme of Part 3 of the book, with the new scholarship designed to take the place of the subsidy scheme. The Equity and Merit Scholarship (EMSS) was short lived, and within three years had been replaced by another scheme (in name at least). Nevertheless, the EMSS laid the foundation for the scholarships that were to follow and several significant design elements of the program have carried through to the present. The chapter, and part, ends in late 1996, with the introduction of (yet another) new scholarship and the election of the conservative government of John Howard.

Dr Ray Anere, Beatrice Mahuru and Samson Akunaii

The first chapter of this part does not focus on a specific scholarship or scheme, as many of the previous chapters have. Nevertheless, scholarships continued to be offered by the Australian Government during the period that the chapter covers. One of the students who studied during this period was Dr Ray Anere. Anere studied in Australia in the early 1980s – from

1982 to 1985 at The Australian National University (ANU) in Canberra. He went to Australia firstly to take a Bachelor of Letters, then a Master of Arts. He then returned to the University of PNG (UPNG), his employer.

He studied in Australia under an Australian Development Aid Bureau (ADAB) scholarship. In an interview,[1] Anere said he chose ANU because of the existing relationships between academics at ANU and UPNG – highlighting the ongoing connections between ANU and universities in the Pacific, including UPNG. In his reflections, Anere recognised the privilege of studying in Australia, and at ANU specifically. In his interview he described how he had maintained connections with these colleagues. In a post marking the death of Anere in 2015, his brother, Davidson Anere, wrote that as brothers they had both managed to gain their education despite few funds being available. Following his ADAB scholarship studies in Australia, Anere completed his PhD in the USA with the support of a Fulbright Scholarship.[2] In an interview conducted the year before his death, Anere was able to point to one of the key conundrums of scholarships. He noted that there was a certain number of awards promised to PNG by the Australian Government, but these come to individuals as once-in-a-lifetime opportunities. Scholarship programs such as the award Anere benefited from 'make a person a very different person' – the individual impact was often life-changing.[3] His sophisticated understanding of the impact of the scholarships on himself and his nation was notable as it is not often so clearly articulated.

Anere's experience, studying under a number of different scholarships in the process of undertaking several degrees, was not uncommon. James Kaiulo[4] completed his PhD at Macquarie University in 1990 after finishing his undergraduate degree at UPNG (and travelling to Australia on a Rotary travelling scholarship), and then his Masters in Hawaii with another scholarship. Because of his advanced degree, Dr Kaiulo was appointed Pro Vice Chancellor of UPNG within a few years of returning to PNG. Dr Anere, Dr Kaiulo and another alumnus of the period, Dr Sergie Bang,

---

1   Ray Anere, interview by Musawe Sinebare, Port Moresby, 17 December 2014, in David Lowe, Jonathan Ritchie, and Jemma Purdey, 'Scholarships and Connections: Australia, Indonesia and Papua New Guinea, 1960–2010', oral history data set, Deakin University, 2015.
2   Davidson Anere, 'The Spirit of Brotherhood: A Tribute', *My Land My Country* (blog), myland mycountry.wordpress.com/2016/10/08/the-spirit-of-brotherhood-a-tribute-by-davidson-anere/, accessed 22 July 2020 (site discontinued).
3   Ray Anere, interview, 17 December 2014, in Lowe, Purdey and Ritchie, 'Scholarships and Connections'.
4   James Kaiulo, interview by Jonathan Ritchie, Port Moresby, 12 February 2015, in Lowe, Ritchie and Purdey, 'Scholarships and Connections'.

all discussed in interviews rapid promotion on return, and how they were all one of the first Papua New Guineans to gain a PhD in their respective fields. While these achievements are laudable, it is also notable that the first PhDs gained by Papua New Guineans in politics, agriculture and horticulture were only achieved in the mid to late 1980s, more than a decade after independence from Australia – highlighting the failure of successive Australian governments to invest in education in the Territory of Papua and New Guinea during their colonial administration.

The latter part of the decade also saw the introduction of a new secondary school scholarship program for Papua New Guinean senior secondary school students. This scheme, which is discussed in the second chapter of this part, was called the Secondary School Students' Project (SSSP).

An interview with a student who came to Australia as part of the SSSP program, Beatrice Mahuru, gives a great insight into the design flaws of the SSSP.[5] Ms Mahuru completed her senior high school years in Australia, sponsored under the SSSP. On returning to PNG following the completion of her scholarship, Ms Mahuru gained entry into her third choice of university degree, which in itself was a perverse outcome of the SSSP program – as students returning to PNG after study abroad were third in the line of priority for university placements (after local students and international students who had studied in PNG). Ms Mahuru failed to complete her degree after she had a baby in her final year; her new husband was an American lecturer at the university. So, while Ms Mahuru was able to successfully complete her secondary schooling in Australia, her return to PNG was marred not only by social judgement, but also by a disconnect between a donor's 'aid' and recipient government policies.

Another alumnus who studied in Australia during the late 1980s, Samson Akunaii,[6] provides another interesting case study in the difficulties in measuring and understanding the impact of a scholarship program, and clearly demonstrates the issue when a scholarship program has no more specifically defined outcome than 'development'. He studied for an MBA at James Cook University between 1987 and 1989. Mr Akunaii saw himself as a positive story from the scholarships, and discussed the skills he had taken home to PNG following his scholarship. But he saw flaws in the scholarship

---

5   Beatrice Mahuru, interview, 16 December 2014, in Lowe, Purdey and Richie, 'Scholarships and Connections'.
6   Samson Akunaii, interview, 9 July 2014, in Lowe, Purdey and Richie, 'Scholarships and Connections'.

program. In an interview, he reserved criticism not for the structure of the scholarship program, but also for his fellow awardees and the choices they made. He indicated a desire to hear more about how alumni are contributing to the development of PNG, but contended that little development has taken place. Mr Akunaii's call for the impact of scholarships to be visible highlights one of the key difficulties in demonstrating the value of scholarships. The building of a dam, or a school, is an obvious, tangible piece of infrastructure as a result of aid funding. The sending away of young people for education is only obvious in their absence. On their return, the outcomes of their study are less clear, and the expense and absence is less easily defended.

In his assessment of the failings of the scholarship program, Mr Akunaii highlighted the many and varied issues that come into play when one is investigating the longer-term impact of scholarship programs. Mr Akunaii saw the problem as the students who receive the scholarships, and their failure to make an impact on development on return, or at the very least their failure to articulate the impact they have made. These perceptions are common within scholarship evaluation.[7] Impact must be articulated within the evaluation framework as proscribed. This can lead to a scholarship program, or a scholarship recipient being deemed a 'failure', when in fact the outcomes are merely outside of what is expected. Beatrice Mahuru is an excellent case of the latter, as she has gone on to have a successful corporate career in PNG and the USA.

---

7   Joan Dassin and David Navarrete, 'International Scholarships and Social Change: Elements for a New Approach', in *International Scholarships in Higher Education: Pathways to Social Change*, ed. Joan Dassin, Robin Marsh, and Matt Mawer, 305–27 (New York, Palgrave Macmillan, 2017), doi.org/10.1007/978-3-319-62734-2.

7

Goldring, Jackson and the fight for the future of international education

The mid-1980s saw the release of two reports that impacted the future of the overseas student subsidy scheme, and influenced the nature of international education in Australia. The first, the Goldring Report, came from the Committee of Review of Private Overseas Student Policy and was tabled in the Australian Parliament in June 1984. The report was titled *Mutual Advantage*. The second report was of the Jackson Review into Australian Overseas Aid Policy, also released in 1984. The two reports came to very different conclusions regarding the future of overseas students in Australia. Put simply, Goldring concluded that the overseas student subsidy system was beneficial to Australia's developing nation neighbours and should be retained. The Jackson Report concluded that the overseas student subsidy system should be removed, a scholarship program put in place for students from developing countries, and full fees expanded for the remaining overseas students.

This chapter diverts slightly from the themes of the previous and subsequent chapters in this book. In part this is because these two reports have proved so consequential to scholarships and international education in Australia, they needed to be addressed at length. However, these two reports also embodied different strands of thinking in political, bureaucratic and academic circles about the place of Australia as an aid donor and international education host nation. Both reports encouraged more consideration and emphasis be given to Pacific policy development, not just in relation to now independent

Papua New Guinea (PNG), but also due to the broader obligations the authors saw Australia as having to the Pacific region. Thus, the reports deserve additional scrutiny given the themes of this book. The reports marked a significant attempt to shift the focus of policymakers towards the South Pacific. They also clearly demonstrate the different ways in which scholarships can be understood and interpreted. Goldring and Jackson each formed their own views about the role that scholarships should play in Australia's foreign aid and foreign policy approach, and those views are clear in these reports.

Additionally, these two reports recommended comprehensive and substantial changes to the way in which international scholarships and international education were implemented in Australia. The reports gave the Hawke Government plans to fundamentally reshape the system. What this chapter shows is that that opportunity was not taken, and iterative change was preferred.

The Goldring Review was chaired by Professor John Goldring of Macquarie University, and determined that 'because of the considerable benefits flowing from the overseas student program and the means of the students to pay, there should be a substantial subsidy'.[1] The report highlighted the intangible nature of many of the benefits of the overseas student program, and was keen to see an *aid* stance taken when it came to international education.

The Jackson Review, however, took a more focused *trade* approach to international education, focused firmly on centring Australia's national interest in the aid program. The Jackson Report's recommendations for a more trade-focused approach were balanced by a significant scholarship program, which was not adopted in the implementation of the recommendations. The scholarship element of the Jackson Review has not been a part of standard recollections, which has led to most contemporary reflections on the Jackson Review noting it as recommending a full-fee model of international education. As this chapter demonstrates, this simplified understanding of the Jackson Review recommendations obscures the report's more nuanced view of international education, and scholarships in particular.

---

1   Howard Conkey, 'Australia Benefits from Taking Foreign Students', *The Canberra Times*, 7 June 1984.

These two reports had significantly different terms of reference and fields of view. International education was one area where they overlapped. This situation was created because international education was, in the mid-1980s, viewed as largely within the realm of aid and development assistance. Broad subsidies were considered 'aid' despite their lack of targeting, and an international education sector that imagined itself to be born of the Colombo Plan encouraged this perspective. So while the Goldring Report was commissioned to look at 'private' students, it quickly strayed into overseas students more broadly. And because Jackson was tasked with reviewing aid, overseas students fell naturally into his remit. Understanding why these reports had significantly different recommendations will be a key focus of this chapter. This is important because these two reports were part of a (still continuing) debate about the role of education and scholarships in Australia's foreign policy and foreign aid conversation.

In the end, a mix of the recommendations from both reports was adopted by the Hawke Government in the years following the tabling of these reports, in an iterative process. In the longer view, however, the recommendations of the Jackson Review dominated the policies implemented. The subsidy scheme had been capped at 13,000 students in 1984, and the Minister for Education, Senator Susan Ryan, made a statement in 1986 explaining the changes to the subsidy scheme over the coming years. In this press release it was noted that 'students from PNG and sovereign states of the South Pacific will continue to have the charge [the Overseas Student Charge, or OSC] paid on their behalf by the Australian Development Assistance Bureau (ADAB)'.[2] The reduction in subsidies was necessary, according to Minister Ryan, due to difficult budgetary pressures, but she also emphasised that 'the Australian Government appreciated the importance of the overseas student program to the Government's international education policy and foreign policy'.[3] This press release could be read as a signal not just to potential overseas students considering coming to Australia for study, but also to a regional government which had become very reliant on the program to supplement their human resource development plans.

---

2   Susan Ryan, 'Changes to Overseas Student Arrangements', news release, 19 August 1986, parlinfo. aph.gov.au/parlInfo/download/media/pressrel/HPR09022017/upload_binary/HPR09022017.pdf;file Type=application%2Fpdf#search=%22media/pressrel/HPR09022017%22, accessed 22 July 2020.
3   Ryan, 'Changes to Overseas Student Arrangements', news release, 19 August 1986.

Nevertheless, subsidies continued into the late 1980s, and by 1988 93 per cent of Pacific students enrolled in formal courses in Australia were subsidised or fully sponsored.[4] Students from the region, particularly South-East Asia and the South Pacific, studied in high schools, vocational colleges and universities. The cap on subsidies, and a slow increase in full-fee places did have some effect on overseas research students in particular, but foreign governments read the signals being sent by the Hawke Government and began to sponsor students to study at the research level.

This chapter outlines the reports of both the Goldring and Jackson Committees, and their recommendations. It also addresses the interdepartmental processes that were necessary given the conflicting recommendations of the two reports. Finally, this chapter also addresses the connections between the Goldring and Jackson reforms, and those implemented for domestic students at a similar time. These reforms, known as the Dawkins Reforms, introduced fees for domestic students in tertiary education for the first time since the Whitlam Government had abolished them in the early 1970s. While not acted on immediately, the reports did set the framework for the next important scholarship program established by the Australian Government, the Equity and Merit Scholarship Scheme, which is discussed in the next chapter. The Jackson Review is often considered a turning point in Australia's engagement with international education, the foundations on which the contemporary sector is based. The oversimplification of the two reports, and a tendency to view international education policy settings as separate from their domestic equivalents, is common to much of the literature about the history of international education in Australia. This chapter is an effort to re-examine the two reports and broader domestic reforms, to better understand their contribution to Australian Government development scholarships, especially scholarships and education aid targeted at the Pacific region.

---

4   Tupeni Baba, *The Business of Australian Aid: Education, Training and Development – The Marjorie Smart Lecture for 1989: Tupeni Baba; and a Summary of the Proceedings of a Subsequent Panel Discussion Edited by D.R. Jones, V.L. Meek and J. Weeks*, ed. David R Jones, V Lynn Meek, and J Weeks (Melbourne: St Hilda's College, University of Melbourne, 1989).

The Goldring Report

Professor John Goldring was commissioned by the Hawke Government in September 1983 to head a committee to undertake a review of the private overseas student policy. The report, *Mutual Advantage,* was released in March 1984. The review was commissioned for a number of reasons. David Lim, a political scientist and member of the Jackson Committee, wrote in 1989 that the report was needed because there were:

> increasing difficulties with administering the program, the concern that the scheme might have severe adverse distributional effects in the sending countries, and the fear that foreign students might displace Australian students.[5]

The committee themselves noted that the 'overseas student program has evolved in a piecemeal fashion over a number of decades and its present problems reflect that unplanned approach'.[6]

Goldring was a Professor of Law at Macquarie University, and had experience working at the University of Papua New Guinea in the early 1970s, where he served in the Faculty of Law from 1970 to 1972.[7] Other committee members were all experienced and respected public servants, except for Frank Hambly, the long-serving Secretary of the Australian Vice-Chancellors' Committee, who had worked with the AVCC since 1966. The other committee members were Charles Beltz, a senior bureaucrat representing the Department of Education and Youth Affairs, Peter Eyles, an experienced public servant representing the Department of Immigration and Ethnic Affairs and Gerry Nutter, who had served as Australian High Commissioner to PNG from 1978 to 1981, representing the Department of Foreign Affairs. The secretariat for the committee was drawn from the departments represented on the committee.[8] The committee's experience and understanding of PNG is of note.

---

5   David Lim, 'Jackson and the Overseas Students', *Australian Journal of Education* 33, no. 1 (1989): 3, doi.org/10.1177/000494418903300101.
6   John Goldring, *Mutual Advantage* (Canberra: Australian Government Publishing Service, 1984), 27.
7   David Weisbrot, 'In Memoriam: Judge John Goldring (1943–2009)', *Australian Law Reform Commission Reform Journal* 63, no. 94 (2009): 63–64.
8   Goldring, *Mutual Advantage.*

The committee's report summary clearly outlined some of the issues faced when it commenced the work of meeting the terms of reference, that is, a Review of <u>Private</u> Overseas Student Policy (my emphasis). The committee broadened its scope after it decided that the 'distinction between private overseas students and overseas students sponsored by the Australian Government under its aid program, was in some respects artificial' and was thus granted permission to expand the review to 'overseas students generally'.[9] Another challenging element noted by the committee was the lack of research available in Australia relating to overseas students. Due to this impediment the committee commissioned its own research, including a survey of overseas students in Australia, an Information Paper (October 1983) and an Issues Paper (December 1983); the latter provided a useful snapshot of the overseas student community in Australia at the time. For example, the committee found that in 1983 there were approximately 3,600 ADAB-sponsored students in the country, 4 per cent of the total number of privately funded students were Fijian, and 2 per cent were from PNG.[10] The survey also yielded valuable contextual information, for example: 'most students come from families which, by Australian standards, are not wealthy, and most have parents with relatively low levels of educational achievement' and 'wealthier students tend to come from the poorer countries'.[11]

Crucially, the Goldring Report made a series of recommendations that argued against a move to a cost-recovery basis for overseas students (the introduction of full fees), instead encouraging the Hawke Government to stick with an Overseas Students Charge. It also outlined a clear objective for Australia's future policy on overseas students to:

1. contribute to the social and economic development of people and institutions in developing countries, and especially those in the Asian and Pacific region, by granting them access to Australia's educational and training resources
2. increase cultural exchange and to improve the quality of Australia's educational and training resources
3. serve Australia's interests by improving communication with and understanding of Australia.[12]

---

9   Goldring, *Mutual Advantage*, 3.
10 Goldring, *Mutual Advantage*, 368.
11 Goldring, *Mutual Advantage*, 4.
12 Goldring, *Mutual Advantage*, 9.

This framing, which was consistent throughout the report, viewed Australia's acceptance of overseas students as a program of development assistance and foreign policy. It also highlighted the presence of overseas students in Australian universities as a crucial element of the education system. The report suggested that the 'overseas student program should be an integral part of Australia's education policy.'[13]

The report also recommended that the Overseas Student Charge (OSC) should continue to be waived for students from PNG and the South Pacific. Goldring recognised this specific subsidy as an element of Australia's aid program, but also saw the broader subsidy scheme as a form of aid. The report recommended that in future budgets, 'specific appropriations should also recognise the subsidy provided to overseas students, and the overwhelming part of this appropriation could be recognised as official aid'.[14] This recommendation highlighted one of the key criticisms of the existing subsidy scheme, that many of those individuals or nations being supported by the subsidies were not considered countries worthy of the aid because the subsidy scheme did not discriminate on the basis of need.

Another key recommendation of the Goldring Report was for the introduction of an Australian Council for Overseas Students. The council, as proposed, was to consist of approximately nine or 10 members who had been appointed by the Minister for Education and Youth Affairs. It was proposed that the council would have representatives from tertiary and secondary education, students and 'a person to reflect the interests of overseas countries', among others.[15] Goldring imagined that this council would set the level of the OSC, and an Overseas Student Office would be established to address issues of administration, policy, liaison and student monitoring. At the time these roles were spread across ADAB, various other government departments and the Coordinating Committees and Councils for Overseas Students that had been established when large numbers of overseas students first began coming to Australia in the 1950s. Goldring's vision laid out a 'one stop shop' for overseas student issues, policies, administration and activities that would deal with both sponsored and private students. ADAB was not entirely happy with this proposal, as many of the small scholarship programs under their management were tied closely to specific country programs within the aid budget. In one document that

---

13   Goldring, *Mutual Advantage*, 5.
14   Goldring, *Mutual Advantage*, 6.
15   Goldring, *Mutual Advantage*, 15.

was prepared to compare the Goldring and Jackson reports the ADAB position is stated thus: 'ADAB must continue to administer [scholarship programs] in accordance with the development assistance function of sponsoring developing country students'.[16]

The report was optimistic about the positive role the Australian Government could play in the development of South-East Asia and the Pacific through education. This reflected the timing of the report, commissioned as it was by the relatively newly elected Hawke Government, who had come to government with a positive mandate about Australia's role in overseas aid and development. It also reflected the submissions that the committee received, focused as so many were on the importance of the welfare of students and the value of the presence of overseas students to Australia and Australians. Goldring and Nutter both had experience in PNG and had undoubtedly come across many alumni of Australian education during their time there. This provided them with an opportunity to see the tangible outcomes of the policies being reviewed by the committee. The report was centred on the student, their needs and the needs of their countries. In this way it was politically naive, which ensured the recommendations failed to garner broad political support.

As mentioned previously, *Mutual Advantage* was also overshadowed because of the release of the Jackson Review of Overseas Aid. There was significant crossover on the subject of private and sponsored overseas students, therefore decisions on policies for overseas students had to be made using both the Jackson and Goldring reports. This process of synthesis is discussed later in this chapter.

In submissions made to the Overseas Student Task Force (described in detail shortly) that was formed to develop a coherent overseas student policy out of the Jackson and Goldring reports, the recommendations of Goldring were more popular. For example, a document titled *Ministerial Representations on Issues Raised by the Jackson and Goldring Reports* summarised 11 responses and representations received by the minister. Only one representation was unequivocal in its support of the recommendations of the Jackson Report whereas many supported the welfare recommendations of the Goldring Report.[17] The Goldring Committee worked much more closely with those

---

16 'The Overseas Student Program – The Jackson and Goldring Reports (ADAB Regional Directors)', B848, V1984/82, 1984, National Archives of Australia (NAA).
17 'Ministerial Representations on Issues Raised by the Jackson and Goldring Reports | 17 August', A4250, 1984/1860, 1984, NAA.

involved with overseas students: 55 recommendations of the report were in line with the status quo. This was a more comfortable position for organisations and institutions not keen to make big changes, which was reflected in their submissions to the task force. Many of these organisations also noted that, by contrast, the Jackson Review Committee did not engage with them, and the Jackson Report made a number of incorrect assumptions about the existing overseas student policy that was in place at the time.

The Jackson Report

The Jackson Report was commissioned in 1982 by the Fraser Government, and like the Goldring Report was handed to the Hawke Government in March 1984, and tabled in Parliament in June 1984. The review was ordered after the Auditor General's Office released a critical report on Australia's aid administration.[18] Sir Gordon Jackson, a well-respected businessman with an international focus was appointed by the Australian Government to review the entire overseas aid program.[19] Jackson began his career with the Colonial Sugar Refining Company (later CSR Limited), and by 1984 had retired from his position as chief executive officer and was serving as deputy chairman. CSR had held a monopoly on sugar production in Fiji until the 1970s, and played a significant role in the exploitation of resources in the Pacific over the twentieth century. Jackson was influential in CSR's move into mining and construction. He was a member of Australia's first trade mission to the People's Republic of China, under Whitlam in 1973, and had advised Whitlam's government on foreign ownership of Australian companies.[20] He had experience running a committee for government, and had extensive experience in international trade, manufacturing and extractive industries. Because of the sectors that CSR was involved in, he had business experience in many of the nations to which Australia was giving aid, which significantly colours the report's recommendations.

---

18   Philip Eldridge, 'The Jackson Report on Australia's Overseas Aid Program: Political Options and Prospects', *Australian Outlook* 39, no. 1 (1985): 23–32, doi.org/10.1080/10357718508444868.
19   The remit for the Jackson Review was far broader than the Goldring Review and addressed the whole of the aid program, not only education aid and scholarships.
20   David Lee, 'Jackson, Sir Ronald Gordon (1924–1991)', in *Australian Dictionary of Biography* (Canberra: National Centre of Biography, Australian National University, 2016), adb.anu.edu.au/biography/jackson-sir-ronald-gordon-23122, accessed 19 April 2023.

The general tone of the report can be seen in the first pages:

> Aid is given primarily for humanitarian reasons to alleviate poverty through economic and social development. It is the response of the wealthy industrial countries to the needs of hundreds of millions of people who live harsh and materially meagre lives. Aid also complements strategic, economic and foreign policy interests, and by helping developing countries to grow, it provides economic opportunities for Australia.[21]

The committee's report touched lightly on different theories of development and what the purposes of government aid should be, deciding that 'in the main, Australian Government aid funds and skills are most effective when applied to removing major constraints to development'.[22] The report also noted the significant proportion of Australia's aid budget that was directed to PNG, at the time of the report it was 36 per cent of the total aid budget.[23] The report criticised the ad hoc nature of Australian aid, and the spread of the program across too many countries (more than 100). Jackson advised that country programs should lead aid allocation. In terms of the geographic allocation, the Jackson Report was clear that 'Australia's geopolitical interests and special relationships with PNG indicate that the main country focus should be on PNG and the small island nations of the Pacific and Indian Oceans'.[24] The report elaborated a little on Australia's 'special relationship' with PNG, and the 'shortcomings in Australia's preparation for Papua New Guinea's independence'[25] and summarised the history of Australia's colonial involvement in PNG. Similarly, the report noted that Australia has 'special responsibilities and interests in the South Pacific'[26] and was somewhat critical of previous colonial administrations, 'the colonial powers did little to train the island people',[27] but did not substantively engage with the ongoing impacts of colonisation on the South Pacific Island states. The report was, however, very clear on the importance (to Australia) of Australia's relationship with the South Pacific states:

---

21 R Gordon Jackson, *Report of the Committee to Review the Australian Overseas Aid Program*, Parliamentary Paper No. 206 of 1984 (Canberra: Australian Government Publishing Service, 1984), 3.
22 Jackson, *Report of the Committee*, 4.
23 Jackson, *Report of the Committee*, 5.
24 Jackson, *Report of the Committee*, 6.
25 Jackson, *Report of the Committee*, 7.
26 Jackson, *Report of the Committee*, 8.
27 Jackson, *Report of the Committee*, 174.

> Australia's international credibility … rests on its ability to be involved in and to understand the region and to have influence with island states on matters of regional and international concern such as de-colonisation and nuclear testing.[28]

Passages such as this in the report demonstrated its position as a pragmatic document, encouraging the giving of aid that leads to a benefit to Australia. The report covered a broad program of aid, outlining the current programs of aid in each area addressed, as well as looking into the activities of other donors. Given the breadth of the review, while the report did engage with debates about aid and development, it could only do so at a superficial level. For some observers, this was problematic. Agricultural economist WR Stent, in a speech in June 1984 at a seminar organised by Community Aid Abroad, expressed his concern that the report would become an authoritative text even though, as he stated 'the Report is never able to come to grips with what development is'.[29] In short, the report failed to grapple with development from a theoretical or practical perspective, other than as a part of Australia's foreign policy outlook. Philip Eldridge described Jackson's 'triple mandate' as balancing equally strategic, economic and humanitarian interests.[30] This was not necessarily a radical change from the way in which aid and development had been practised by the Australian Government over the previous decades, but it was certainly far more explicitly stated in the Jackson Report than it had been previously. It was also starkly different from the perspective taken in the Goldring Report, wherein supporting developing countries was considered a responsibility.

In terms of tertiary education, the report noted:

> the Committee found that developing countries have a high regard for many aspects of Australian education, but that Australia is missing out on some of the best overseas students because university and immigration procedures are overly bureaucratic.[31]

---

28 Jackson, *Report of the Committee*, 177.
29 WR Stent, 'Comments on Jackson Committee Report', A4250, 1984/2194, 1984, NAA.
30 Philip J Eldridge, *The Politics of Human Rights in Southeast Asia*, Politics in Asia Series (Routledge, 2002).
31 Jackson, *Report of the Committee*, 10.

This focus on high-calibre students hinted at Jackson's contention that Australia should benefit from overseas students in the country. This further fuelled the critique that the committee's recommendations were more focused on benefits to Australia than the potential benefits overseas students could enjoy through their study in Australia.

The Jackson Report also explicitly called for the 'hidden subsidy' funding to be counted as Overseas Development Assistance (ODA), noting that this would 'raise official aid as a share of GNP by about 0.04%'.[32] In the context of a goal of ODA to be equal to 0.7 per cent of GNP, this was not an inconsequential increase. The Director-General of ADAB, Bob Dun, agreed with this approach, and wrote to Foreign Minister Hayden in June 1986 asking that he request the subsidy contribution be made explicit in financial documentation, in part because this 'fix' allowed for Australia to demonstrate a greater commitment to aid funding at the Organisation for Economic Co-operation and Development (OECD).[33]

The report was very explicit about one of the key concerns around the existing scholarship scheme that was troubling scholarship and aid administrators. It noted that students from developing countries

> must be approved by their own government and are often selected on grounds other than academic merit. The criteria of the more influential government departments in developing countries tend to prevail.[34]

This sentence, tucked away in the report, called attention to a significant issue in the selection of students for scholarships funded by the Australian Government. Scholarship administrators suspected that favouritism and nepotism played a part in the awarding of scholarships. This issue was critically important to the designers of the next significant Australian Government development scholarship, the Equity and Merit Scholarship Scheme (discussed in the next chapter), who were very keen to avoid nepotism and favouritism in selection of scholarship awardees.

---

32 Jackson, *Report of the Committee*, 94.
33 The timing of this was especially useful to coincide with a visit to the OECD by an Australian representative – Mr Corkery. RB Dun, 'The Hidden Subsidy in Education in Australia of Overseas Students: Counting as ODA | Note for Minister Hayden | 5 June', A4250, 1984/1427, 1984, NAA.
34 Jackson, *Report of the Committee*, 92.

7. GOLDRING, JACKSON AND THE FIGHT FOR THE FUTURE OF INTERNATIONAL EDUCATION

The report did recommend a scholarship program, to 'improve the balance of student intake and offset rising charges'[35]. The three-tiered scholarship program was substantial. Committee member and academic David Lim explained that:

> The first tier is the existing Australian government-to-government sponsorship scheme, which should be retained at the current level. The geographical distribution of these scholarships should be in line with that recommended for other bilateral aid programs. However, the adoption of country programming will help to improve the coherence of the disciplinary mix of the scholarships. The second tier is the provision of merit scholarships, to be awarded directly by Australian tertiary institutions. Students would be selected entirely on merit, unlike those in the first category who have to be approved by their own governments and who may have been selected on non-academic grounds. To ensure that these scholarships have an impact on economic development generally, they should be offered in areas where Australia has a competitive advantage and to the poorer of the targeted aid recipient LDCs [Least Developed Countries]. Special scholarships for students from disadvantaged groups in LDCs would form the third category of scholarships.[36]

The plan for scholarships was for the government to move to a target of 10,000 scholarships by the mid-1990s, a massive increase in the number of scholarships available at that time.[37] If there were students who were unable to gain one of the 10,000 scholarships available, then under the Jackson plan they were to apply to study in Australian institutions based on available places and pay a full fee to that institution. The committee's report also recommended that the administration of overseas students, both their placement and support in Australia, should be handled by education institutions, rather than ADAB and other volunteer organisations, as was the practice at the time.

The comments by Lim, going into depth about the scholarship program proposed by the Jackson Committee, were published in 1989, well after decisions about the recommendations of the Jackson Report had been translated into policy. He was, perhaps, responding to an observation made that it was the Jackson Report that reoriented Australia's overseas student policies from aid to trade. As will be made clear in subsequent chapters, at

---

35 Jackson, *Report of the Committee*, 11.
36 Lim, 'Jackson and the Overseas Students', 9.
37 Lim, 'Jackson and the Overseas Students', 9.

no point did the planned 10,000 award scholarship scheme come into being, whereas the market-oriented export approach to international education became a mainstay of Australia's tertiary education sector.

The Committee of Review consulted widely, although, as mentioned earlier many involved in the overseas students sector felt ignored by the report. The report recommended that Australia's aid program be allowed to mature, and:

> [the] Jackson Committee accepted that in Australia, as in other donor countries, there is more than one mandate for giving aid for development. It also recognised that the humanitarian, political and economic mandates can give rise to quite different groups of LDCs being helped.[38]

This is the triple mandate as discussed earlier.

After the report was tabled it received coverage in many newspapers across Australia and the world.[39] There was a recognition that Australia's responsibilities to different countries came from our historical and geographical connections to those nations, an article in the PNG newspaper *Niugini Nius* reported that Jackson 'harshly criticises the management of the Australian aid programme to Papua New Guinea'.[40] Reporting also focused on Jackson's conclusions about the thin spread of Australian aid, and possible opportunities for education to become an export industry.[41] An article by Niki Savva in *The Australian* focused on how the report recommended a reduction in aid to PNG, and framed the report as criticising Australia's present aid policies.[42]

Many critics of the report disagreed with the strong focus on the growth model of development adopted by the committee, including a number of economists. According to Phillip Eldridge, the 'Jackson Report ignores the radical critique [of aid and development] entirely'.[43] It did not engage with the idea of a basic needs approach, or Marxist and structuralist discussions around aid and development. The Jackson Report safely resided in the theories of modernisation that dominated development practice

---

38   Lim, 'Jackson and the Overseas Students', 5.
39   See, among others, Stuart Inder, 'Fiji's Progress Praised', *The Fiji Times*, 9 June 1984, 3.
40   'Aussie Attack on Aid Misuse', *Niugini Nius*, 8 June 1984.
41   Patrick Walters, 'Australian Aid Spread Too Thinly, Report Says', *The Sydney Morning Herald*, 8 June 1984, 11.
42   Niki Savva, 'PNG Aid Should Be Cut, Jackson Tells Gov', *The Australian*, 8 June 1984.
43   Eldridge, 'The Jackson Report on Australia's Overseas Aid Program', 23.

in the 1980s. Other organisations were also dissatisfied with the report. In October 1984 Community Aid Abroad (CAA) reported that its position had 'hardened' following months of intensive analysis of the report. CAA's main concern with the report was that 'when they come into conflict, Australia's self-interest must take priority over the needs of the poor'.[44]

There were other broad critiques of the Jackson Review Committee's report. The Fijian academic and politician Tupeni Baba believed that the 'Jackson Committee saw aid largely in terms of furthering Australia's interests'.[45] Historian Elizabeth Cassity noted that it was perceived as having a 'neo-classical and authoritarian view of development'.[46] The focus on the potential of developing a full-fee overseas student market was often noted as one of the key elements of the report that elicited these critiques. But the report itself did not stress this element, especially as it called for a massive scholarship program.

While the committee had a broad scope – all of Australia's overseas aid program – significant attention was paid to policies regarding overseas students, which by virtue of the OSC (and its waiving for students from PNG and the South Pacific) was part of the aid budget. This element featured in reporting in newspapers, including a report by Ian Davis in *The Age*:

> Sir Gordon Jackson said yesterday that there should be 'a lot more overseas students. The present student intake is neither big enough, nor balanced enough'. He said overseas students should not be considered part of Australia's education policy, but rather as part of its foreign aid policy. They should be financed under the aid program and thus would not displace Australian students seeking places in universities and colleges.[47]

This was a fascinating quote from Jackson, given that much of the critique of his proposals relating to overseas education was in opposition to the trade focus, preferring Goldring's aid focus. It was also in direct contradiction to the call from Goldring to make overseas student policy an integral part of Australia's education policy rather than a separate and distinct element.

---

44   'CAA Attitude Hardens', *Community Aid Abroad Review*, October 1984.
45   Baba, *The Business of Australian Aid*, 8.
46   Elizabeth Cassity, 'Cast the Net a Little Wider: Australian Aid in the South Pacific', *International Journal of Educational Development* 28 (2008): 254, doi.org/10.1016/j.ijedudev.2006.12.003.
47   Ian Davis, 'Report Seeks More Foreign Student Aid', *The Age*, 8 June 1984.

Eldrige's critique of the recommendations, published in 1985, highlighted the difficulties of the scholarship proposal, particularly in relation to ideas around brain drain, with policies like 10,000 scholarships having the potential to embed 'biases against local training and research or collaboration with third countries'.[48] Eldridge noted that without clear equity criteria and with assumptions that the benefits of education to development materialise with the education itself, development outcomes might not be forthcoming.

ADAB itself was open to the scholarship concept. A paper prepared in March 1984 outlined a way of implementing the scholarship program. The plan involved the establishment of Australian Scholarship Advisory Committees in each recipient nation – committees that would be responsible for initial vetting of applications, and providing advice on placements. Responsibility for placements would be with the institutions, and as part of the plan outlined in this paper, Australian educational institutions would apply to be a part of the scholarship scheme. It was felt that this approach would 'encourage institutions to develop suitable courses/research degrees for developing country students'.[49]

Overseas Students Task Force

As noted earlier in this chapter, the Goldring and Jackson reports released in 1984 overlapped in the key area of overseas students and education aid. This presented the Australian aid and education bureaucracy with the difficult task of synthesising and understanding the recommendations of two reports which suggested the Australian Government take very different approaches to the same issue.

In March 1984 the Director-General of ADAB, Bob Dun wrote to the Minister of Foreign Affairs, Bill Hayden, seeking his advice on how to reconcile the two reports for a Cabinet submission. The process was being hurried by the Department of Education and Youth Affairs, which was hoping to have new policies in place for the intake of overseas students

---

48   Eldridge, 'The Jackson Report on Australia's Overseas Aid Program', 25.
49   'Australian Overseas Student Scholarship Scheme Possible Method of Handling (within Jackson Committee Approach | 15 March', A4250, 1984/897, 1984, NAA.

in 1985. Dun saw this rush as unnecessary, especially because he saw the reports as having 'important philosophical differences of approach which may not be fully reconcilable [his emphasis]'.[50]

The efforts of the Department of Education for haste were not misplaced. The Australian High Commission in Fiji were inundated with enquiries in 1984, with over 1,000 would-be students approaching the High Commission in a three-day period in June 1984. There were only 225 places allocated to Fijian students for the 1985 academic year.[51] The demand for access to Australian universities from Fiji, at least, was clear.

At the time the reports were released, ADAB had a significant role in managing the overseas student cohort (not only the sponsored students), after the reshuffle of responsibilities out of the review in 1977/78 discussed in the previous chapter. ADAB employed social workers who provided pastoral care for students, and also supported the Coordinating Committees for Overseas Students that had, since their establishment in the 1950s, coordinated support for overseas students from non-government and community organisations such as the Country Women's Association, Rotary and Apex.

As the Goldring and Jackson reports were digested, Bob Dun asked his staff to consider the reports in conjunction with each other. A report of the ADAB Regional Directors provides an insight into the thinking of ADAB staff. The report was not complimentary of either Goldring or Jackson, concluding:

> It is the considered view of the Regional Directors that neither the Jackson nor the Goldring Reports has produced satisfactory findings in relation to the Overseas Student Program.[52]

This submission to ADAB senior leaders outlined the ways in which both committees had failed to understand the existing program, and how the administrative, welfare and foreign policy burden was shared. The Regional Directors were particularly scathing of the limited insight provided by the Jackson Report (which was tasked with a much greater remit than that of the Goldring Committee). They wrote:

---

50   RB Dun, 'Overseas Students – Reconciliation of the Recommendations of the Goldring and Jackson Reports | March 1984', A4250, 1984/897, 1984, NAA.
51   'Flood of Inquiries on Study in Australia', *The Fiji Times*, 8 June 1984, 14.
52   'The Overseas Student Program – the Jackson and Goldring Reports (ADAB Regional Directors)', B848, V1984/82, 1984, NAA.

> The Jackson Report … limits its findings on overseas students to a few broad and seemingly simple ideas. It does not go into detail or make any attempt to follow through the full administrative, financial, welfare or foreign and domestic political impact of its ideas.[53]

The Regional Directors expressed concern about the manner in which the overseas student program was dealt with, either by the conflation of the sponsored and non-sponsored cohorts (Goldring Report) or to a greater split between them (the Jackson Report).

In order to deal with the difficulties posed by the two alternative policy proposals, outside of the ADAB internal considerations, an interdepartmental Overseas Student Task Force was convened. The decision to establish an Overseas Student Task Force was made at a special meeting of 'relevant' ministers held in May 1984 which involved the Minister for Foreign Affairs (Bill Hayden), the Minister for Education and Youth Affairs (Susan Ryan) and the Minister for Immigration and Ethnic Affairs (Stewart West). This meeting made a number of decisions outlining the scope of the task force, but also regarding future decision-making. Minister Hayden had requested that the Goldring and Jackson reports were to be considered together, thus it was accepted that any policy changes would be influenced by both reports. Reports of this meeting show that the 'ownership' of overseas student policy was contested. A meeting report summarising the decisions made noted that 'portfolio responsibility in the future for overseas student matters was a matter for the Prime Minister's prerogative under the administrative arrangements'.[54] ADAB staffers had discussed this issue prior to the meeting, and had agreed that, with the subsidy and increases recommended by Jackson equal to approximately 20 per cent of the total aid budget, the 'loss of policy control over so large a component of the aid program would be a very serious matter'.[55] Before the meeting a number of submissions and internal documents from ADAB and the Department of Foreign Affairs had noted the importance of overseas student policy to aid and diplomacy. Nevertheless, after this meeting Charles Terrell (First Secretary) wrote that Hayden:

---

53 'The Overseas Student Program – the Jackson and Goldring Reports (ADAB Regional Directors)', B848, V1984/82, 1984, NAA.
54 'Meeting of Ministers on the Jackson and Goldring Reports | 4 May', A4250, 1984/897, 1984, NAA.
55 'Overseas Student Policy: The Goldring and Jackson Reports, Briefing Note for Minister Hayden', A4250, 1984/1427, 1984, NAA.

Indicated that he felt that student matters should be the responsibility of the Education and Youth Affairs portfolio and I gained the impression that he would be glad to be rid of his present responsibility in regard to scholarship, etc. policy.[56]

The bureaucrats of the Department of Foreign Affairs and ADAB were far more attached to the policy levers of overseas students and scholarships than their minister was, adding an additional layer of difficulty to the task force process.

The task force had representation from the Department of Prime Minister and Cabinet, the Department of Education and Youth Affairs, the Department of Foreign Affairs, the Department of Finance, the Treasury Department and the Department of Immigration and Ethnic Affairs.[57] While ADAB was able to provide advice to the task force, it was decided by the Department of Education and Youth Affairs, who chaired the task force, that only one representative of each portfolio was able to be a full member of the task force. This created special difficulties for ADAB and the Department of Foreign Affairs, who had different priorities and concerns related to the policy settings for overseas students. They sought advice from their minister, Bill Hayden, about the conflicts. The Department of Foreign Affairs was 'interested in a range of foreign policy implications of the overseas student program' whereas ADAB was 'interested in the implementation of the Jackson Report on the Aid Program'.[58] This conflict between Foreign Affairs and ADAB mirrored the internal conflicts within the scholarship programs and the broader overseas student polices. There were many foreign policy implications, and benefits, of scholarship programs. But they did not always sit comfortably with the development goals that those scholarship programs were created to address, or within the normal bureaucratic structures of the Commonwealth government.

The task force was given tight deadlines, with ministers asking for the Cabinet submission to be prepared by August 1984. Responsibility for policies in relation to the 1985 intake of overseas students had been given to the Department of Immigration and Ethnic Affairs, but there were pressures coming from other sources, such as a planned visit of the Prime Minister

---

56 'Meeting of Ministers on the Jackson and Goldring Reports | 4 May', A4250, 1984/897, 1984, NAA.
57 It is interesting to note that the ministers involved had asked in the meeting in May 1984 that Treasury was not to be involved in the Task Force.
58 PGF Henderson, 'Task Force on Overseas Students – Note to Mr Hayden | 6 July', A4250, 1984/1428, 1984, NAA.

of Malaysia, Dr Mahathir, in August 1984. Minutes from a meeting held in early July 1984 noted 'the importance of the overseas student issue in Australia's relations with Malaysia'.[59] Given the complicated policy that was being addressed these timelines were always unrealistic. In reality the policies in relation to overseas students were still being reformed and changed over subsequent years, and the scholarship program advocated by Jackson (in a significantly reduced form) was not announced until 1989.

The task force planned for its main output to be a Cabinet submission recommending the proposed policy approach for overseas students. Papers prepared for meetings of the task force, along with other internal ADAB briefings, made clear the difficulties that each of the reports raised. For example, the suggestion of transitioning to full-cost-recovery (rejected by Goldring and supported in part by Jackson) was also advised against by the Commonwealth Standing Committee on Student Mobility, which was a part of the Commonwealth Secretariat.[60] It was expected that if a Commonwealth country such as Australia did introduce a full-cost-recovery system, they would then be at a disadvantage in comparison to other countries such as Canada and the United Kingdom. How fees could be set, depending on the institution, was also up for discussion by the task force. There was an expectation that introducing full fees for overseas students would be negatively received by developing country governments. One paper noted that Malaysia in particular would be expected to react poorly 'because the effects of increased fees would be felt immediately, long before the scholarship program grew to the extent that it was a counteracting force'.[61] Given that the survey conducted by Goldring had found that 50 per cent of overseas students in Australia were from Malaysia, the focus on the reception of the policy changes in Malaysia was critical.

Consultations around the two reports also included the Metropolitan Coordinating Committees, who were largely supportive of the recommendations in the Goldring Report, but scathing of the Jackson Report. A record of a meeting notes the group 'unanimously dismissed the directions for education advocated in the Jackson Report'.[62] The Melbourne Council for Overseas Students (MELCOS) also wrote a submission on the Overseas Student Task Force, pointing out specific issues around welfare

---

59 'Meeting Minutes: Overseas Student Task Force | 2 July', A4250, 1984/897, 1984, NAA.
60 'Overseas Student Task Force – Papers for Meeting on 10 July 1984', A4250, 1984/897, 1984, NAA.
61 'Overseas Student Task Force – Papers for Meeting on 10 July 1984', A4250, 1984/897, 1984, NAA.
62 'Submission from Metropolitan Coordinating Committees, 18 August 1984', B848, V1984/93, NAA.

7. GOLDRING, JACKSON AND THE FIGHT FOR THE FUTURE OF INTERNATIONAL EDUCATION

and fees for overseas students,[63] issues that MELCOS felt had not even been addressed by the Jackson Report. MELCOS also discussed at a meeting in July 1984 that it was resigned to full cost fees being introduced, in part because 'Professor Goldring in conversation with Stephen Gan UNSW [University of New South Wales], reportedly stated that as the Jackson Committee's "power base" was in Canberra it was in a strong position to lobby for its own recommendations'.[64] MELCOS was also aware that the Department of Education was looking to introduce fees for domestic students, making fees for overseas students inevitable.

The outcomes of the Jackson and Goldring reports are often oversimplified, particularly in the context of the history of Australia's international education sector.[65] However, as files, briefings and the reports themselves make clear, the response to these reports was not a simple matter. The implementation fell short of what the Jackson Committee imagined. In the short term, the policy change more closely mirrored the Goldring recommendations. Lim wrote in 1989 that the new policy announced in 1985 'was a compromise between the Goldring and Jackson recommendations but more towards the former than the latter'.[66] The OSC was retained, although increased from 25 per cent of the cost of a tertiary place to 35 per cent and quotas were introduced at both the institutional level (the number of overseas students in each institution) and the national level (the number of overseas students from individual nations). Under these settings the number of subsidised students continued to grow: over twice as many subsidised overseas students were in Australia in 1986 as were in 1980.[67] In many ways the choice made by the Hawke Government in 1985 to only tinker with the status quo, and to continue with the OSC and subsidies, delayed more substantial reforms only for a few years. By 1988 the budget was being stretched by the attractiveness of the subsidy scheme to overseas students, and plans were

---

63   'Melbourne Council for Overseas Students – Submission to Overseas Student Task Force | 18 July', A4250, 1984/1860, 1984, NAA.
64   'Melbourne Council for Overseas Students Committee of Presidents | Meeting Minutes | 12 July', A4250, 1984/1941, 1984, NAA.
65   Much documented history of the Australian international education sector mentions the reports of 1984 in passing, concluding that the Jackson Report recommends a move of the overseas student program to a trade footing, rather than the aid footing recommended by Goldring. Examples include: Paula Dunstan, 'Beyond the Campus: Students Engagement and Community Responses', in *Making a Difference: Australian International Education*, ed. Dorothy Davis and Bruce Mackintosh (Sydney: UNSW Press, 2011); Anna Kent, 'Australian Development Scholarships and their Place within Diplomacy, Development and Education', Master's thesis, University of Melbourne, 2012. This oversimplistic approach is notable given the discussions in this chapter, and other work such as Lim, 'Jackson and the Overseas Students'.
66   Lim, 'Jackson and the Overseas Students', 13.
67   Lim, 'Jackson and the Overseas Students', 14.

Dawkins Reforms

There were also significant influences on policy development coming from domestic reforms. As the policies for overseas students were still being redesigned and reshaped (although at this point behind closed doors), the Hawke Government began what became known as the Dawkins Reforms. Precipitated by a 1987 Green Paper titled *Higher Education: A Policy Discussion Paper*, a White Paper was released by the Minister for Education John Dawkins. The process was aimed at addressing the 'capacity and effectiveness of the higher education sector'.[68] The conditions that led to the call for reforms were similar to those that had led to the Goldring Report. Access to tertiary education was seen as vital (in the case of Goldring it was vital in a diplomatic and development sense), but it was becoming clear that the Hawke Government felt it could no longer afford to subsidise education at the level it did.[69] The reforms were also influenced by changes occurring in other parts of the world. Simon Marginson wrote that the policy conversation was 'inspired by the neo-liberal "revolution" and policies of privatisation and deregulation set in train by the Thatcher government in the UK'.[70] The Higher Education Access Charge, a flat rate of $250 per full-time domestic student, was introduced in 1986, and was followed in 1988 by the Higher Education Contribution Scheme (HECS).[71] These changes, in many ways mirroring the OSC that had been increased earlier in the decade for overseas students, changed the settings around equity of access to higher education that had been key to the reforms made by the Whitlam Government in the 1970s. Marginson argues that it was these changes that led to the marketisation of higher education in Australia for Australian

---

68 Department of Education and Training, *Higher Education in Australia: A Review of Reviews from Dawkins to Today* (Canberra: Department of Education and Training, 2015), 11.
69 According to Elizabeth Humphrys, the abolition of free tertiary education for domestic students was in direct contravention of the 'Accord' struck by the Hawke Government shortly after the election of Bob Hawke as prime minister. This provides a potential explanation for the hesitation within the Hawke Government to remove the subsidy scheme as it would mark the beginning of a process that ended free tertiary education for both international and domestic students. See Elizabeth Humphrys, *How Labour Built Neoliberalism: Australia's Accord, the Labour Movement and the Neoliberal Project* (Leiden, The Netherlands: Brill, 2018), doi.org/10.1163/9789004383463.
70 Simon Marginson, 'National and Global Competition in Higher Education', *The Australian Educational Researcher* 31, no. 2 (2004): 2, doi.org/10.1007/BF03249517.
71 Marginson, 'National and Global Competition in Higher Education'.

students, in the same way that critics felt the policy settings recommended by Jackson would lead to the marketisation of higher education for overseas students.[72]

These changes were not a surprise to the sector. As discussed earlier, the MELCOS Committee of Presidents noted in 1984, when the Jackson and Goldring reports were being synthesised, that the Department of Education and Youth Affairs was investigating the possibility of introducing fees for domestic students on a means-tested basis.[73]

Fees were introduced for domestic students in 1988, albeit via the HECS program, which was an income-contingent loan. This created the politically unsustainable position whereby overseas students were able to access tertiary education in Australia with extremely low fees while domestic students were paying higher fees via the HECS program. Thus, despite the wishes of Goldring and his committee, more substantive changes to the policies relating to international students, and fees for study, were needed. Eugene Sebastian argued that one of the reasons overseas students were the constituency that suffered more acutely from the changes during this period was because there was little political organisation of overseas students prior to the 1980s.[74]

By 1988 the end of the subsidy scheme was assured, and by 1990 it was over. Thousands of students from South-East Asia and the South Pacific, and even further afield, had made use of the subsidy scheme during the 16 years it was in place. At this time the demand for Australian education in the South Pacific was high, with applications far exceeding allocated places from some nations such as Fiji. The scheme also allowed other governments to sponsor their nationals to study in Australia, only having to pay a stipend or living costs. It was for this equity of access that Goldring supported the continuation of the scheme. But in the end the forces of neoliberalism and domestic financial pressures could not be resisted; the Jackson-influenced approach was more in line with the prevailing political and economic winds.[75]

---

72 Marginson, 'National and Global Competition in Higher Education'.
73 'Melbourne Council for Overseas Students Committee of Presidents | Meeting Minutes | 12 July', A4250, 1984/1941, 1984, NAA.
74 Eugene F Sebastian, 'Protest from the Fringe: Overseas Students and their Influence on Australia's Export of Education Services Policy 1983–1996', PhD thesis, University of Sydney, 2009.
75 Marginson, 'National and Global Competition in Higher Education'.

In commissioning the Goldring Review of Overseas Students, and having it report at the same time as a report commissioned by the previous Fraser Government, the Hawke Government created unexpected complications for itself. Significant time and energy was spent by departments, charities, non-government organisations (NGOs) and other community groups in trying to interpret and understand the reports in tandem. The Goldring Report was more thoroughly embraced by NGOs, with Jackson's neoliberal tendencies putting many organisations, including CAA and MELCOS, offside.

As explained earlier, while Australia's 'new' policy on overseas students, coming out of the two reports, was announced in March 1985, this was not the end of the matter. The initial decision to retain the OSC, with an increase, maintained a level of status quo that reassured regional countries, such as Malaysia and Singapore. These nations continued to rely on the subsidy scheme, which in turn influenced the next major policy shift. After an election in 1987, Minister for Foreign Affairs Bill Hayden was offered the position of Governor-General. His replacement as foreign minister was Gareth Evans, who took control of the problems that the overseas student policy continued to create, both financially and politically. Thus, the scholarship program recommended by the Jackson Committee report was reshaped to become the Equity and Merit Scholarship Scheme, which is discussed in detail in the next chapter.

This chapter provides us with a new interpretation on what has, over intervening decades, been perceived as a turning point in Australian international education policy. The accepted 'understanding' that the Jackson Report is the point at which Australian international education turned from aid to trade is not nearly as simple as that. There was not a binary division, where Goldring recommended aid and Jackson recommended trade. There is no doubt that when reforms were made to the policies governing overseas students and international development scholarships, the Jackson Report provided more of the inspiration for the reforms than the Goldring Report did. The reality is, however, that the nature and pace of policy change was far more complex, influenced by more than simply a report issued by Sir Gordon Jackson. International economic pressure and domestic budget constraints, a neoliberal approach to policymaking coming from the UK, domestic higher education reforms and activist community organisations such as MELCOS were all involved in the reforms to overseas student policies over the late 1980s.

Major decisions were put off by the Hawke Government, following the lines of the Goldring Report, until the budget pressures could no longer be ignored. But by failing to fully adopt the recommendations of either of these reports, the Hawke Government continued a long tradition of iterative policymaking in the realm of international education and scholarships. Big reforms were rare to this point, and changes to policy were made 'around the edges' so as not to upset the status quo. The previous 'big reform' was the introduction of the subsidy scheme by a prime minister remembered for many of his reforms, Gough Whitlam. That scheme was allowed to continue, with small changes, for 16 years because it proved so popular with regional partners and domestic supporters. Changing the policy drastically after the release of Goldring and Jackson would have created problems domestically and internationally, and the Hawke Government chose to put off those problems. In the realm of scholarships, the Development Training Scheme also continued, along with small changes, over the decade of the 1980s, not dramatically or substantially changed by either Jackson or Goldring. While the turning-point narrative is appealing, in practice the iterative nature of policy change was continued through this period.

And while both Jackson and Goldring called for a more concerted focus on the Pacific, reflecting what they saw as Australia's obligations to the region, the Pacific remained a secondary policy focus. This failure to shift development and aid focus to the Pacific did not represent a complete lack of focus in the Pacific, which was far more likely to be viewed through a security lens during the 1980s as nuclear testing and other security concerns, such as coups in Fiji, came to the fore. These issues were all present as the Hawke Government implemented a significantly different scholarship late in the decade, discussed in the next chapter.

8

Centring the power

With the Dawkins Reforms 'bedded down' and international education policy settings adjusted after the Jackson and Goldring reports, the late 1980s were a time of significant change within Australian higher education. This is a period often marked as the turning point, where the international education in Australia moved from being a sector to an 'industry' – from aid to trade.[1]

This chapter discusses in depth one of the outcomes of the negotiations between the Jackson and Goldring reports: the Equity and Merit Scholarship Scheme (EMSS), which was also influenced by an international economic environment that put stress on the Australian Government's budget. The focus of the EMSS was not the Pacific. The design was far more focused on managing the flow of students from Malaysia, and seeking to mitigate the possible diplomatic damage from ending the subsidy scheme. While the focus of scholarship designers was on South-East Asia, the political and security situation in the Pacific became far more tumultuous, with missile tests and military coups drawing the attention of the foreign policy community. The previous approaches that had marked much of Australia's foreign policy towards the Pacific could not continue in the face of these challenges. It was these issues that forced the designers of the EMSS to make the scheme regionally led, as discussed throughout this chapter, while shifting important levers of control to Canberra.

---

1   Eric Meadows, 'From Aid to Industry: A History of International Education in Australia', in *Making a Difference: Australian International Education,* ed. Dorothy Davis and Bruce Mackintosh (Sydney: University of New South Wales Press, 2011).

The EMSS was a significant 'new' scholarship scheme. It differed in approach, theory of change and implementation mode from all other schemes the Australian Government had designed or participated in since the 1940s. It was short lived but, much like the Colombo Plan, it laid the foundations for subsequent schemes, and elements of the scheme were genuinely novel in their approach to scholarship design. It bucked the trend of iterative adjustments that had marked scholarship implementation for most of the period covered by this book.

The contours of the Cold War shifted during the 1980s, as the relationship between the USSR and the USA evolved, and the USSR loosened its grip on its satellite states. The Pacific's position in global affairs was also changing. The period was marked by difficulties in many of Australia's bilateral relationships with Pacific nations. Two coups in Fiji in 1987 tested the relationship between Australia and an independent Fiji, which had been relatively strong to that point. The coups themselves were motivated by various political, social and ethnic conflicts that had existed in Fiji for decades, certainly since independence in 1970, where many issues had been papered over rather than addressed. In the area of education, there was a perception that Indigenous Fijians were less able to access education than their Indian Fijian contemporaries.[2] These issues of access were driven by a Fijian narrative contending that Indigenous Fijians have been disadvantaged in education by virtue of their unpreparedness for Western life and Western education. This narrative persisted into the 1980s, with stereotyping by race leading to some government scholarship programs only being open to ethnic Fijians, and higher university entrance scores required by ethnic Indian students.[3] According to Carmen White:

> this is indicative of a conventional wisdom in Fiji that seeks an explanation for educational disparities in innate Fijian characteristics and suggests that Fijian childrearing practices and customs fail to stimulate academic interests and achievement.[4]

---

2   Padmini Gaunder, *Education and Race Relations in Fiji 1835–1998* (Fiji: Padmini Gaunder, 1999).
3   Carmen M White, 'Affirmative Action and Education in Fiji: Legitimation, Contestation, and Colonial Discourse', *Harvard Educational Review*, no. 2 (2001): 240–68, doi.org/10.17763/haer.71.2. p1057320407582t0.
4   White, 'Affirmative Action and Education in Fiji', 251.

These broader narratives of disadvantage were part of what led to the coups, with other issues such as a rebalancing of political power away from chiefly leadership playing perhaps a more important role. But as Sanjay Ramesh noted, these coups ensured 'a majority of the population, particularly Indo-Fijians, were politically marginalised and socially ostracised'.[5]

The Hawke Labor Government decided in 1987, in response to the first coup, to stop aid.[6] That decision was reversed quickly, and aid was flowing again by 1988. These coups not only impacted on Australian (and other nations') aid to Fiji, but importantly, affected higher education delivery and access in Fiji and by extension (because of the University of the South Pacific, or USP), across Pacific Island countries.

Pacific stability was also challenged in 1988 with the beginnings of a separatist conflict in Bougainville and what was been described as an 'incipient civil war' also occurring in New Caledonia.[7] Australia did not provide direct military aid to Papua New Guinea (PNG) to support its efforts to maintain control in Bougainville, but indirect military aid and significant non-military aid continued to PNG during the period.[8] In the case of New Caledonia, Australia maintained a level of support for self-determination.

The issue of nuclear testing in the Pacific continued to haunt a number of relationships the Hawke Government had in the Pacific, with concerns being raised about Australia's loyalties to both the USA (via the Australia, New Zealand and United States ANZUS treaty) and commitments to its Pacific neighbours. This was very clear in the case of the MX missile tests, where the Hawke Government allowed the USA to test MX missiles in the waters of the Western Pacific off the coast of Tasmania. This military activity had first occurred in 1981 under the Fraser Government. The decision to allow the tests, and perhaps more importantly not to inform the Australian public about them, was blamed for a significant drop in the popularity of

---

5   Sanjay Ramesh, 'Reflections on the 1987 Fiji Coups', *Fijian Studies: A Journal of Contemporary Fiji* 5, no. 1 (2007): 164–78.
6   Jeannie Zakharov, 'Cabinet Decides to Stop Aid to Fiji', *Canberra Times*, 30 September 1987.
7   Denise Fisher, 'New Caledonia's Independence Referendum: Local and Regional Implications', *The Lowy Institute* (blog), 8 May 2019, www.lowyinstitute.org/publications/new-caledonia-s-independence-referendum-local-regional-implications, accessed 31 March 2023.
8   The use of helicopters donated by the Australian Government was especially controversial.

the Hawke Government in 1985.⁹ New Zealand's nuclear ban was a marked point of difference between Australia and New Zealand in their policies in the Pacific, which put strain on Australia's relationship with the USA under the ANZUS treaty. The nuclear ban, which meant that New Zealand refused to allow nuclear-powered submarines to visit its ports, led to the USA suspending its ANZUS treaty obligations to New Zealand in 1986. For the Pacific Island countries themselves, regionalism was a key focus as they sought to establish themselves as independent states and manage the militarisation of their region.

In an overview of Australian education aid to the Pacific during this period, Elizabeth Cassity notes that decision-making processes within the Australian Hawke Government and bureaucracy at the time were 'ruptured by political instability'.¹⁰ This sense of instability created circumstances where Australian policymakers were often overly keen to exercise more decision-making power than their bilateral aid partners were comfortable with. This is explored further in this chapter.

First, however, this chapter examines the Equity and Merit Scholarship Scheme, which was designed within the Australian International Development Assistance Bureau (AIDAB, formerly known as ADAB, the Australian Development Assistance Bureau), with input from other departments including the Department of Education and the Department of Immigration. The scheme represented a significant shift in the delivery and administration of Australian Government development scholarships, and in many ways established the underpinning infrastructure of both scholarship administration and student recruitment that exists in Australia to the present day.

The Equity and Merit Scholarship Scheme

After it failed to fully address the issues raised in 1984 after the Goldring and Jackson reports, the Hawke Government decided the budget could no longer sustain the growing number of overseas student subsidies and the program

---

9   David Lee, 'Australia's Ambassadors in Washington, 1982–89', in *Australia Goes to Washington: 75 Years of Australian Representation in the United States, 1940-2015*, ed. David Lowe, David Lee, and Carl Bridge, 183–207 (Canberra: ANU Press, 2016), doi.org/10.22459/AGTW.12.2016.10; and Steve Lohr, 'MX Reversal by Australian Isn't Popular', *The New York Times*, 24 February 1985, 12.
10   Elizabeth Cassity, 'Cast the Net a Little Wider: Australian Aid in the South Pacific', *International Journal of Educational Development* 28, (2008): 255, doi.org/10.1016/j.ijedudev.2006.12.003.

had to end. This was also in line with recommendations from the Jackson Report (as discussed in the previous chapter). This was a difficult decision from both diplomatic and development perspectives. Diplomatically, the subsidy program had helped to develop and strengthen ties with countries in the region, in particular Malaysia. Developing countries in South-East Asia and the Pacific had also appreciated the program, which allowed them to send students to study in Australia on government scholarships for a fraction of what it might have otherwise cost. This was an indirect contribution to human resource development programs across the Pacific and South-East Asia. The EMSS was pitched to these nations, especially Malaysia, as the transitional program to ease the pain of the removal of subsidies.

As this chapter outlines, the introduction of the new scholarship scheme took time and was not without problems. The removal of the subsidy scheme represented a tangible cut in funding for universities, with fewer students coming from overseas after the subsidy scheme was ended; the EMSS was designed to soften that blow.[11]

Most importantly, however, the scheme marked a significant change in the way the Australian Government administered scholarships, and the way in which they were viewed in Australia and in recipient nations. Where schemes in the past had used the themes and frameworks provided by the Colombo Plan, and had stuck to a similar script, the EMSS marked a shift. These variations reverberated through subsequent scholarship programs implemented by Australian Governments, both Coalition and Labor.

In moving from a subsidy program to a scholarship program, the government justified the change by pointing to significant issues in the broad nature of the subsidy scheme. Foreign Minister Gareth Evans was quoted in the *Canberra Times* in 1988, at the time of the EMSS announcement, as saying 'this has caused aid funds to be channelled to relatively prosperous countries at the expense of those demonstrating greatest need'.[12] By framing the program as a shift, rather than a reduction, Minister Evans provided

---

11   The subsidy scheme allowed for universities to seek full cost recovery from the government, while the government in turn passed only approximately 25 per cent of that on through the Overseas Student Charge (OSC). The OSC was waived entirely for students from Pacific Island countries. Thus, a reduction in the number of students coming to Australia for study was going to have a tangible impact on the financial health of Australian universities and colleges.
12   'Scholarships Replace Subsidies', *Canberra Times*, 19 December 1988, 2.

a rationale for the new scholarship program that highlighted its benefits. He noted that the scholarship program was going to cost the same amount as the subsidy program.[13]

Prior to the ending of the subsidy scheme, the Department of Foreign Affairs and AIDAB were aware that ending the scheme was going to cause problems for many neighbouring countries. The subsidy scheme widened access to higher education for many who did not have access to university study in their own country and it had become a part of long-term planning for many families. Parents of students from Malaysia who had sent their children to study in Australia for high school under the subsidy system were suddenly facing the prospect of full fees for university education. The National Liaison Committee for Overseas Students Australia wrote to Foreign Minister Gareth Evans to complain about the changing policy:

> The long-established subsidised programme has made it possible for overseas students to gain entrance into tertiary education at prices that an average middle-class family could afford.[14]

This was well understood by the designers of the EMSS; much of the impetus behind the 'equity' element of the EMSS stemmed from this concern.

The Equity and Merit Scholarship Scheme (EMSS),[15] a working title which was then chosen as the final name, was workshopped over the course of a few years, almost longer than the scheme itself existed. Overseas posts were consulted by the Department of Foreign Affairs and AIDAB. The Department of Education, Austrade and the Department of Industry, Technology and Commerce were also part of the working group. The working group also consulted with the Australian Vice-Chancellors' Committee (AVCC). The scholarship program was not the only scholarship program being managed by AIDAB; Development Training Awards continued as they had since the 1970s. However, there was a sense within AIDAB that the new scheme represented 'a major improvement in training assistance in the Australian aid program'.[16] This was not only because of the design elements within the scholarship scheme, but also because the

---

13 This represented a smaller subsidy program that the one that had existed earlier in the decade as cuts to the subsidy program had begun around 1986.
14 'Letter from National Liaison Committee Overseas Students' Australia to FM Evans, 18 May 1989', A4250, 1989/792, National Archives of Australia (NAA).
15 EMSS was the working title for the scheme. Despite a number of other suggestions for names, including the Sir Percy Spender Scholarships, the EMSS name was retained for the implementation of the scheme.
16 'EMSS Progress Report to 31 July 1989', A4250, 1989/792, NAA.

subsidy scheme it was replacing was un-targeted and did not address specific development needs of recipient countries. AIDAB bureaucrats also felt that the scheme offered an opportunity for the bureau to demonstrate its value. A document prepared for the AIDAB Executive by the AIDAB Policy Branch noted that AIDAB would be under scrutiny about the scholarship scheme from parliament, the public and ministers, but 'we have fought for the opportunity, now we have to show we can deliver the goods'.[17]

The key features around which the scheme was designed were what set the program apart from other scholarship programs that the Australian Government had implemented in the past. These features included gender parity, the selection of awardees being independent of partner governments, and students being allowed to pursue any field of study.[18] The attention of the program on being open to all, and very much focused on the individual and their needs, was significantly different to all previous schemes. Partner governments had been significantly involved in selection, and individuals were selected on the basis of how their skills could be part of a broader country development plan. It is clear that the EMSS represented a very significant diversion from the normal practice of government-funded scholarship schemes. The scheme also aimed to have students treated in Australia in the same way as private overseas students, a 'mainstreaming' of students rather than being singled out as part of the Australian Aid Program.

The scheme diverted from its foundational principles only slightly during the final stages of design, largely due to changing circumstances and political and diplomatic calculations. A temporary cohort of 'Year 12' scholarships was introduced by AIDAB, where students in their final year of schooling in Australia were able to apply for EMSS scholarships. This was to cater for students who had commenced high schooling in Australia with the expectation of continuing to university with subsidised fees. The belief was that once that cohort was cleared from the system, that scholarship category would no longer be necessary.[19]

The scheme itself was framed by the designers within the bureaucracy as being directly linked to the recommendations of the Jackson Review, which had called for a significant scholarship program to ensure Australia's obligations to its developing country neighbours were met if the subsidy

---

17   'Notes for Executive on Getting the EMSS up and Running | 16 December', A4250, 1990/801, 1988, NAA.
18   'EMSS Progress Report to 31 July 1989', A4250, 1989/792, NAA.
19   'EMSS Progress Report to 31 July 1989', A4250, 1989/792, NAA.

program was removed. A close reading of documents recording the planning and implementation of the program shows that this is only partially true. Diplomats and bureaucrats within AIDAB expressed significant concerns for how the removal of the subsidy scheme would be received by developing nations, particularly those nations that had made use of it for their own government scholarships. Staff within AIDAB were aware that removing the subsidy scheme would, at the very least, look like a cut to Australia's aid activity. It was noted in a Cabinet submission regarding the ending of the subsidy scheme, and introduction of the scholarship program: 'The aid component of the new scholarship scheme would enable the Government to announce a major aid initiative focused on our region.'[20] This concern was acute in the Pacific region: while the program was intended to 'cover' the same number of students as the subsidy scheme, a cablegram to the High Commission in Fiji noted the government 'may not have wished to be seen to be reducing its support for Pacific students at this time'.[21] Fiji had been a significant source of students under the subsidy scheme, both with private students and students sponsored by the Fijian Government,[22] so the ending of subsidies was likely to have a noticeable impact.

In a significant shift in the nature of Australian development scholarships, a decision was made by the EMSS designers that the scholarship program would involve candidate selection by the Australian Government and their representatives, rather than relying on nominations from recipient countries. A note regarding the details of the program as of February 1989 stated that while recipient governments were to be involved in the Memoranda of Understanding outlining the programs within each country, they were 'not to be involved in final selection of students'.[23] This significant change to the status quo came out of concerns from, among others, diplomats[24] who had noticed discriminatory policies in scholarship selection. For example, the ethnic mix of students from Fiji was of concern, given the fact that government scholarships were largely restricted to Indigenous Fijian students, not Fijians of other ethnic groups such as Fijian Indians. Australian diplomats based in the Pacific during the coups in Fiji in 1987 saw the rhetoric around race,

---

20 'Overseas Student Policy Review Cabinet Submission | Draft | 21 November', A4250, 1990/801, 1988, NAA.
21 'Aid: Equity and Merit Scholarship Scheme (Cablegram Canberra to Suva) 22/03/1989', A4250 1989/792, NAA.
22 'Aid: Equity and Merit Scholarship Scheme (Cablegram Canberra to Suva) 22/03/1989', A4250 1989/792, NAA.
23 'EMSS: Design Issues for Task Force Meeting, 7 February 1989', A4250, 1989/792, NAA.
24 'Aid: Malaysia: Programming Visit (Cablegram), 11 February 1989', A4250, 1989/792, NAA.

and preferential treatment based on race, as it was discussed openly. These discussions continued in Fiji after the coups, a letter to the editor in the *Fiji Times* in 1988 wrote of how iTaukei had been:

> branded as failures in business, lazy workers, suitable only for "labour" jobs, constantly filling the prisons, failures in high schools and university, and this degradation has formulated a negative self-image in us.[25]

A cablegram from diplomats in Malaysia noted that concerns about the Fijian program would be replicated in Malaysia, 'it is possible that a similar concern could arise in respect of the Malaysian program',[26] which had similarly discriminatory selection policies based on race, giving preference to ethnic Malays over Chinese or Indian Malays. These concerns were further compounded when the Prime Minister of Malaysia visited Fiji in 1988, stressing to Indian Fijians that they should accept the realities of the coup, and accept the draft constitution, with its embedded discrimination. Dr Mahathir Mohamad claimed that 'the Malays, like Fijians, were not successful in business but the Malaysian government had set out programmes of participation that Fiji could learn from'.[27]

The working group was fully aware of this rhetoric. They were also bound by Australian legislation regarding equal opportunity and concerns for the development outcomes that could be jeopardised by a racially prejudiced selection policy.

As noted earlier, the scheme was designed around a number of fundamental principles. These were explained by a consultant (WL Mellor) in his administrative review of the program in 1990 as being:

a. an 'open to all' approach
b. academic merit as the primary selection criterion within both the Merit and Equity categories
c. a focus on the needs of individuals and on their choices in terms of courses of study and institutions
d. a new administrative approach which treated aid-funded students as far as possible as private students within Australia.[28]

---

25   Samisoni Tiko, 'Letters to the Editor: Alien System', *The Fiji Times*, 11 November 1988, 6.
26   'Aid: Malaysia: Programming Visit (Cablegram), 11 February 1989', A4250, 1989/792, NAA.
27   'Fiji Indians Must Accept Reality – Malaysian PM', *The Fiji Times*, 4 November 1988, 1.
28   WL Mellor, 'Equity and Merit Scholarship Scheme, 1990 Administrative Review', A4250, 1990/1349, NAA, 7.

That the design included the concept of self-nomination by candidates was seen as an 'innovative approach to development and training in the Third World context'.[29] There was an assumption that this less rigid approach to selection of candidates, and the subjects they studied, would lead to development within the recipient nations. This positive assumption, as has been noted in other research, is endemic in scholarship design and can be problematic.[30]

Rather than being entirely managed from Canberra, the scheme was operated out of diplomatic posts in target countries. This practical necessity allowed for tailoring of each country's cohort, and also fit well within the changing structure of Australian aid into 'Country Programs', as recommended by the Jackson Report. However, the close involvement of posts was not part of the original design, which had sought to:

> distance the control of the scheme from the Australian Government so that it would be perceived to be more in the hands of Australian educational institutions than of the Australian Government.[31]

The diverse cohort of students from across many countries and development contexts was better managed through the involvement of posts. However, depending on the national setting, this also gave partner governments more influence on selection.

A foundational element of this new scholarship program was the notion of equity. The bureaucrats designing the scholarship believed that this element was the key development aspect of the scholarship, and would ensure it achieved individual and societal development outcomes once the student returned home. The design of the scholarship program meant that those on 'Merit' awards were supported through fee-only scholarships, while those on 'Equity' scholarships were supported by fee and stipend scholarships.

---

[29] WL Mellor, 'Equity and Merit Scholarship Scheme, 1990 Administrative Review', A4250, 1990/1349, NAA, 7.
[30] For discussion about the problematic nature of the assumptions of positive outcomes from scholarships see: Joan Dassin, Robin Marsh, and Matt Mawer, 'Introduction: Pathways for Social Change?', in *International Scholarships and Higher Education: Pathways for Social Change*, ed. Joan Dassin, Robin Marsh, and Matt Mawer, 3–21 (New York: Palgrave Macmillan, 2017), doi.org/10.1007/978-3-319-62734-2; and Anna Kent, 'Australian Development Scholarships and Their Place within Diplomacy, Development and Education', Master's thesis, University of Melbourne, 2012; and Anna Kent, 'Recent Trends in International Scholarships', in Dassin, Marsh and Mawer, *International Scholarship in Higher Education*, 23–42.
[31] 'EMSS Progress Report to 31 July 1989', A4250, 1989/792, NAA.

To this end, the selection criteria around equity were determined by each post, allowing the factors important in each country to be considered. In the Pacific, the concept was applied in different ways. In New Caledonia, family income was assessed and gender equity was a key element across the Pacific.[32] In PNG, deciding on the equity criteria involved the PNG Government. A record of a meeting was recounted by an Australian diplomat in a cable to Canberra, noting that the discussion around equity criteria had been difficult, in part because:

> … we suggested applicants who had graduated from a (government) National High School (as opposed to International High Schools or overseas high schools as one equity criteria). Officials reluctantly agreed (several had students at Port Moresby International High School).[33]

This incident mirrors the conversations at the time of independence, discussed in an earlier chapter, wherein Australian diplomats were trapped between obligations to support the stated PNG education policy and the desires of senior politicians for their family members to be educated in Australia.

As the program was implemented, it was clear that the Equity cohort had higher needs in Australian universities. They often required more English language training, bridging and foundational courses and other support. A 1990 administrative review of the EMSS noted that as these students progressed through their studies it was important to monitor them, not least because:

> an unduly high failure rate could give rise to concern both for the individual student and for relationships with those Governments that expressed disquiet at their exclusion from the nomination and selection process.[34]

The inclusion of equity was important to make the scheme truly a part of the program of Overseas Development Assistance. There was uneven application of the concept of equity. This was considered important to ensure the country-specific issues were addressed, but it also caused

---

32 WL Mellor, 'Equity and Merit Scholarship Scheme, 1990 Administrative Review', A4250, 1990/1349, NAA.
33 'Cablegram Port Moresby to Canberra, 9 May', A4250, 1989/735, NAA.
34 WL Mellor, 'Equity and Merit Scholarship Scheme, 1990 Administrative Review', A4250, 1990/1349, NAA, 8.

difficulties for bureaucrats, diplomats, educational institutions and the students themselves. A draft review report in 1990, reflecting on the first cohort of students, noted that in the 'definition and application of Equity criteria a balance needs to be struck between an acknowledgement of social and economic disadvantage and their ability to cope with tertiary studies in Australia'.[35] This tension of different rules, and country-specific elements, did however offer a new approach for the Pacific Island nations. All previous scholarship programs were designed with other nations in mind (for example the Australian International Awards Scheme which was designed for South-East Asia) and did not necessarily meet the specific needs of Pacific Island nations. The EMSS design was adaptable to some of the unique needs of these smaller states.

At the other end of the spectrum, there was disquiet about the possibility of those with means being awarded Equity (rather than Merit) scholarships because of their countries of origin. This was of concern to the working group developing the next iteration of the scholarship scheme, 'the fact that wealthy Filipinos, Thais and Indonesians benefit from this arrangement has not passed without comment'.[36] Only Hong Kong and Singapore were restricted to fee-only scholarships, while other countries including Nepal, Pakistan and Malaysia offered both Equity and Merit awards.

As noted earlier, the EMSS was intended to provide support to Australian universities as they managed the transition from the overseas student subsidy program to the full fee–paying international student system. The EMSS program costs were framed around spending the 'savings' from the overseas subsidy scheme on fees (replacing the income lost by universities). However, because the EMSS students were able to choose their destination institution, the funds were distributed unevenly across the sector. Some institutions, such as the University of New South Wales and the University of Melbourne were able to gain significant revenue from the EMSS program, while other universities were unable to make up for the loss of the Commonwealth subsidy program through the EMSS.[37] These adjustments were occurring at the same time as the changes to the

---

35 'Draft Report of the EMSS Review', A4250, 1990/1349, NAA.
36 'Report of Working Group – JCSS – Integration into Country Programs', A4250, 1991/2160, 1991, NAA.
37 WL Mellor, 'Equity and Merit Scholarship Scheme, 1990 Administrative Review', A4250, 1990/1349, NAA, 9.

university sector via the Dawkins Reforms were being implemented.[38] As discussed in the previous chapter, this included the imposition of fees onto the domestic student population and the growth in number of full fee–paying international students. This added a layer of complexity to the implementation of a new scholarship scheme.

The EMSS was a much larger scholarship program than many of its predecessors, particularly in the Pacific. In the planning, the goal was to provide 600 scholarships (Equity and Merit) allocated across particular countries, and 350 scholarships (Merit only) for students from 20 eligible countries who were completing their Year 12 in Australia by the middle of 1989.[39] In the early phase of designing the EMSS program, bureaucrats believed that after the subsidy scheme was removed, for the 'South Pacific the new program would provide the same student numbers in Australian higher education as under the subsidised scheme'.[40] The first round of the awards included 198 scholarships for Pacific Island nations, including 55 for Fiji, 50 for PNG and 20 for both Tonga and Western Samoa.[41] There were also 19 regional scholarships awarded to scholars from the Cook Islands, Kiribati, Niue and Tuvalu. A cablegram from Canberra to the Australian High Commission in Fiji explained the decisions around numbers in this way:

> The number of scholarships for the South Pacific was drawn up with a close eye on the existing numbers of private students from the South Pacific in Australian Higher Education Institutions. In the past AIDAB has paid the overseas student charge for every private student from the South Pacific. The total number which was set for the South Pacific in the first year would in fact have delivered a smaller number of students from the South Pacific into Australia in 1990 than had started higher education courses in 1989, if no students had purchased places on their own account.[42]

---

38 In addition to fee changes and the introduction of the Higher Education Contribution Scheme (HECS), the Dawkins reforms included the consolidation of Colleges of Adult Education (CAEs) into universities.
39 'Meeting of National Liaison Committee Overseas Students Australia', A4250, 1990/801, 1989, NAA.
40 'Overseas Student Policy Review Cabinet Submission | Draft | 21 November', A4250, 1990/801, 1988, NAA.
41 WL Mellor, 'Equity and Merit Scholarship Scheme, 1990 Administrative Review', A4250, 1990/1349, NAA.
42 'Aid: Equity and Merit Scholarship Scheme (Cablegram Canberra to Suva) 22/03/1989', A4250 1989/792, NAA.

The 1992 intake included 80 awards for Fiji and PNG respectively, each representing 9 per cent of the total number of awards in that intake. The following year was significantly smaller in number, with 34 awards each; however, it still represented a 9 per cent share each.[43]

These numbers did not rival those available to other larger countries such as Indonesia and Malaysia, but both Malaysia and Indonesia had much larger populations than any Pacific states. However, they represented a large number of students to be taken out of the education systems of the Pacific Island states. This was an issue for both the Australian Government and the recipient governments. The regional university system, the USP and other universities in the region were undermined by the EMSS, especially as students were able to choose their own courses, even if that course was being offered in the region.

The shaping and administration of the EMSS was as part of the aid program, and remained an element of bilateral aid funding. However, by the nature of its implementation and design it was at times interpreted by recipient governments as outside the normal government-to-government approach to aid funding. Rushed implementation without Memoranda of Understanding between the Australian Government and the recipient governments led some local authorities to view it as 'a "private" matter, rather than a government-to-government project'.[44] The foundational element of the scheme, the idea that 'all comers' were welcome, was a key issue of concern for some partner governments, who were unused to being cut out of selection decisions when it came to scholarships. Posts were given substantial freedom to make decisions around the scholarships, without the imposition of the partner government viewpoint. This represented a significant change. It was an explicitly stated element of the program that the scholarship was focused on 'individual needs and personal development'[45] rather than broader sector development.

Some partner governments were happy to participate in the program on this basis, but there were others who did not share the view that 'enhancing the individual development of "all comers" necessarily enhances national development' and met this development 'with polite scepticism in many

---

43 'Overseas Students Programs – New Arrangements | Ministerial Submission | 19 December', A4250, 1991/2160, 1991, NAA.
44 WL Mellor, 'Equity and Merit Scholarship Scheme, 1990 Administrative Review', A4250, 1990/1349, NAA, 11.
45 'EMSS Progress Report to 31 July 1989', A4250, 1989/792, NAA.

cases'.⁴⁶ The impact of the program on recipient government training and human resource development plans was of significant concern to some small Pacific nations.

For some recipient nations the objections were vague and unspecific, while others were able to point to specific reservations. The PNG Government reported that:

> the design and operation of the EMSS scheme had actually caused some disruption of manpower plans and introduced negative 'ripple effects' upon the training of other individuals whose programs could be delayed or jeopardised.⁴⁷

The Tongan Government was disappointed with the EMSS programs, and noted in a joint review of scholarships in 1991⁴⁸ that three highly trained medical practitioners (from a very small population of qualified personnel) were going to Australia under the EMSS, against the wishes of the Tongan Government.⁴⁹

The involvement of recipient governments was worrying to the designers of the scheme for a number of important reasons. It was clear that racially discriminatory policies like those employed by the Malaysian and Fijian governments were in mind when the EMSS designers removed selection from recipient governments. The designers also understood that issues of gender equity and nepotism had at different times been noted in the selection of scholarship students in the decades leading up to the EMSS implementation, as has been explained in previous chapters.

Nevertheless, many recipient governments resented the distance inbuilt into the EMSS. Many posts did keep their host governments informed of activities and selections, but recipient governments wanted, and in some cases felt they needed, a louder voice in the process. But always in the minds of the administrators of the scheme, and the posts implementing it, was 'the capacity of Government to propose names of potential awardees on

---

46 WL Mellor, 'Equity and Merit Scholarship Scheme, 1990 Administrative Review', A4250, 1990/1349, NAA, 11.
47 WL Mellor, 'Equity and Merit Scholarship Scheme, 1990 Administrative Review', A4250, 1990/1349, NAA, 12.
48 The joint review was an Australian, New Zealand and Tongan government review that looked at both Tongan and Australian Government scholarships, including the EMSS.
49 'Tonga Scholarships Scheme Review – Background Briefing | March 1991', A4250, 1990/4203, NAA.

some other basis than merit or equity'.⁵⁰ Nevertheless, the reviews of the program after the first year of implementation noted 'EMSS was generally welcomed by participating countries although some insist on some degree of involvement in the selection of candidates for scholarships'.⁵¹ AIDAB reluctantly conceded that some involvement of partner governments would be inevitable.

With the program operating somewhat separately from the recipient governments, there was concern that it would lead to brain drain: the exodus of well-educated and trained individuals from the developing countries of the Pacific. This was an acute issue, especially in light of the development of higher educational institutions such as USP. This worry was voiced by Fijian academic and politician Tupeni Baba in 1989 when he wrote that selection being undertaken in Australia:

> means that Australian institutes through AIDAB machinery would cream off the best Pacific students who could have gone to universities in the region. This ... would have the effect of undermining local institutions.⁵²

This issue was not new, but the significant shift of moving selection to the donor, rather than the recipient, highlighted the issue. The 'brain drain' impact of the EMSS on Fiji was greater than other parts of the South Pacific, as the candidate pool for Fiji was larger than expected in the early intakes of the EMSS. This was in contrast to the rest of the South Pacific, where the candidate pools were smaller. This was met with disquiet by scholarship administrators, who thought that the 'situation may deteriorate in future years as the pool of potential candidates is drained by the numbers of awardees'.⁵³

The EMSS lasted only three intakes, nevertheless it was reviewed a number of times. This reflected the growing trend for aid evaluations, and the nature of the program, which was so different to previous scholarship programs. The first review was undertaken following the arrival of the first students in

---

50   WL Mellor, 'Equity and Merit Scholarship Scheme, 1990 Administrative Review', A4250, 1990/1349, NAA, 13.
51   'Draft Report of the EMSS Review', A4250, 1990/1349, NAA.
52   Tupeni Baba, *The Business of Australian Aid: Education, Training and Development – The Marjorie Smart Lecture for 1989: Tupeni Baba; and a Summary of the Proceedings of a Subsequent Panel Discussion Edited by D.R. Jones, V.L. Meek and J. Weeks*, ed. David R Jones, V Lynn Meek, and J Weeks (Melbourne: St Hilda's College, University of Melbourne, 1989), 14.
53   WL Mellor, 'Equity and Merit Scholarship Scheme, 1990 Administrative Review', A4250, 1990/1349, NAA, 13.

Australia in 1990. It was undertaken by an external consultant and a review team who travelled to a number of posts.[54] This was accompanied by an internal review.[55] These were largely positive, the external review concluding that the 'EMSS has succeeded, and will continue to succeed, because of the commitment of institutions and personnel both in Australia and overseas'.[56]

The EMSS was again reviewed as it was renamed, and slightly redesigned, as the John Crawford Scholarship Scheme in 1993, and again in 1994. The review in 1994 was designed to provide an 'end of program' review, looking at administrative aspects of the program and their implementation as well as the success of students.[57] It was intended that this review would go towards supporting the new Australian Development Cooperation Scholarship (ADCOS) program, with the 'best' elements of the EMSS being carried forward into the design of the ADCOS.

Scholarship programs by their very nature are difficult to measure. Long-term outcomes cannot be measured for decades after the activity of the scholarship is complete. In the case of the EMSS, which was over sooner than a student could complete an undergraduate degree, it was particularly difficult. This was noted in reviews: 'It remains to be seen what the advantages or disadvantages are of the scheme being so diverse in design.'[58]

The EMSS program had been designed to utilise funding made available by the abolishing of overseas student subsidies, and to cushion the blow of that policy change for Australian universities. In 1992 a new program, utilising many of the same policy and design settings, was introduced. The name change was not the only alteration (and was incidentally very short lived). The John Crawford Scholarship Scheme (JCSS)[59] was in operation for only a year (1993), and was replaced/renamed with the ADCOS program. At the same time of the change of name, AIDAB made the decision to move the scholarship programs into the bilateral country programs, rather than in its own scholarship-focused area. In addition, the ongoing Sponsored

---

54 WL Mellor, 'Equity and Merit Scholarship Scheme, 1990 Administrative Review', A4250, 1990/1349, NAA.
55 'Draft Report of the EMSS Review', A4250, 1990/1349, NAA.
56 WL Mellor, 'Equity and Merit Scholarship Scheme, 1990 Administrative Review', A4250, 1990/1349, NAA, 33.
57 'Terms of Reference for an Evaluation of the EMSS and a Review of the Administrative Arrangements of the Australian Development Cooperation Scholarships | 28 July', A4250, 1990/1583, 1994, NAA.
58 'EMSS Progress Report to 31 July 1989', A4250, 1989/792, NAA.
59 John Crawford played an important role in the development of Australia's aid program. His name is now attached to a specific scholarship funded by the Australian Aid program and managed by the Australian Centre for International Agricultural Research (ACIAR).

Training Program (STP) (sometimes known as the Development Training Program (DTP)) was renamed as the Australian Sponsored Training Assistance Scheme (ASTAS), and in-Australia management was merged with ADCOS.[60]

This move represented a shift in thinking within AIDAB, with decisions about the quantum and style of scholarships to be delegated to the country programs, and much of the in-Australia management delegated to AIDAB Regional Offices, rather than within AIDAB Central. Some concerns about this shift remained; AIDAB was keen to retain gender equity across the whole program,[61] which became more difficult with the devolution into country programs. This, however, did allow for country programs that were struggling to achieve gender equity to be 'saved' by the broader program. Officials recommending these changes appear to have accepted that devolution to country programs would lead to 'an increased degree of involvement of recipient country officials in JCSS targeting and selection'.[62] Given the EMSS's strong position on barring the involvement of recipient governments in selection, this was a significant concession.[63] The ministerial submission requesting the administrative changes is blunt: 'we believe that once JCSS is integrated into country programs, recipient officials will put pressure on us to clear scholarships with them'.[64]

There were some positives expected from the move in responsibility. AIDAB staff felt that the change to a more 'country-specific' element within the scholarship would allow for a flexibility in level of study that was not in the original EMSS design. AIDAB described the JCSS as being 'more closely aligned to the development priorities within individual country programs'.[65] This was a particular issue in the Pacific, where officials expressed concern that there were not enough 'quality' candidates to sustain

---

60 'Overseas Students Programs – New Arrangements | Ministerial Submission | 19 December', A4250, 1991/2160, 1991, NAA.
61 'Overseas Students Programs – New Arrangements | Ministerial Submission | 19 December', A4250, 1991/2160, 1991, NAA.
62 'Overseas Students Programs – New Arrangements | Ministerial Submission | 19 December', A4250, 1991/2160, 1991, NAA.
63 While the EMSS had been designed to have little to no input from recipient governments, this had not always worked in practice during implementation. The Chinese scheme involved the recipient government (who selected all the students) and some other limited or significant involvement was present in a number of countries.
64 'Overseas Students Programs – New Arrangements | Ministerial Submission | 19 December', A4250, 1991/2160, 1991, NAA.
65 'Aid – John Crawford Scholarship Scheme (JCSS) | Cablegram to All Student Posts | 4 October', A4250, 1991/2160, 1991, NAA.

the scholarship in its designed form, focused as it was on university-level study. The devolution to country programs would allow for a transition to technical and vocational level training where appropriate.[66]

The shift to the JCSS also included another significant amendment to the program: the move to a two-tiered stipend amount where students with accompanying families received a higher rate. This represented another policy change with lasting implications for the access, equity and gender diversity of Australian Government scholarships. This was a policy difference that resonated through subsequent iterations of the scholarship.

As the EMSS transitioned to the JCSS, bureaucrats within AIDAB discussed the geographic spread of the scholarship program. The program had been put in place to soften the blow for many stakeholders following the abolition of the subsidised higher education for overseas students. Malaysia, Hong Kong and Singapore had been included in the EMSS program for this very reason, and as the 'cushion' was to be removed, their inclusion was considered. A working group in 1991 concluded that while Singapore and Hong Kong should be removed from the program, Malaysia was a more complicated prospect, due to some strain on the political relationship. It was noted by the working group that:

> Malaysia represents a major supply of 'commercial' scholars to Australian tertiary institutions; we probably need to hold out JCSS scholarships as part of the publicity program for selling Australian education abroad as an 'aid-trade' activity.[67]

These issues were of less concern in the Pacific, with Equity programs dominating. However, as discussed earlier, some Pacific posts such as New Caledonia had instituted a level of income assessment to ensure that students were not 'of means', to ensure that it was Kanak students rather than white students eligible for the scholarships. Despite the concerns of the working group, a decision was made to continue offering the (fee-only) JCSS to Hong Kong and Singapore in the first intake, with a decision on their future to be decided at a later time.[68]

---

66 'Report of Working Group – JCSS – Integration into Country Programs', A4250, 1991/2160, 1991, NAA.
67 'Report of Working Group – JCSS – Integration into Country Programs', A4250, 1991/2160, 1991, NAA.
68 'Report of Working Group – JCSS – Integration into Country Programs', A4250, 1991/2160, 1991, NAA.

The JCSS was short lived as a name because of a decision to make the programs 'more appropriately reflect the Australian nature of the program'.[69] Bureaucrats felt that the Australian Development Cooperation Scholarships more clearly labelled it as an Australian program, hence the change to the ADCOS. The first intake of ADCOS students commenced in 1994. The move from JCSS to ADCOS included some administrative amendments, as the scholarships moved more firmly into the bilateral aid programs. But perhaps more important was the shift to more clearly identify the program as an Australian scholarship to allow the Australian Government more easily bask in the reflected glow of the program. In contemporary discussions around international scholarships this is known as the soft power outcomes of scholarship programs.

Concurrent to the design and launch of the EMSS program, a far more specialised and focused scholarship scheme was initiated by the Australian Government. While the focus of much of this book is tertiary-level scholarships, this award offers an interesting case study on the role of Australia's aid program and scholarships offered during an earlier, perhaps more formative period of a young person's life. It also demonstrates, by its very existence, some of the limitations of the education aid delivered in PNG by successive Australian governments up to that point. As part of the Australia–PNG Treaty of Development Cooperation, in 1988 a Secondary School Students' Project (SSSP) was launched. As part of the project, 'academically high achievers who scored A and B grades in Year 10 in PNG high schools were eligible to apply for the scholarship'.[70] The scholarship involved them travelling to Australia, boarding at an Australian high school, and completing their senior schooling (Years 11 and 12), although many students also needed to repeat Year 10 to achieve the necessary results to continue into Year 11.

This scholarship scheme was framed as necessary because, in part, there was still extremely limited access to secondary schools in PNG. This was despite the presence of a number of universities in PNG in 1988, including the University of PNG. According to education researcher Juliana McLaughlin, most of the secondary schools in PNG:

---

69 'Terms of Reference for an Evaluation of the EMSS and a Reivew of the Administrative Arrangements of the Australian Development Cooperation Scholarships | 28 July', A4250, 1990/1583, 1994, NAA.
70 Juliana Mohok McLaughlin and Anne Hickling-Hudson, 'Beyond Dependency Theory: A Postcolonial Analysis of Educating Papua New Guinean High School Students in Australian Schools', *Asia Pacific Journal of Education* 25, no. 2 (2005): 196, doi.org/10.1080/02188790500338187.

offered only a Year 7–10 level of education with an approximate enrolment of 33% of primary school graduates. The majority of these left before Year 10, and very few proceeded to higher education.[71]

Some of the graduates of the SSSP program had significant difficulties on their arrival in Australia, unsurprising given the education system from which they came. Unmet expectations about adjustment and capacity in many ways mirror the issues faced by students from PNG during the 1960s and 1970s, which were discussed in an earlier part of this book. Research about this program has also demonstrated that students also had significant difficulties on return to PNG. Juliana McLaughlin's research indicated that:

> the social identities that they had developed during their three years in Australia were rejected by the PNG communities, thus pressuring returnees to recreate an appropriate identity which supported their acceptance into PNG society.[72]

This rejection was experienced by returning students at a community level, but also at a systemic level. The existence of the SSSP highlights the failures of Australia's colonial and postcolonial education policies in PNG.

The policy conflicts emerging out of the SSSP are illustrative of broader concerns with Australian international development scholarships during this period. The Hawke Government, through AIDAB, was making decisions about aid delivery that were in many ways divorced from the recipient governments; seeing the aid recipient as the individual rather than the state. This move was linked to broader conversations occurring at the time about the uses and methods of aid. The role of the individual was given priority, a process Corinna Unger describes as a trend to 'redefine the role of the state in the development process'.[73] The EMSS was an experiment in redefining the function of the recipient state in scholarship aid. Tupeni Baba was particularly critical of this approach to aid delivery in the Pacific:

> It is obvious in my view that the kind of relationship that has been struck is one-sided. It has been devised to meet Australian needs and interests. This type of relationship can be described as paternalism and not partnership.[74]

---

71 Mohok McLaughlin and Hickling-Hudson, 'Beyond Dependency Theory', 195.
72 Mohok McLaughlin and Hickling-Hudson, 'Beyond Dependency Theory', 197.
73 Corrina R Unger, *International Development: A Postwar History* (London: Bloomsbury Academic, 2018).
74 Tupeni L Baba, 'Australia's Involvement in Education in the Pacific: Partnership or Patronage?', *Directions: Journal of Educational Studies* 11, no. 2 (1989): 51.

The charge of paternalism was not new, and the alternative that the EMSS represented did little to address the perception, despite the adaptability of the EMSS to specific country needs and conditions.

The EMSS, and the scholarship programs that came after it, represent a significant shift in approach by the Australian Government in the way it managed scholarships to foreign countries. While the outcomes sought by the scholarship program remained the same – development of recipient countries and development of the recipients of scholarships themselves – one of the key elements shifted: selection. In part, this shift reflected technological advancements of the time. Up until the 1980s, the process of accepting, assessing and shortlisting applications would have needed to be conducted by post, a time-consuming activity. Access to computers, and the capacity to transmit data, either via disk or over emerging internet networks, changed the dynamic significantly. Rather than relying on those 'in-country' to make the selections, it was possible to move the responsibility to Australia.

AIDAB was also grappling with the significant domestic pressures that equal opportunity legislation caused on internationally focused policies. By bringing selection in-country it was better able to fulfil the obligations of the Hawke Government. The experiment of the EMSS did allow AIDAB to reset scholarship selection to be the responsibility of the donor, but the freedom for students to choose their own courses from the full range on offer was short lived. As discussed in the next chapter, successive scholarship programs moved to a far more instrumentalist approach, with 'priority areas of study' identified by recipient governments. Recipient governments also wrested back some of the control of selection, or at least a seat at the scholarship selection table. Development scholarships also became a part of country programs, allowing them to be integrated into broader aid activities within a country.

This chapter has engaged with the design and implementation of a scholarship program that can be seen as a turning point in Australian international development scholarships. The design process involved many departments and bureaucrats, but there is little evidence to suggest that it was undertaken by specialists in scholarship design. Nevertheless, the process involved a significant number of external parties, including the Australian Vice-Chancellors' Committees, and a growing network of Australians working to educate those within the region about the Australian education sector. These foundations have grown significantly since that time, with the

AVCC International Development Program (IDP) organisation becoming a significant influence on the growth of the Australian international education sector over subsequent decades.

The EMSS represented an attempt by aid bureaucrats to make the management of scholarship selection easier for themselves, failing to recognise the controlling and paternalistic message that decision made. The EMSS also represented an effort to see education as a broader social good, rather than an instrumentalist activity designed to effect 'development'. This view was not shared by partner governments and was also not in line with the broader neoliberal approach to education that the Dawkins Reforms were putting in place.

As the recommendations of both the Jackson and Goldring reports were synthesised, digested and implemented, or ignored and rejected, Australian universities were forced to develop processes for recruiting, engaging with and supporting a changing cohort of international students. The EMSS provided them with a taste for the requirements, and for many institutions these students compensated for the massive drop in numbers of international students following the abolishing of subsidies. AIDAB itself was also able to test itself in its capacity to design and implement a scholarship program, essentially from scratch. Rather than being a tweaked existing program, the EMSS represents a significant break in approach. AIDAB challenged Australian diplomats across the region to have difficult conversations around equity, access, nepotism, and gender equality. It was a bold experiment that helped Australia to meet its own obligations, and it appears that no diplomatic relationships was terminally damaged by the EMSS. It also laid out the framework for each scholarship program that has come since.

PART 5: 1997–2018

This is the final part of this book, covering two major scholarship schemes and just over 10 years. The first chapter covers the period in government of John Howard, and the Australian Development Scholarships scheme (ADS). Howard and his government became fixated on the security threat posed by small and unstable states in the Pacific. This preoccupation came about because of two key events: the Timor-Leste independence referendum and subsequent conflict from 1999, and the September 11 attacks in the USA in 2001 and a growing perception that Australia was surrounded by an 'arc of instability' in the Pacific. Terrorism and security concerns shaped aid allocations and decisions around scholarships, and the Australian Government became bolder when it came to intervention in conflicts.

The second chapter of this part addresses the final scholarship scheme of this book, the Australia Awards. The Australia Awards did not diverge from the ADS significantly in design, but the name change signifies a broader change in the scholarship program. Development was no longer at the centre of the name, nor the centre of the scholarship program. The diplomatic outcomes of the scholarship became far more significant. This chapter addresses this change, and other important changes in aid administration and scholarship management. The chapter, and this book, concludes in 2018, at a time when policy focus was beginning to shift back to the Pacific, in large part to counter the influence of the People's Republic of China.

MANDATES AND MISSTEPS

Paulus William Kei, Lavarah Haihavu and Jakapi Arigo

The stories of students of this more recent period are easier to find, less like the puzzles and snippets from previous parts of this book. This is in part due to investments made by the Department of Foreign Affairs and Trade into a Global Alumni Strategy in the 2010s, which involved a website profiling students who have completed, or are completing, their studies. Universities were also keen to profile their Australia Awards students as part of their marketing efforts. But crucially, these alumni have completed their studies more recently, which means that the long-term impact of their studies are either yet to be felt or not yet obvious. Unlike alumni such as Judy Annemarie Wong, we cannot see the full trajectory of their life. There are immediate impacts for most of these alumni, but their reflections will change over the course of their lives. Their recorded stories are also more likely to be, in part, a marketing tool that is edited for public consumption. These examples will rarely give the unvarnished version of their experiences, including the difficulties and setbacks as well as the positives and happy experiences. Nevertheless, issues that have been part of the students' stories of the previous part remain present. This includes the ability to use the agency gained during a scholarship to choose a life and home, and the nature of status and privilege.

Paulus William Kei studied in Australia between 2006 and 2007, at Southbank Institute of Technology in Brisbane.[1] In an interview about his experiences he clearly identified the positives of the scholarship – on the face of it, he epitomises the 'poverty reduction' element of a scholarship program. He had a difficult childhood, finished school at the end of Year 10 and had a number of jobs until he became a lab technician. He was promoted in the lab when he returned from his studies in Australia, and had been able to undertake project consultancies for additional income. However, some members of his family struggled to reintegrate into Papua New Guinea (PNG) when they returned, and he noted in his interview that he was now saving money to send his children to Australia for a 'better life'. By utilising the skills he developed in Australia he was working to subvert, perhaps unconsciously, one of the goals of the scholarship program.

---

1   Paulus William Kei, interview, 14 December 2014 in David Lowe, Jemma Purdey, and Jonathan Richie, 'Scholarships and Connections: Australia, Indonesia and Papua New Guinea, 1960–2010', data set, Deakin University, 2015.

But in doing so was supporting another outcome of the scholarship – an ongoing connection to Australia. In addition, the pressure he felt to return home despite a job offer in Australia demonstrated the conflict that the scholarship can create within an individual. Kei had been given a level of agency through his program, but he was not able to exercise this agency with freedom because of the restrictions of the scholarship, and thus returned home, a process made especially difficult for his family.

Agency is a key memory for Lavarah Haihavu, who was interviewed in December 2014 about her experience as a PNG ADS student in Australia.[2] Studying in Australia was a difficult and complicated experience for Haihavu, who found her Masters program challenging. Nevertheless, in her reflections she notes that during her time in Australia she had fewer responsibilities, and was able to live free from the perceived burden of her extended family. Haihavu's experience, and reflections, also demonstrate how the scholarships place barriers to access. She was able to gain a scholarship from a position of relative privilege, as she had an undergraduate degree and was working at a university when she applied for her first scholarship. When she applied for a second scholarship, a research degree, she was unsuccessful. Haihavu interpreted this as being the result of her lack of 'insider' status – she was not connected to the aid program sufficiently to be awarded a scholarship.

These two examples represent a great number of the benefits of the ADS scholarship program. The two students successfully completed their degrees, and their experiences were life altering in largely positive ways. However, they also embody a number of the complications and drawbacks that scholarship students over the decades experienced. They attained a level of independence and agency during their study, but were unable to convert that into action in part due to restrictions on returning home.

From the Global Alumni website we are able to find the story of Jakapi Arigo, who first studied for a Masters in IT with an Australia Awards scholarship.[3] She returned home to PNG, but has returned to Australia for a second Masters. Her profile focuses on her choice of Queensland as a destination, unsurprising given the profile was commissioned by Study

---

2   Lavarah Haihavu, interview by Jemma Purdey, Port Moresby, 16 December 2014, in Lowe, Purdey and Richie, 'Scholarships and Connections'.
3   'PNG's Jakapi Arigo on IT, Masters, Queensland and Rugby League', Australia Global Alumni, Department of Foreign Affairs and Trade (Australia), 2019, www.globalalumni.gov.au/alumni-stories/pngs-jakapi-arigo-on-it-masters-queensland-and-rugby-league, accessed 15 July 2020.

Queensland. Arigo's case is interesting in the context of the Australia Awards, given her preference for gaining work experience in Australia after her second Masters. Because she is not an Australia Awards scholar for her second Masters program, she is not bound by a return home requirement. She noted that she would like to 'ultimately' return home to PNG, but her short-term plan is to work in Australia. She has been able to make the choice to stay in Australia, a choice not available to Paulus Kei.

While these stories, and the others collected by the Australian Government, state governments, universities and other educational institutions purport to tell us the stories of success of the Australia Awards, their positive framing and brevity give very little insight into the experiences the students and alumni have had. This reflects the reality of scholarships, where outcomes can take years and sometimes decades to manifest. Finding the stories of recent Pacific scholarship alumni is relatively easy, but the insights to be gained from these snippets do not provide significant depth. The puzzles constructed from archival material telling the stories of students from the 1950s also fail to provide the full story, but the benefits of time and reflection do allow for greater understanding.

9

Multiple objectives for scholarships and aid

This chapter focuses on a raft of scholarships that emerged from the late 1990s and across the 2000s. These awards were primarily based around what will be termed the 'anchor' award, the Australian Development Scholarships (ADS). The ADS was created in 1998, coming out of the Australian Development Cooperation Scholarship (ADCOS) and Australian Sponsored Training Assistance (ASTAS) schemes discussed in the previous chapter.

This chapter examines developments in Australian development scholarships over the 12 years following the introduction of the ADS, up until 2010. The period this chapter covers also marked the introduction of a new regional educational institution, the Australia Pacific Training College, announced by the Howard Government in 2006. The college, based in Fiji, was designed to deliver vocational training and qualifications to fill skills gaps in the Pacific region.

The aid bureaucracy through which these scholarships were managed also remained relatively stable across the turn of the century and into the beginning of the new millennium. This is in part due to the continuity of government across the period, with John Howard elected as prime minister in 1996, and his Coalition Government remaining in place until 2007. The Australian Aid Agency (AusAID) was for the most part an entity of its own, within the portfolio of the Department of Foreign Affairs and Trade (DFAT). In 2010 it was created as an executive agency, still within the DFAT portfolio, but with a measure of greater independence. Reforms were introduced in relation to scholarship management over a period from 1995 to 1997, prior to the 'creation' of the ADS that affected the administration of scholarships, which included the introduction of contracts for educational institutions in an effort to provide a minimum level of service to the students.

While the aid bureaucracy may have been relatively calm over the end of the twentieth century and into the twenty-first, Australia's role in the Pacific was changing. The election of the Howard Government in 1996 ended a long period of Labor rule, and began more than a decade of Coalition Government. In 1999, after Timor-Leste voted to become independent from Indonesia, Australia led a United Nations peacekeeping force to protect the people of Timor-Leste from the departing Indonesian military and militia. This became the first of Australia's forays into Pacific regional security under Prime Minister Howard. In 2003, unrest in the Solomon Islands, and encouragement from US President George W Bush led to Prime Minister Howard 'signalling that he wants to be the region's policeman, promoting Australia as a "long-term guardian" which would take a more "interventionist" role'.[1] As part of its responsibilities as 'Deputy Sheriff' in the Pacific',[2] Australia led the Regional Assistance Mission to Solomon Islands (RAMSI), which began in 2003. A coup in Fiji in 2006 heightened a sense of an unstable political environment in the South Pacific. The end of the Cold War had changed the dynamics of aid and foreign policy for nations across the Pacific. But the rise of Al Qaeda, particularly after the September 11 attacks in New York, and a focus on the threat and risk of Islamic extremism coloured aid, foreign affairs and security considerations for the Howard Government across the world, including the Pacific. Fear of the potential chaos created by political and social instability governed the behaviour of the Australian Government. Foreign Minister Alexander Downer noted in a speech in 2006 that:

> since September 11, 2001 we have come to face a new challenge for national and international security ... The September 11 attacks changed the way we think about weak states and their possible effect on international security.[3]

---

1 Alex Spillius, 'Bush Entrusts "Deputy Sheriff" Howard with Pacific Policing Role', *The Telegraph*, 15 August 2003.
2 Spillius, 'Bush Entrusts "Deputy Sheriff" Howard'.
3 Alexander Downer, 'Inaugural Lecture on National and International Security: 16 May 2006, Wollongong', 2006, webarchive.nla.gov.au/awa/20060601232535/http://pandora.nla.gov.au/pan/25167/20060602-0000/www.foreignminister.gov.au/speeches/2006/060516_national_international_security.html, accessed 28 July 2020.

He used this same speech to frame Australia's role in the Solomon Islands and Timor-Leste (along with Afghanistan and Iraq) as nation-building conducted by Australia, saying the RAMSI mission 'marked a new willingness of the Government to become more actively engaged in nation building in the Pacific'.[4] This more interventionist approach played out not only in peacekeeping and policing, but also in the provision of scholarships, as is demonstrated throughout this chapter.

In this chapter it is not possible to use the archival sources that have been a feature of previous parts of this book. The timeframes involved preclude the use of government archival documentation. Nevertheless, it is possible to gain a comprehensive understanding of the situation through other sources, including audit reports, publicly released reports, and internal documents released under a freedom of information process. A close reading of these documents, particularly with the knowledge of the schemes that preceded those addressed in this chapter, can provide significant insight.

Another useful source to understand the attitude and understanding of both the Commonwealth government, and many of those Australians working in the Pacific Island states, are two Senate inquiries. The first, an Inquiry into Australia's Relationship with Papua New Guinea and other Pacific Island Countries was tabled in August 2003 and received 87 submissions from government departments, non-government organisations, unions, churches, individuals, research organisations and businesses. The second inquiry was in 2009, this time into the security and economic challenges facing Papua New Guinea (PNG) and the south-west Pacific. The range of submissions from across the community provides a useful insight into Australia's sense of itself in relation to the Pacific at the beginning of the twenty-first century. The second round of submissions also allows for a greater understanding of how much of Australia's policy had changed (or not) in the intervening six years.

This chapter investigates the ADS and what role it played in Australian foreign policy and foreign aid at the end of the twentieth century and into the twenty-first century. The program had become more rigidly focused on priority areas of study, and focused on measurable outcomes. The number of sub-awards specifically focused on certain areas was a feature of this period, and much of this chapter is shaped around those awards and the way in which they represent the priorities of the Australian Government,

---

4   Downer, 'Inaugural Lecture on National and International Security'.

signals of the intentions of broader aid and foreign policy. This included a growing focus on security and anti-terrorism measures, and concern about the capacity of small states to manage the risks the Australian Government saw as acute.

Over this decade the desire to measure outcomes was not restricted to the scholarship component of aid and became an intrinsic part of all aid delivery. This, along with government priorities and a focus on governance and security, had significant impact on the way the scholarship programs were implemented across the world, and in the Pacific specifically.

This period also marked an effort on behalf of the Australian and New Zealand governments to work collaboratively on scholarship implementation. Australia's support for Pacific regional scholarships continued over the period, and is examined in more detail in this chapter.

Many nations within the Pacific, and other donors, had scholarships of their own to offer during this period. An Australian and New Zealand review of scholarship provision in the Pacific (which is discussed in more detail later in this chapter) also included a 'competitor scan' of major donors offering scholarships in the Pacific.[5] Two of the larger donors across the decade from 2000 include China and Taiwan, who used aid and scholarships as part of a long-running effort to gain recognition in global forums such as the United Nations. In 2007/08 it was estimated that China offered between nine and 20 long-term awards per country to a number of Pacific nations including Vanuatu, Tonga, Samoa, PNG, the Federated States of Micronesia, Fiji and the Cook Islands. In 2009 they also began offering a small number of regional scholarships through the Pacific Islands Forum Secretariat.[6] Over the same period, Taiwan offered approximately 60 awards across the Pacific, but in 2001 it established a scholarships scheme in collaboration with the Pacific Island Forum, the Forum Islands Scholarship Scheme, which offered scholarships for study in Taiwan and in regional universities.[7] Taiwan also gave the Solomon Islands Government funding to create the Taiwan Solomon Islands Government National and Overseas

---

5   *Joint Australia/New Zealand Pacific Scholarships Review, Final Draft Report* (Canberra: Department of Foreign Affairs and Trade (Aus), Ministry of Foreign Affairs and Trade (NZ), 2010).
6   *Joint Australia/New Zealand Pacific Scholarships Review.*
7   *Joint Australia/New Zealand Pacific Scholarships Review.*

Training and Education Awards, which subsidised the existing Ministry of Education and Human Resource Development budget, providing scholarships for Solomon Islanders to study in regional universities.[8]

Cuba was also a large donor in the region with scholarships focused on health training. Between 2006 and 2010 the Cuban Government offered 400 Cuban Government Medicine Scholarships in the Pacific, although not all of those had been taken up by 2010.[9] The scholarships were part of a broader aid effort by Cuba dating back to the socialist regime that took power in 1959. By the 2000s, medical training was being provided to students from a number of developing countries in Africa, Asia and the Pacific.[10]

There were also scholarships offered by Japan, the UK, Germany, Canada, Netherlands, France, the EU, Norway and the USA. But these scholarships were estimated to be between only 100 and 200 scholarships per year in the Pacific region.[11]

Scholarships were also offered by the governments of the Pacific Island countries themselves. The Fijian Government had three main scholarship programs on offer (in 2008) for study in Fiji, but only one scheme, the Fijian Affairs Scholarship, for which only iTaukei Fijians were eligible, allowed for study outside of Fiji.[12] The Solomon Islands Government also had a scholarship scheme, in part funded by the Taiwanese Government.

The 12 years covered by this chapter was also a period of time wherein the focus of the global aid and development sector was trained on donor harmonisation and aid effectiveness. Via the Paris Declaration on Aid Effectiveness, signed in 2005, and the Cairns Compact on Strengthening Development Cooperation in the Pacific of 2009, successive Australian governments committed to these concepts. Harmonisation between Australian and New Zealand scholarships, particularly the Regional Development Scholarships, was possible to achieve without significant issues, as is discussed later in this chapter. But cooperation with other donors, such as Cuba, China and Taiwan, was less straightforward. The role

---

8   *Joint Australia/New Zealand Pacific Scholarships Review*, 7.
9   *Joint Australia/New Zealand Pacific Scholarships Review*.
10 Sabine Lehr, 'Cuba's Scholarship Tradition: The Perspective from Ghana', *NORRAG News* 45 (April 2011): 89–91, www.researchgate.net/publication/256375092, accessed 24 April 2023.
11 'Submission to the Standing Committee on Foreign Affairs, Defence and Trade by the Acting Fiji High Commissioner to Australia: Mr Kamlesh Kumar Arya' (Canberra: 2008), 9.
12 'Submission to the Standing Committee on Foreign Affairs, Defence and Trade by the Acting Fiji High Commissioner to Australia: Mr Kamlesh Kumar Arya', 9.

of partner governments in the awarding and management of scholarships was linked to the concept of harmonisation. The Australian Government accepted that the partner governments would have a significant role in the 'public' category of scholarships – those awarded to public servants – but was unwilling to hand over control when it came to the 'open' category. A report published in 2010 noted that this was 'particularly important ... where there have been concerns over PG [partner government] agency resourcing or their capacity to manage merit-based and transparent pre-award processes'.[13] The Australian Government was not prepared to transfer responsibility of scholarships to governments in the Pacific, because it felt it could not trust the processes for the awarding of these scholarships. It was couched in the terms that these governments were not 'ready' for the responsibility of scholarship ownership, but the underlying distrust remained.

The push to make universities more responsible for the support and management of all international students, and sponsored students particularly, played out in a number of ways in the late 1990s. In 1995 a series of reforms intended to make the scholarship program more efficient were introduced, although not fully implemented until 1997. As part of these reforms, a select group of universities and Technical and Further Education (TAFE) colleges were contracted by AusAID to host scholarship students. These institutions were across the country, and covered a number of different types of institutions, not just the high-prestige Group of Eight institutions. This limited approach allowed AusAID to work closely with a smaller number of institutions, building relationships with teaching, welfare and support staff.

A review of the ADCOS program in 1995 had led to yet another scholarship scheme proposal. At that point, this was the fourth scheme (or at least the fourth name for a similar scheme) within less than a decade. This scheme, the Australian Development Scholarship Scheme (ADS) was approved by the Minister for Foreign Affairs, Alexander Downer, in 1996. It was expected that this 'new' scheme would 'would deliver more effective scholarship assistance and realise some cost savings'.[14] Maintaining an important element of the Equity and Merit Scholarship Scheme (EMSS), the ADS scheme also required Australian involvement in the selection of awardees.

---

13 *Joint Australia/New Zealand Pacific Scholarships Review*, 31.
14 *Management of the Australian Development Scholarships Scheme*, Audit Report No. 15 1999–2000 (Canberra: Australian National Audit Office, 1999), 41.

9. MULTIPLE OBJECTIVES FOR SCHOLARSHIPS AND AID

The ADS was introduced formally in 1998. It replaced two schemes, the ASTAS and the ADCOS, as discussed in the previous chapter. The Australian National Audit Office (ANAO) reviewed the management of the ADS scheme in 1999.[15] This audit report provided a useful overview of the scholarship program administration from the very beginning of a particular iteration of ADS, with later reviews providing information about how the program was implemented over the following decade.

The 1999 audit is of note, because the scheme it addresses, the ADS, only formally commenced in the academic year of 1998. However, given the ADS was an iteration of schemes in place since the introduction of the EMSS, it was possible to audit the overall scholarship operations of AusAID. While there is some specific data available in the audit reports, the documents also provided insights into the process of scholarship implementation prior to the design of the ADS, and the process of the introduction of the ADS. It is clear from this report that the introduction of the ADS was not the result of a comprehensive and detailed 'new' scholarship design, but could be more accurately described as a rebranding exercise. For example, the 1999 ANAO report noted that in relation to the benefits paid to students (stipend and other financial support), there had 'not been an in-depth review of the benefits structure since it was implemented some years ago, before the ADS scheme came into existence'.[16] This indicates that when the ADS scheme was designed, there was no expectation that the benefits to be paid to students would be changed from those already being paid to students under the scholarship scheme at the time. This further supports the contention that following the introduction of the EMSS, itself an entirely different scheme to those that existed before it, there was little wholesale redesign of the 'new' scholarships introduced, rather small iterative changes made to the scheme and the introduction of a new name.

The 1999 audit reported that there were 3,700 ADS students at the time of audit, and the program cost '$128 million in 1997–98'.[17] The summary of the report condensed the scholarship process into one dot point:

> Applicants compete for ADS awards through annual selection processes conducted in their home countries. Students receive stipends and have their academic fees paid by AusAID. They are expected to complete their studies in minimum time, return home

---

15 *Management of the Australian Development Scholarships Scheme*, 41.
16 *Management of the Australian Development Scholarships Scheme*, 52.
17 *Management of the Australian Development Scholarships Scheme*, 12.

and apply their qualifications to contribute to their country's development. Each scholarship costs about $100 000 over the award period.[18]

The ANAO concluded that the ADS scheme was administratively, 'a substantial improvement on those that existed for previous scholarship schemes',[19] with better arrangements with educational institutions and partner governments. The report also called for the ADS to be even more aligned with the needs of partner governments, representing a decisive shift from the 'open to all' approach of the EMSS.

As had been mooted in almost every review of the various scholarship schemes over previous decades, the ADS scheme was intended to be more closely connected with the bilateral aid program, aligning with the needs of partner governments more than previous scholarship schemes. The ADS design stipulated 'high Australian involvement in student selection'.[20] In these ways, the scheme was adopting elements of the EMSS and its subsequent schemes to best fit the needs of the Australian Government at the time. An understanding of the difficulties experienced by the Australian Government after the implementation of the EMSS can be seen in the way in which the ADS was formed, and what elements of the scheme were considered important.

From the ANAO report it is possible to see the issues that the designers of the scholarship programs were attempting to address. While a large proportion of students completed their studies and returned home, '10 per cent of students assisted under scholarship schemes from 1987–88 to 1996–97 discontinued their studies and another two per cent did not return home'.[21] This was a significant issue for students coming from South Pacific nations. In the 1996–97 period assessed by the audit report, nearly 30 per cent of Tongan students discontinued their studies or failed to return home after their scholarship concluded. Western Samoa and Vanuatu were both over 25 per cent, and PNG, Fiji and the Solomon Islands were all well over the scholarship program average of 12 per cent.[22] While these statistics clearly indicated issues with a number of the country program scholarship schemes, they were not at the rate of the domestic student population,

---

18   *Management of the Australian Development Scholarships Scheme*, 12.
19   *Management of the Australian Development Scholarships Scheme*, 13.
20   *Management of the Australian Development Scholarships Scheme*, 14.
21   *Management of the Australian Development Scholarships Scheme*, 17.
22   *Management of the Australian Development Scholarships Scheme*, 59.

where a dropout rate of 40 per cent was estimated. AusAID believed that stricter selection processes would work to reduce the number of students who did not complete their course of study, or failed to return home after their award. AusAID also introduced other policies in an attempt to compel students to complete and return home. Students began incurring a debt to the Commonwealth if they failed to return home (or leave Australia) after the completion of their scholarship.

As an external review of the scholarship program, rather than an internal or AusAID commissioned review as most previous reviews had been, the ANAO report had a different lens. It hinted at the unspoken element of scholarships, the desired outcomes outside of those 'development' outcomes expected and the way in which the scheme was being manipulated by various stakeholders. It noted that there was not sufficient evidence to support the allocations between open and public sector awards in many countries. It also noted that in one country, 'almost 80 per cent of students were studying for undergraduate degrees' despite the human resource development plan of that nation not reflecting a need for undergraduate training.[23]

The outsider view, however, was not always helpful, as some elements of the review failed to comprehend the complexity that multiple country programs presented. Each country program had its own version of the selection process, which was criticised by the ANAO but reflective of the needs expressed in the design of the EMSS and subsequent schemes where flexibility to meet individual country needs was considered important.

Understanding the scale of the scholarship program, in a financial context, was analysed as an overall figure ($128 million as noted above) but also as a proportion of each bilateral program. Because of the shift, over the course of the 1990s, to a scholarship scheme more integrated into country programs, this figure demonstrated how much of the bilateral aid relationship was committed to scholarships. In 1997–98, the scholarship program only represented 6 per cent of the funding committed to PNG, whereas it was 35 per cent of the commitment to Fiji.[24]

In student numbers, the first year of the ADS (1998) represented a diverse cohort of students from across 50 countries. There were 403 students from PNG, representing 11 per cent of the total cohort and 188 from

---

23   *Management of the Australian Development Scholarships Scheme*, 19.
24   *Management of the Australian Development Scholarships Scheme*, 34.

Fiji (5 per cent). The largest single cohort was from Indonesia, with 666 students.[25] The gender balance of that 1998 cohort, 43 per cent female and 57 per cent male, was far more even than the balance of the 1980s, although still not equal.

One other key change to scholarship management implemented over the course of the 1990s reflected a shift that had taken place over the aid program across the previous decades. Two of the major scholarship programs, Indonesia and PNG, were both partially outsourced to managing contractors. This outsourcing moved much of the responsibility for selection and placement of the students to a third party. With the concurrent move of student support to educational institutions, AusAID was divesting itself of the day-to-day management of the scholarship program, ostensibly to focus on the strategic direction of the program.

The AusAID response to the 1999 ANAO report was broadly positive. AusAID responded that the 'benefits students derive from studying in Australia under the scheme are difficult to quantify'[26] but claimed that it was accepted by AusAID, and the World Bank, that the 'scheme makes a substantial contribution to domestic governance in partner countries as many of these individuals take up positions in central government agencies, civil society and businesses'.[27] This 'acceptance' of impact, without quantitative or qualitative evidence was considered acceptable to both the Australian Government and many other scholarship administrators during this period. As subsequent reviews demonstrate, as the ADS continued and the quest to justify all and any taxpayer funding became more intense, the Australian Government was required to seek more concrete answers to the questions of 'impact' that scholarship schemes raised.

While the ANAO audit report went into great detail about the scholarship scheme in its first year, it also offered an outsider view of the implementation of scholarships. It was clear from the report that the scholarship was not being implemented according to the design in a number of different recipient countries. Certain country programs were able to implement elements of the ADS scholarship in different ways, and there was much that went unspoken and undocumented when it came to both the development impact and effectiveness, and the 'needs' of the partner governments. It was difficult

---

25 *Management of the Australian Development Scholarships Scheme*, 37.
26 *Management of the Australian Development Scholarships Scheme*, 13.
27 *Management of the Australian Development Scholarships Scheme*, 13.

to ensure that a scheme as large as this (across 50 countries) was applied uniformly and it is clear that politics played a part in decision-making. It was also not in the best interests of each of the bilateral relationships that it was implemented uniformly.

It is perhaps this quest for specificity and relevance that led to a proliferation of scholarship schemes over the 2000s – each specifically shaped around a foreign or domestic policy concern of the Australian Government. Discussion of these schemes and their varied (but similar) natures takes up much space in an internal review commissioned by AusAID in 2008. The review was conducted by Margaret Gosling, who had significant experience managing AusAID scholarship programs both in Australia and overseas. She was a long-time Team Leader in the ADS East Timor program.

Part One of the Scholarship Effectiveness Review by Gosling notes that in 2007/08 there were 27 scholarship schemes being administered by AusAID,[28] over a total of 36 countries, including 10 in the Pacific. By 2008 a large majority of students were undertaking Masters-level study. Students were still required, as was recommended in the Fraser Government in the 1970s, to return home for two years following completion of their study program. While the spirit of the scholarship program was to encourage students to return home and contribute to development, in fact the Australian Government could only prevent students from returning to Australia for those two years, thus there was no restriction on students working or living in a third country. In practice, this occurred more often in smaller nations in the Pacific where there were fewer job opportunities.

An Annexe to the Scholarship Review lists the major scholarship programs as being the ADS, Australian Leadership Awards (ALAs), Allison Sudradjat Awards, Australian Regional Development Scholarships (ARDS), Carnegie Mellon University Awards,[29] Centre for Transnational Crime Prevention Scholarships, Australia–IMF Scholarship Program for Asia, ACIAR John Allwright Scholarships and Australian Pacific Technical College Scholarships.[30] This list of scholarships demonstrates the use (arguably

---

28 *Management of the Australian Development Scholarships Scheme*, 13.
29 The description of the Carnegie Mellon Awards is revealing, demonstrating another example of the scholarship program being used for political aims. The program was introduced by Foreign Minister Alexander Downer, and guaranteed 20 ADS scholars to the newly opened Australian campus of the US Carnegie Mellon University, over a period of four years. This represents a considerable investment by the Commonwealth Government in the activities of a foreign university opening in Australia. No students from the Pacific were part of the scheme.
30 'Annexe Two: Outline of Major Programs by Scheme' (Canberra: AusAID, 2008).

overuse) of scholarships for similar aims. The ALAs were introduced to add a level of prestige to the standard ADS program, and the Allison Sudradjat Awards were part of the ADS Indonesia program, and were selected from those already awarded an ALA scholarship, in memory of an AusAID staff member who had been killed in a plane crash in Indonesia. A significant program not included in this extensive list is the Australian Partnership Scholarship program, which was a scholarship for Indonesian students and was funded as part of a massive tranche of aid promised by Prime Minister Howard after the tsunami in the Indian Ocean in December 2004.[31] The proliferation of subcategories, and other very specific scholarships with very small numbers created more administrative difficulties than it solved. Nevertheless, by this proliferation it is possible to gain insights into the thinking of AusAID and the Howard and Rudd governments at the time.

The 2003 Senate Inquiry into Australia's relationship with PNG and Pacific Island countries had simple terms of references. The inquiry sought to understand these relationships in political, economic and development terms, and what implications they had for Australia.[32]

The inquiry was convened before Australia committed to the RAMSI mission,[33] which is discussed in more detail shortly, and Australia's relationship with the South Pacific was largely focused on aid and development. Nevertheless, the title of the committee's report provides an interesting insight into the committee's understanding of the status of the relationships between Australia and Pacific Island countries: *A Pacific Engaged* allows the reader to decide if that title is indicative of Australia's future, current or historical relationship with the South Pacific. The committee's report noted that the one common understanding that came from their own investigation, and the submissions received, was that 'Australia has an obligation to assist the Pacific states to protect their security and stimulate their economies'.[34] This obligation came not only from colonial ties, but also from a growing sense that the security situation of the South Pacific was deteriorating. In a speech to the Menzies Research Centre in February 2003, Australian journalist and author Graeme Dobell, said that while 'the

---

31 Rizal Sukma, 'Indonesia and the Tsunami: Responses and Foreign Policy Implications', *Australian Journal of International Affairs* 60, no. 2 (June 2006): 213–28, doi.org/10.1080/10357710600696142.
32 Defence and Trade Senate Standing Committee on Foreign Affairs, ed., *A Pacific Engaged: Australia's Relations with Papua New Guinea and the Island States of the Southwest Pacific* (Canberra: Parliament of Australia, 2003), 1.
33 Which led to a strong security focus on Australia's political relationships in the Pacific.
34 Defence and Trade Senate Standing Committee on Foreign Affairs, *A Pacific Engaged*, 8.

"arc of instability" started off as a polite way to refer to Indonesia … it is the Pacific part of the arc that has really been living up to the name'.[35] Dobell pointed to two Pacific Island countries as failed states, the Solomon Islands and Nauru, and many other nations and territories in difficulties: East Timor, West Papua, PNG, Vanuatu and Fiji. And while the 'arc' may have been particularly unstable in the early 2000s, the concept of an arc of instability in the region goes back much further. Dobell himself points to the Second World War, and the fall of Singapore, as the point that the concept became part of Australia's understanding of the Pacific region.[36]

This developing sense of instability, and the growing number of failing or 'failed' states in the Pacific influenced Australia's aid delivery and scholarship design in the Pacific. The interventions in Timor-Leste and the Solomon Islands were part of a move to a greater focus on security and 'governance'[37] as areas of focus in aid and scholarships. This can be seen by the development of these topics within priority areas of study in the Pacific ADS programs.

The report of the 2003 Senate Committee also helped to highlight a debate within the aid community about aid to the Pacific. The AusAID submission to the committee argued that the region faced 'considerable development challenges including rural poverty, political instability and government structures that were inherited from colonial powers which are no longer affordable'.[38] Their solution was economic and governance reform, including a focus on police forces, financial management and civil society participation, among other efforts. However, a prominent submission that is extensively quoted in the committee's report, made by Professor Helen Hughes, claimed that aid had failed the Pacific.[39] Her argument was that aid was 'not the solution to Pacific development, but a major part of the problem'.[40] Hughes wrote that she believed that Australian aid to the Pacific should be suspended. She recognised that this was unlikely, and thus advised

---

35 Graeme Dobell, 'The South Pacific: Policy Taboos, Popular Amnesia and Political Failure (Speech)', part of the Menzies Research Centre Lecture Series: Australian Security in the 21st Century (Canberra: The Menzies Centre, 2003).
36 Graeme Dobell, 'The "Arc of Instability": The History of an Idea," in *History as Policy: Framing the Debate on the Future of Australia's Defence Policy*, ed. Ron Huisken and Meredith Thatcher, 85–104 (Canberra: ANU Press, 2007), doi.org/10.22459/HP.12.2007.06.
37 Dobell, 'The "Arc of Instability"'.
38 Defence and Trade Senate Standing Committee on Foreign Affairs, *A Pacific Engaged*, 82.
39 Helen Hughes, 'Aid Has Failed in the Pacific', Submission to the Inquiry into Australia's Relationship with Papua New Guinea and Other Pacific Island Countries, submission no. 61, 2002, www.aph.gov.au/Parliamentary_Business/Committees/Senate/Foreign_Affairs_Defence_and_Trade/Completed_inquiries/2002-04/png/submissions/sublist, accessed 28 March 2023.
40 Defence and Trade Senate Standing Committee on Foreign Affairs, *A Pacific Engaged*, 94.

that the government 'empower AusAID to impose real aid conditionality under the principle of mutual obligation'.[41] This approach could easily have been interpreted as paternalistic and was, not surprisingly, rejected by AusAID and not supported by the committee. They did, however, agree with Professor Hughes' contention that 'the fundamental problems of Pacific societies can only be tackled in the Pacific'.[42] By increasing the participation of the governments of the Pacific Island countries in aid decision-making and implementation, change was expected by AusAID and the committee. But as will be explained later in this chapter, that control over decision-making in the realm of scholarships was difficult to cede. Scholarship administrators did not feel able to hand decision-making on scholarships to governments when they could not be sure that the processes of selection and awarding scholarships would be free of corruption.

The social and political situation in the Solomon Islands had been fraught for a number of years, Sinclair Dinnen described it as a 'debilitating internal conflict between 1998 and 2003'.[43] Clive Moore wrote in 2007 that, 'although the disturbance did not affect the rural majority, Honiara was tense, and law and order was out of control'.[44] Requests had been made to Australia for intervention over the period of the conflict, but the Howard Government rejected these requests, Howard himself wrote that 'each time we firmly but politely declined'.[45] In April 2003, the Prime Minister of the Solomon Islands, Sir Allan Kemakeza again requested urgent assistance from Australia. By this time Howard and Foreign Minister Downer had 'formed the view that the internal conflict in the Solomon Islands had become so serious that it posed a risk to Australia's interests'.[46] Whether this change in policy truly came from a realisation of the risk to Australia posed by a failed state in the Solomon Islands, or the need to demonstrate to the USA that Australia could keep the peace in the Pacific, is still an

---

41 Hughes, 'Aid Has Failed in the Pacific', 3.
42 Hughes, 'Aid Has Failed in the Pacific', 2.
43 Sinclair Dinnen, 'RAMSI Ten Years On: From Post-Conflict Stabilisation to Development in Solomon Islands?', *Journal of International Peacekeeping* 18, Issue 3–4 (2014): 195, doi.org/10.1163/18754112-1804005.
44 Clive Moore, 'Helpem Fren: The Solomon Islands, 2003–2007', *The Journal of Pacific History* 42, no. 2 (2007): 141, doi.org/10.1080/00223340701461601.
45 John Howard, 'John Howard: RAMSI Ends with its Mission Accomplished for Solomon Islands', *The Sydney Morning Herald*, 28 June 2007.
46 John Howard, 'John Howard: RAMSI Ends with its Mission Accomplished'.

area of debate between scholars, politicians and others.[47] Nevertheless, in July 2003, the month before the Senate Committee reported, the Solomon Islands Parliament unanimously supported legislation to authorise the incoming Regional Assistance Mission in Solomon Islands (RAMSI). The RAMSI mission was sponsored by the Pacific Islands Forum, with a lesser relationship to the United Nations. The operational personnel were overwhelmingly Australian and New Zealanders.[48]

The RAMSI intervention marked the second significant regional intervention of the Howard Government, after the INTERFET intervention in Timor-Leste in 1999. Australia was also involved in military interventions in Iraq and Afghanistan over this period.[49] This security lens came to guide many areas of scholarship design. In many ways this focus on security and defence (against 'terrorists' rather than state actors) shows the Australian Government taking a more active role in determining the security and military ground rules in the Pacific – rather than waiting for the USA to make its own moves. While this demonstrates a level of independence from the USA in relation to questions of security and militarisation in the Pacific, the agenda was still being set by the USA as highlighted by the 'Deputy Sheriff' nickname assigned to Prime Minister John Howard.[50]

It was in this security-focused environment that Minister for Foreign Affairs Alexander Downer launched the Centre for Transnational Crime Prevention Scholarships (CTCPS). The CTCPS scheme was announced by the Minister Downer in 2005 with a discrete award for 15–20 students from South and South-East Asia to study at the University of Wollongong Centre for Transnational Crime Prevention. The scheme was expanded to become a broader AusAID-funded program in 2006. The program differed from the rest of the ADS cohort, in that students were recruited in consultation with the educational institute (the Centre for Transnational Crime Prevention), with Foreign Minister Downer saying in a speech to the University of Wollongong that 'places will be directed to priority countries and agencies in our region in consultation with the Centre'.[51] Only two students from

---

47   The debate is succinctly outlined by Graeme Dobell in an article on the Australian Strategic Policy Institute blog, *The Strategist*: Graeme Dobell, 'Australia, Solomon Islands and RAMSI', *The Strategist*, 13 October 2017, www.aspistrategist.org.au/australia-solomon-islands-and-ramsi/, accessed 26 July 2020.
48   Moore, 'Helpem Fren', 141.
49   Scholarships were also offered to students from Afghanistan in a small program that was difficult to manage due to the complex security situation.
50   Spillius, 'Bush Entrusts "Deputy Sheriff" Howard'.
51   Downer, 'Inaugural Lecture on National and International Security'.

the Pacific, one from Fiji and one from PNG, were awarded scholarships under this scheme,[52] but the message sent by the focused scholarship was clear; security and crime prevention in the region were of fundamental importance to the Australian Government.

Only six years later, long after RAMSI was well entrenched, another Senate inquiry was commenced in June 2008 during the first year of the Rudd Government. Adding to the instability narrative, there had been a coup in Fiji in 2006. This inquiry into the major economic and security challenges facing PNG and the island states of the south-west Pacific was conducted by the Senate Foreign Affairs, Defence and Trade References Committee. The title alone – *Inquiry into the Economic and Security Challenges Facing Papua New Guinea and the Island States of the Southwest Pacific* – demonstrates a pivot towards security. Again, submissions came from a wide variety of sources, including the Fijian Government, unions, think tanks and government departments. The committee wrote two reports, one volume focused on the economic challenges facing PNG and the south-west Pacific, and the other focused on the security challenges. Again, the committee wrote that they had 'identified a range of impediments to economic growth in Pacific island Countries'.[53] The Executive Summary is remarkably similar to the committee report from 2003, although it hints at the fact that a focus on governance in aid is not having the expected impact:

> although over 50 per cent of Australia's bilateral ODA [Overseas Development Assistance] to the region goes to governance, one of the main weaknesses remains the inability of bureaucracies in Pacific Island countries to deliver essential services on the ground – whether it relates to resource management, education or economic infrastructure.[54]

The report noted that the Rudd Government had recently taken a new approach to aid relationships with the Pacific region, signing a series of Pacific Partnerships for Development over the course of 2008.

Two chapters in the first volume focused on education and training: the first, an overview of the education and training situation in Pacific Island countries; the second focused on Australia's assistance in that area. The report noted a number of impediments to expanding the standard of

---

52 'Annexe Two: Outline of Major Programs by Scheme'.
53 Defence and Trade References Committee Foreign Affairs, ed., *Economic Challenges Facing Papua New Guinea and the Island States of the Southwest Pacific* (Canberra: Parliament of Australia, 2009), xvii.
54 Defence and Trade References Committee Foreign Affairs, *Economic Challenges*, xviii.

education (from basic education all the way through to higher education) in the Pacific; these included affordability, physical access, facilities, the training and supply of teachers, curriculum and standards.[55] A number of submissions to the committee, and World Bank reports, raised concerns that education targets in the Pacific would be difficult to achieve given that a disproportionate amount of education budgets across the nations of the Pacific were spent on tertiary education.[56] Despite this, the levels and standards of higher education were not adequate.

In outlining Australia's assistance in education, the committee noted that a number of submissions were keen to see the scholarship scheme expanded. The Lowy Institute recommended post-study work placements and Qantas wanted the scheme expanded to the aviation industry.[57] The committee noted there were reports that the Rudd Government was intending to expand the scholarship scheme to approximately 19,000 awards within the next five years. This would have represented an extraordinary expansion of the scheme as it stood at the time.

The committee came down in support of 'the Australian Government's extensive scholarship program and draws attention to the various suggestions on how Australia could enhance this program', while recognising that the OECD had recommended the scholarships be more targeted and connected to the aid program.[58] This piece of advice was, as previous reviews had demonstrated, not new, nor was it the last time in the decade that this advice was received by the Australian Government.

This focus on governance and leadership was intrinsic to the development of another key 'subcategory' scholarship implemented in the 2000s: the Australian Leadership Award Scheme (ALAS). The ALAS selection scheme was similar to the ADS selection process, but the ALAS aimed to be an 'academically prestigious award'.[59] Prestigious in comparison to what is not

---

55 Defence and Trade References Committee Foreign Affairs, *Economic Challenges*, 166.
56 Defence and Trade References Committee Foreign Affairs, *Economic Challenges*, 167. This was not a new problem. An AusAID report reviewing aid to PNG between 1975 and 2000 noted that in 1993 only 2 per cent of students attended university but 37 per cent of public funding for education was focused on the tertiary sector. *The Contribution of Australian Aid to Papua New Guinea's Development 1975–2000*, Evaluation and Review Series No. 34 (Canberra: AusAID, June 2003).
57 Defence and Trade References Committee Foreign Affairs, *Economic Challenges*, 182.
58 Defence and Trade References Committee Foreign Affairs, *Economic Challenges*, 183.
59 Defence and Trade References Committee Foreign Affairs, *Economic Challenges*, 6.

clear, but efforts to create a 'prestigious' award with name recognition similar to the Fulbright had formed a part of Australian Government scholarship design over decades.

An ALAS award included the standard scholarship, fees and a stipend, but also involved a leadership program which AusAID noted was worth an additional $17,000 per award.[60] The program was open to candidates across the Indo-Pacific region. Many students from the Pacific were involved in the program, including students from Tuvalu (one award in 2008), Tonga (awards in 2007 and 2008), Samoa (awards in 2007 and 2008), 11 Solomon Islanders over 2007 and 2008, PNG (27 awards in 2007 and 2008), Kiribati (three awards in 2007 and 2008) and 12 Fijian students over 2007 and 2008.[61]

The ALAS, in contrast to most of the ADS country programs, had no input from partner/recipient governments. This, along with the CTCPS, distinguished it from the ADS program. Students selected as part of this award were encouraged to study in areas considered important to the development of their home country or region, and aimed to 'develop a cadre of leaders advancing regional reform, development and governance'.[62] However, they were not limited by their own country's human resource development plan.

The focus on 'governance' was both encouraged by Senate inquiry and a key plank of the RAMSI intervention in the Solomon Islands. The ALA Scholarships were another effort to signal Australia's clear policy focus when it came to the Pacific. While the Howard Government had rejected the proposal by Professor Hughes that Australian aid to the Pacific should be tied to mutual obligation expectations, it was clear it was improvements in leadership and governance that the Australian Government sought in the region.

As mentioned previously, Margaret Gosling was very experienced in the implementation of scholarship programs and was working at AusAID in the late 2000s. The Gosling Review and attachments she wrote were internal documents, written with the expectation that they would remain within AusAID. Because of this they were more candid and straightforward

---

60 Defence and Trade References Committee Foreign Affairs, *Economic Challenges*, 6.
61 'Annexe Three: Scholarship Programs by Region/Country (Draft)', (Canberra: AusAID, 2008). One Palauan student was also awarded an ALAS, but discontinued their study after a short time.
62 'Annexe Two: Outline of Major Programs by Scheme', 6.

than the documents prepared for a public audience, such as the ANAO report. The report was able to articulate some of the 'unspoken' elements of scholarship programs – for example clearly explaining why scholarships remain popular:

> Partner governments tend to be keen on scholarships, perhaps because they give the impression of building capacity of public institutions and, in some places, may provide 'rewards' that can be granted to chosen candidates. Travelling politicians also find scholarships handy 'announcables' and there is a general feeling that they help to build linkages between Australia and partner countries at the 'people-to-people' level.[63]

The review and its annexes revealed tensions between the Australian Government and its bilateral government partners. Redactions in an annexe to the review, released as part of a freedom of information request, highlighted lingering tensions between Australia and Fiji, following the coup in 2006. Allowed past the censor is a line that demonstrates the tension: 'whilst there are constraints in the current political climate, GOF [Government of Fiji] participate jointly with Australia in the final selection process'.[64] A candid assessment of the Government of PNG is also documented, noting that public service departments were hesitant to nominate 'their best … employees, as to do so would mean they would have to make do without a productive member of their team for a year at the least'.[65] The document repeatedly referred to disconnection between the scholarship schemes and the human resource development needs of the recipient nations, particularly in the small island states of the Pacific. These were the same issues that were raised by the nations of the South Pacific after the introduction of the EMSS program in the late 1980s and in the ANAO report in 1999. It is clear that 20 years of scholarship provision had failed to fully address the problems.

The review report noted several times that one of the aims of the scholarship program is to promote 'friendships and linkages'[66] throughout the region as part of both the ADS and ARDS. This effort to develop people-to-people linkages was common across many of the scholarship schemes, but the term 'friendships' was less common. In the French Pacific territories,

---

63   Margaret Gosling, 'Scholarship Effectiveness Review Part 1', ed. AusAID (Canberra: Commonwealth of Australia, 2008), 16.
64   'Annexe Three: Scholarship Programs by Region/Country (Draft)', 19.
65   'Annexe Three: Scholarship Programs by Region/Country (Draft)', 24.
66   'Annexe Three: Scholarship Programs by Region/Country (Draft)', 19.

the friendships were to be part of an effort to 'enhance the integration of French Pacific territories (New Caledonia, French Polynesia, and Wallis and Futuna) into the predominantly Anglophone South Pacific region'.[67] But Annexe Three to the report repeatedly noted that there had been no proper evaluation of the impact of the scholarships. This was in part because the scholarship programs were comparatively small. The evidence of 'success' or 'failure' is largely anecdotal, with the fact that alumni of the scholarship program were in senior positions counted as success.

The report does demonstrate that over the period since the 1999 ANAO report, many measures had been introduced when it came to administering the scholarship programs. Institutions were required to meet key performance measures, and databases that were used across posts (Australian diplomatic missions endowed with the decision-making authority to grant scholarships), AusAID Canberra and educational institutions allowed for more coordinated student management.

Some of the recommendations made in the Scholarship Effectiveness Review were strikingly similar to those made by most of the reviews of scholarships and international education over previous decades. Gosling recommended that scholarships should be better integrated into country programs of aid,[68] a recommendation made by Jackson more than 24 years before, in 1984. Gosling also recommended that more attention should be paid to developing capacity at local institutions,[69] in addition to the scholarships taking students away from those institutions. Gosling wrote these recommendations with the expectation that the Australian Government scholarship scheme was going to grow, with an understanding the program would be at 19,000 scholarships within five years.[70] It was with this in mind that AusAID was working to develop a clearer blueprint for what form scholarships would take under the Rudd Government. The proliferation of scholarships only made the program more complex to run, and it was this consideration that Gosling recommended that the design of 'future scholarships should be guided by a set of common principles'.[71] The creation of 'new' scholarship schemes, by Foreign Minister Downer in particular, to support specific elements of Australia's foreign policy was not consistent with the outcomes sought by AusAID or the Australian Government.

---

67 'Annexe Three: Scholarship Programs by Region/Country (Draft)', 20.
68 Gosling, 'Scholarship Effectiveness Review Part 1', 7.
69 Gosling, 'Scholarship Effectiveness Review Part 1', 7.
70 Defence and Trade References Committee Foreign Affairs, *Economic Challenges*.
71 Gosling, 'Scholarship Effectiveness Review Part 1', 8.

9. MULTIPLE OBJECTIVES FOR SCHOLARSHIPS AND AID

The Gosling Review also addressed a specific Pacific scholarship, the Australian Regional Development Scholarship (ARDS) program, which provided:

> scholarships to students from Pacific countries to study in several regional institutions, including the University of the South Pacific (USP), the Fiji School of Medicine, Fiji Institute of Technology, Fiji School of Nursing, National University of Samoa and three institutions in PNG.[72]

Because of the third country nature of the ARDS program, it was often not considered in reviews or overviews of the scholarship program, as demonstrated in the 1999 ANAO report. Thus, the detail in the Gosling Effectiveness Review and Annexes offered a rare insight into the program.

According to Gosling, in 2008 there was an intake of 190 students in the ARDS scheme, taking the total number of students on award in the middle of the year to 490. The number of graduates in 2007 was 133. The largest cohort on award in 2008 was from Vanuatu, with 109 students. The smallest was Niue and Tokelau with 20 students.[73] The program was primarily focused on undergraduate study, with an expectation that the ADS would be used for postgraduate study. The program had an added, explicit, goal and that was to support regional institutions.

This support was twofold, according to Gosling. Firstly, the ARDS provided these institutions with a consistent flow of students. Secondly, the scholarship program required a level of student support not necessarily common in those institutions, thus the scholarships required 'levels of student services and administrative accountability that might otherwise not be achieved'.[74]

The scholarships therefore provided funding to universities of the South Pacific, albeit in an indirect way. There was also an argument that by placing students who have achieved the standards required to gain a scholarship in the higher education system, the system itself is improved. Where this argument became less sustainable was in the realm of postgraduate

---

72   'Annexe Two: Outline of Major Programs by Scheme'.
73   'Annexe Two: Outline of Major Programs by Scheme'.
74   Gosling, 'Scholarship Effectiveness Review Part 1', 20.

scholarships. By directing high-calibre students out of a regional university, towards postgraduate study in Australia, the efforts of the ARDS were undermined.

The growth in regional scholarships was not universally accepted by recipient governments. In a submission to the 2009 Senate Inquiry into the security and economic needs of PNG and the countries of the South-West Pacific, the Fijian Government wrote that one of its key concerns with Australia's aid to the region was the increase in the number of in-Fiji scholarships provided by the Australian Government. It also sought an increase in the number of in-Australia awards as part of its submission.[75] This was despite a concern expressed by the Fijian Government in its submission that:

> a good number of Fijian citizens who studied under Australian Government sponsorship either did not return to Fiji, or came back to Australia after having served their bond obligations in Fiji.[76]

This is explained, in part, by a recognition that the Fijian diaspora, including those in Australia, were a key 'partner in development' of Fiji through remittances, and concerns around employment in Fiji. The submission proposed two options to address the issue that local institutions did not offer the courses required to meet the manpower needs of Fiji that the Fijian Government considered pressing. Option one was to refrain from sponsoring students to study in Fiji and increase the number of in-Australia awards and option two was to spend the funds to increase investment in local institutions, such as the University of the South Pacific (USP).[77] This bolsters the argument, stated above, that by diverting funds and students to Australia, the Australian Government was undermining its own aid spending.

Other issues about regional scholarships were raised during this period, including concerns around personal safety and political security. Given that a large cohort of the ARDS scholars was based at USP, the 2006 Fijian coup created significant issues for the scheme. Scholars were evacuated, only returning to their studies in the following year.[78] A review of Australian

---

75 'Submission to the Standing Committee on Foreign Affairs, Defence and Trade by the Acting Fiji High Commissioner to Australia: Mr Kamlesh Kumar Arya'.
76 'Submission to the Standing Committee on Foreign Affairs, Defence and Trade by the Acting Fiji High Commissioner to Australia: Mr Kamlesh Kumar Arya'.
77 'Submission to the Standing Committee on Foreign Affairs, Defence and Trade by the Acting Fiji High Commissioner to Australia: Mr Kamlesh Kumar Arya'.
78 *Joint Australia/New Zealand Pacific Scholarships Review*, 24.

and New Zealand Pacific Scholarships noted in 2010 that PNG was also of concern to administrators of the regional scholarships. Not only were there issues of personal security, but 'instability has also on occasion flowed over to PNG educational institutions, affecting the continued delivery and quality of education provided to awardees'.[79] This situation would have only fed into the instability narrative that was driving much of the Coalition Government's policy approach at the time.

New Zealand, as another major donor in the region and a close Australian ally, was an ideal partner for the Australian Government when it came to increasing the 'efficiency' of the scholarship program, particularly in the very small Pacific Island states. Its scholarship program was similarly oriented, with the majority of scholarships in the New Zealand Regional Development Scholarships (NZRDS) of over 300 awards, and less than 90 New Zealand Development Scholarships (NZDS) for study in New Zealand.[80] The biggest difference was quantity: Australia offered more than 1,500 awards to the region in an average year at the time, 1,200 as ARDS and 300 as ADS.

Both scholarships had similar broad aims: 'capacity development, interpersonal linkages, and regional institutional strengthening to support long-term social and economic development'.[81] As such, a report commissioned by both AusAID and the New Zealand Ministry of Foreign Affairs (MFAT) reviewing the scholarships, the Joint Australia/New Zealand Pacific Scholarships Review (JPSR), reported in early 2010 that it recommended the nations collaborate to create a single Pacific Regional Development Scholarship Scheme.[82]

Australia and New Zealand agreed on other aspects of scholarship design, both being concerned with equity of access to the scholarships. The JPSR report noted that in some Pacific states this was a difficult element of the implementation:

> While there is gender balance of award offers in PNG, anecdotal evidence suggests that the initial screening by PNG agencies, with male-dominated management structures, is prohibiting the advancement of many female applications.[83]

---

79   *Joint Australia/New Zealand Pacific Scholarships Review*, 24.
80   *Joint Australia/New Zealand Pacific Scholarships Review*.
81   *Joint Australia/New Zealand Pacific Scholarships Review*, ii.
82   *Joint Australia/New Zealand Pacific Scholarships Review*.
83   *Joint Australia/New Zealand Pacific Scholarships Review*, 11.

A lack of policies to target disadvantaged communities within the scholarships provided by Australia or New Zealand was also of concern to the JPSR team. The JPSR team, through their review, also acknowledged the difficulties faced by women not only in gaining a scholarship, but also in their return to their home country. The report noted that 'the culture shock of returning to a more restrictive society can be greater for women than for men'.[84]

Perceptions of unfair selection processes dogged both national scholarship schemes. It was noted by the JPSR that 'public perceptions that selection is merit-based, fair and equitable are a crucial aspect to the integrity of the schemes and in demonstrating good governance and accountability'.[85] The JPSR noted that this was possible to demonstrate in the case of New Zealand and Australian schemes, but less obvious in the Pacific Island government schemes, where 'agencies face considerable difficulties in undertaking merit-based ranking without clear methodologies', among other problems.[86] The JPSR reported on the difficulty of conducting interviews of prospective scholarship candidates, indicating that interviews were not commonly used at the time. Including interviews in the selection of candidates had been recommended by a 2008 Tracer Study of Tongan AusAID scholarship alumni.[87]

Where the Australian and New Zealand schemes differed was intrinsically connected to their separate colonial histories in the Pacific. It was an obligation, under the Australian schemes, that students were required to return home on completion of their scholarship. In practice, this could only be enforced by not allowing the alumni to return to Australia for two years, or by bonding requirements put in place by home country governments. New Zealand, on the other hand, allowed for dual citizens from the Cook Islands, Samoa, Niue and Tokelau to apply for the NZDS scheme. Following completion of their scholarships, these students were able to remain in New Zealand.[88] The deep historical and cultural connections between New Zealand and the Pacific Islands, deeper than those between Australia and the Pacific Island countries, are pronounced in this policy setting. New Zealand is unable to divorce itself from the Pacific Islands, whereas Australia's policy

---

84 *Joint Australia/New Zealand Pacific Scholarships Review*, 17.
85 *Joint Australia/New Zealand Pacific Scholarships Review*, 13.
86 *Joint Australia/New Zealand Pacific Scholarships Review*, 13.
87 *Joint Australia/New Zealand Pacific Scholarships Review*.
88 *Joint Australia/New Zealand Pacific Scholarships Review*, 16.

was that dual citizens could not even apply for an ADS, let alone stay in Australia following completion. Dobell made this argument in his 2003 speech to the Menzies Centre:

> Australia still sends out the same message to the Pacific, we do not want them. And much of the time we don't even realise the way the negative signals are interpreted.[89]

Australia's scholarship policy settings merely reinforced a perception that Australia was only prepared to partner with Pacific Island countries to a point, but not further.

This chapter has shown that the 2000s marked a time of review and consolidation for Australian Government development scholarships. With the introduction of the ADS in 1998, the scholarship program had a new name and by 1999 had already been audited by the ANAO. Reviews continued, with a comprehensive internal review of all the AusAID scholarships undertaken in 2008, and a review of both Australian and New Zealand scholarships to the Pacific drafted in early 2010. These, along with other country program specific reviews, added to the increasing load of monitoring and evaluation that scholarship schemes were being subjected to, as part of a broader aid effectiveness push across the world.

There was also a proliferation of Australian Government scholarships over this period, in part because of an increasing focus by the Australian Government on demonstrating its position as the guardian of security, stability and nation-building in the South Pacific. These 'new' scholarships, the CTCPS and the ALAS among others, were focused on developing a cadre of security specialists and leaders across the region, and were not only focused on the Pacific. However, the fact that they were outside the normal ADS selection processes placed them even more firmly outside of the ADS realm. Their distinctiveness and difference allowed them to be viewed as clearer signposts to the Australian Government's foreign policy objectives and policies during the 2000s. These scholarships also indicated to those within AusAID that the Howard Government supported scholarships as a mode of aid. However, while it was clear that the Pacific loomed large in the minds of both politicians and policymakers, evidenced by two Senate inquiries into Australia's relationship with PNG and the Pacific, this was only translated into scholarship design through the ARDS. None of the

---

89   Dobell, 'The South Pacific', 16.

other proliferating scholarship schemes of the time was designed or imagined with a Pacific applicant pool in mind. This is despite the fact that the aid and development focus for the government was security (or insecurity), a quest for 'good governance' and leadership in Australia's interests, all issues intimately linked to the status of Pacific Island nations in the 2000s.

The election of the Rudd Labor Government in 2007 did not diminish the feeling within AusAID that scholarships were 'in vogue' with politicians. In the Gosling Scholarship Effectiveness Review, it was noted that AusAID needed to 'respond to the new government's trend to scaling up of scholarship programs'.[90] It was this final part of the Gosling Review that recommended to the government the rebadging of all the proliferating scholarships under a new single umbrella, Australian Development Awards. By 2010 part of this recommendation was being introduced, with the creation of the Australia Award brand. This is discussed in the next chapter.

---

[90] Margaret Gosling, 'Scholarship Effectiveness Review Part 3', ed. AusAID (Canberra: Commonwealth of Australia, 2009), 1.

10

Diplomacy or development?

The final phase of activity that this book addresses covers the period from 2010 to 2018. Successive Australian governments wrestled with the role of scholarships, and indeed the purpose of aid more broadly over this period. Reviews were conducted into acknowledged areas of concern, especially in the case of a review of Papua New Guinean higher education. Where this period differs from others discussed in this book is the more overt use of scholarships as a tool of diplomacy. The connections between scholarships and diplomatic outcomes were especially clear in the case of the Australian Government's quest to gain a seat on the United Nations Security Council (UNSC). The focus on diplomatic outcomes of aid more broadly was also clear in the decision by the Abbott Government to integrate AusAID into the Department of Foreign Affairs and Trade (DFAT). This led to the loss of jobs, and expertise, in aid delivery and design and changed the way in which aid was viewed within and outside of the government. The changes made it difficult to retain development at the centre of the scholarship scheme, as they were then managed in conjunction with non–aid focused programs. Given the branding and name change that had been put in place by the Rudd/Gillard Government, moving from Australian Development Scholarships to Australia Awards, it was difficult for the focus on aid and development to be maintained, in perception or reality.

The Rudd Government put in train a number of the changes and reviews that started the decade, including efforts to gain a temporary seat on the UNSC. The shift of focus of the Abbott Government in 2013 had a greater impact on the progress and implementation of development scholarships, as discussed later in this chapter. In a shift from the previous decade, there was little policy focus on scholarships, as policy and political attention was drawn to a new outbound scholarships scheme, the New Colombo Plan. This was a favourite project of the Foreign Minister from 2013 to 2018, Julie Bishop. This, along with a shift to a more private sector-oriented aid program, left the Australia Awards vulnerable and they suffered the same budget cuts that the Abbott and Turnbull governments wrung out of the aid program.

Meanwhile, from an Australian Government perspective, 2010 to 2018 in the Pacific was a period of relative political calm. The security focus that had characterised Australia's engagement over the 2000s slowly dissipated. While the Regional Assistance Mission to Solomon Islands (RAMSI) continued, the focus of the Australian Government drifted elsewhere. The Australian political situation over the same period became tempestuous; between 2010 and 2018 Australia had five separate prime ministers, with one, Kevin Rudd, serving twice. The period in domestic Australian politics was marked by leadership spills, leaking, policy changes and instability.

Some elements of the recommendations that had been articulated by Margaret Gosling in 2008 (as outlined in the previous chapter) were implemented by the Rudd/Gillard/Rudd governments between 2007 and 2013. The scholarships were consolidated, in part, under the umbrella term of Australia Awards. But, as with much of the activity of the time, this was a stylistic change, not a substantive one. While Australian Government international scholarships were all now known as Australia Awards, they were each still their own separate programs. This caused significant confusion, given the vast differences in processes, designs and goals of these awards. For example, the Endeavour Awards became known as the Australia Awards Endeavour. These awards were run by the Department of Education and had a significantly different remit to the Australia Awards (development).[1] The Endeavour Awards were focused on academic excellence and offered both inbound and outbound scholarships.

The Australia Awards (AA) of the development kind were expanded quite substantially with this new branding. Two new, multinational programs were introduced: Australia Awards Africa and Australia Awards Latin America. The Latin America program was almost entirely focused on fellowships, but the AA Africa was more in line with other AA programs.

---

1   For an excellent brief history of the Endeavour Awards, see Kent Anderson and Joanne Barker, 'Vale Endeavour, Long Live the New Endeavour: The End of Australia's World Leading Commitment to Internationalism and the Opportunity to Reassert Ourselves', *Australian Policy History*, 28 May 2019, aph.org.au/2019/05/vale-endeavour/, accessed 20 April 2023.

The introduction of the AA Africa program was an enormous undertaking covering nations across the continent, involving a significant logistical and funding investment to establish.

These two new programs, largely de-linked from the broader bilateral or existing multilateral aid programs that existed in those regions, were implemented in the service of a larger goal that serves to highlight the role of scholarships as a diplomatic tool. They were created to demonstrate the generosity of the Rudd Government rather than out of a need for an investment of Australian aid in the recipient nations. Scholarships were as malleable as they have been over the decades covered by this book, used for a multitude of purposes by even a single actor – in this case, an investment in gaining votes at the UN.

The AA Africa and AA Latin America scholarships were part of an ambitious attempt by Kevin Rudd and his government to gain election to one of the rotating seats of the UNSC. As this position is elected by the General Assembly of the UN, Australian diplomats were tasked with gaining the support of a majority of nations within the UN. This effort coincided with a significant expansion of Australian aid,[2] and the introduction of the AA program into geographic areas where Australian aid was not normally focused, namely Africa and Latin America. There were reasonable rationales for Australia to engage with Africa in particular. In a report prepared as part of an Aid Effectiveness Review in 2011 by academics Joel Negin and Glen Denning, they noted that there was a need for aid, but also, 'a strong commercial rationale exists for engaging with Africa'.[3] Negin and Denning acknowledged that the number of countries in Africa, and Rudd's stated commitment to cementing Australia's position as a middle power, necessitate 'active relationships with African nations. This may include, but is not limited to, efforts to secure a United Nations (UN) Security Council seat'.[4]

Negin and Denning's report noted that scholarships formed the largest component of Australia's aid to Africa, but the scholarships offered opportunities for Australians to learn more about Africa. They outlined the risks of the large program, the rapid ramp up and the amount of human

---

2   Joel Negin and Glen Denning, *Study of Australia's Approach to Aid in Africa: Commissioned Study as part of the Independent Review of Aid Effectiveness* (Canberra: Department of Foreign Affairs and Trade, 2011).
3   Negin and Denning, *Study of Australia's Approach to Aid in Africa*, 4.
4   Negin and Denning, *Study of Australia's Approach to Aid in Africa*, 4.

resources required to undertake the expansion.[5] The risk that was not addressed by the report was the reputational risk the Australian Government took on by expanding a program quickly, and then reducing it quickly just a few years later.

And while the focus on Africa was not clearly related to the provision of scholarships to the Pacific, what the massive new scholarship component did was divert attention from all other scholarship country programs, as a huge and multinational scholarship program was designed and implemented. The first iteration of the AA involved 27 countries across Africa. The program was run from a central office in Pretoria, South Africa, but involved promotion, coordination of applications, shortlisting, interviews, selection and pre-departure briefing across a huge number of national contexts. This required huge resources, financial and human, in a short period of time. This diversion of attention to Africa also highlighted to all of Australia's other bilateral partners, including those in the Pacific, that one of the most important aspects to Australia's aid provision at the time was a seat at the UNSC.

Australia was elected to a two-year term on the UNSC, commencing on 1 January 2013. In September of that year the Abbott-led Coalition Government was elected in Australia, changing the trajectory of Australian aid, and the AA scholarship program.

In one of its first major moves,[6] the Abbott Government announced that AusAID was to be closed, and its functions moved into DFAT. This surprise move was a shock to the aid community. Scholar Jack Corbett wrote that those within AusAID, even Coalition insiders, were shocked by the decision.[7] It was more than just moving the aid program into DFAT – different elements of the aid program were themselves split across DFAT. According to Corbett, it was 'difficult to imagine how the administration of the aid program could have been more thoroughly dismantled'.[8] These significant administrative moves were coupled with significant cuts to staffing levels, and cuts to program funding over several budgets. It also signalled very clearly to the Australian and international community that the Abbott Government saw aid very clearly as a tool of diplomacy, firmly

---

5   Negin and Denning, *Study of Australia's Approach to Aid in Africa*, 26.
6   The decision was announced on the same day that Tony Abbott was sworn in as prime minister.
7   Jack Corbett, *Australia's Foreign Aid Dilemma: Humanitarian Aspirations Confront Democratic Legitimacy*, Routledge Humanitarian Studies (Abingdon, Oxon: Routledge, 2017), doi.org/10.4324/9781315523491.
8   Corbett, *Australia's Foreign Aid Dilemma*, 136.

part of Australia's foreign policy, with the Australian-centric focus that came with that. Given the Australian focus on scholarship programs, not only the name of the scheme but the way in which much of the benefit flowed to Australian institutions and individuals,[9] this signal was relevant in the context of scholarships.

The cuts to the budget that the Abbott Government introduced impacted on scholarship numbers across the world, but owing to the manner in which scholarship programs are implemented and the long lead time for students to arrive in Australia, these cuts were not obvious until 2015. In 2016 the impact was clear, with 1,000 fewer scholarships offered that year than were offered in 2014. The reduction was not even across the world, with the AA Africa program suffering enormous cuts and the program shrinking its reach across the African continent. Numbers in the Pacific were reduced by over 80 awards. This was a significant cut in the context of the numbers offered in the Pacific, at the time just under 300 long-term awards.[10]

While there was a sudden and dramatic drop in the number of awards in the years following the election of the Abbott Government, the number of awards increased year on year from 2016. Scholarships became a little more politically popular, easily coopted into the new aid outlook promoted by Foreign Minister Julie Bishop that was focused on developing the private sector and encouraging economic growth, with 'promoting prosperity' coming first in the aid tagline, ahead of reducing poverty and enhancing stability.[11].

In addition to the push to gain a seat on the UNSC, and in line with the reforming zeal of the early years of the Rudd Government, a review of Papua New Guinea (PNG) universities was commissioned. The review was part of a frenetic round of reviews and policy ideas that characterised the first iteration of the Rudd prime ministership and was commissioned by Rudd and PNG Prime Minister Sir Michael Somare. The report was handed down in 2010. The review was conducted by Professor Ross Garnaut and Sir Rabbie Namaliu. Garnaut and Namaliu were both distinguished academics and public sector experts. Namaliu also had a long career as a

---

9   Scholarships include fees paid to educational institutions and stipends spent largely in Australia. The benefit of the education is felt by the individual and the recipient nation, but much of the immediate financial benefit is experienced by Australian organisations.
10 Austrade, ed., *Australia Awards Data (2002–2018)* (Canberra: Australian Trade Commission, 2018).
11 Corbett, *Australia's Foreign Aid Dilemma*; Department of Foreign Affairs and Trade, *Australian Aid: Promoting Prosperity, Reducing Poverty, Enhancing Stability* (Canberra: Department of Foreign Affairs and Trade, 2014).

politician including a period as prime minister of PNG and was also the first Papua New Guinean graduate to be appointed to the academic staff at the University of PNG.

Garnaut and Namaliu were asked to:

> review the condition of the Papua New Guinea Universities, to assess whether they were performing the roles required of them in Papua New Guinea development and to make recommendations on steps that could be taken to strengthen their contributions.[12]

The report was effusive about the contribution of PNG universities to the development of PNG in the lead-up to, and soon after, independence. According to Garnaut and Namaliu, 'students in that first generation played leading roles in dismantling the institutionalised racial discrimination that had been a feature of life in the territories of Papua and New Guinea'.[13]

The report was commissioned as part of an effort to address the growing critical skill gaps in PNG, such as the number of trained teachers, health professionals and workers in the resources sector. The authors noted that over the decade prior to the report, aid to PNG had been shifted from budget support to project aid, altering the way in which the country was able to manage aid inflows. This had impacted on the manner in which universities had been funded and reduced the ability for the Papua New Guinean Government to allocate funds where it saw fit.

Garnaut and Namaliu found that the university sector in PNG, as it was in 2010, would not be able to address these skill gaps. The report was highly critical of the standards, funding and provision of university-level education in PNG, they wrote that they 'have reluctantly come to the conclusion that a high proportion of the courses in Papua New Guinea State universities are not taught at an adequate standard'.[14] They explained that these low standards came from quality control, a lack of funding, governance and ethical failures and pressure to expand numbers, among other reasons. The report's authors made recommendations relating to all of these issues, including how Australian aid should be used to support PNG universities. The authors recommended the introduction of an income-contingent loans system, similar to the Australian Higher Education Contribution Scheme (HECS),

---

12   Ross Garnaut and Rabbie Namaliu, *PNG Universities Review: Report to Prime Ministers Somare and Rudd* (Canberra: AusAID, 2010), 6.
13   Garnaut and Namaliu, *PNG Universities Review*, 7.
14   Garnaut and Namaliu, *PNG Universities Review*, 12.

twinning arrangements with Australian universities, and other support mechanisms.[15] Garnaut and Namaliu suggested that these commitments be made in addition to the continuing scholarship program. However, they suggested that the existing scholarships be reoriented to support university development: 'we suggest that the scholarships allocations be concentrated on training of staff and potential staff members of universities and research institutions, mostly at PhD and some at Master's level'.[16]

The report recognised that these scholarships represented a key tool for demonstrating, both in the source country (PNG) and the donor country (Australia), what was important. If the scholarships had been reoriented to support the higher education sector, that would have been a clear indication that Australia was deeply invested in developing a high-quality higher education sector in PNG. Unfortunately, like much of the reformative zeal of the Rudd Government, the review served more as a snapshot in time than as a comprehensive blueprint for development within the PNG universities sector. Despite it containing significant substance, there were limited outcomes from the report for scholarships.

Over the period beginning in 2010 there was a large increase in the number of international students coming to Australia. This came after the Global Financial Crisis of 2008, the collapse of a number of private providers and a number of racially motivated attacks on students had led to a reduction in the number of students coming to Australia.[17] Students sponsored by the Australian Government were only a tiny percentage of the overall number of students.[18] As discussed earlier, the number of Australia Award Scholarships from 2010 to 2018 fluctuated, the highest being 2,112 in 2013, and the lowest being 971 awards in 2016.[19] These high and low points correlate with the expansion of the AA into Africa and Latin America, and the rapid reduction in awards after the election of the Abbott Government in 2013 (as discussed). In contrast, the number of awards offered in Pacific Island countries was relatively consistent, albeit at a fairly low level, reaching a high of 303 in 2011 and a low of 201 in 2016.

---

15   Garnaut and Namaliu, *PNG Universities Review*, 56.
16   Garnaut and Namaliu, *PNG Universities Review*, 57.
17   For an assessment of the issues raised during this period see Michael Wesley, 'Australia's Poisoned Alumni: International Education and the Costs to Australia', Policy Brief (Sydney: Lowy Institute for International Policy, 2009).
18   In 2010, according to Austrade data, there were around 444,000 international students in Australia. In 2018 that figure was nearly 640,000.
19   Austrade, *Australia Awards Data*.

Table 10.1: Australia Award Scholarships in the Pacific

Pacific Island countries (recipients)	2010	2011	2012	2013	2014	2015	2016	2017	2018
Cook Islands	1	-	-	-	-	-	-	-	-
Fiji	16	44	41	38	46	43	7	34	47
French Polynesia	2	4	3	3	4	5	-	-	-
Kiribati	4	9	9	8	10	12	13	19	19
Marshall Islands	1	-	2	1	-	-	-	-	-
Federated States of Micronesia (FSM)	-	1	-	1	1	1	-	-	-
Nauru	1	-	-	-	3	5	4	5	7
New Caledonia	6	4	4	4	4	12	1	-	-
Niue	1	-	-	-	-	-	-	-	-
Papua New Guinea	135	174	152	158	154	147	137	103	87
Samoa	14	15	23	24	19	21	13	20	29
Solomon Islands	17	29	29	29	25	22	16	18	26
Tuvalu	4	4	6	6	4	7	3	3	6
Vanuatu	17	16	22	24	12	12	7	12	11
Wallis and Futuna	-	3	-	2	1	-	-	-	-
Grand total per year	219	303	291	298	283	287	201	214	232

Source: Austrade, ed., *Australia Awards Data (2002–2018)* (Canberra: Australian Trade Commission, 2018).

The figures in Table 10.1 are only for students who were awarded scholarships to study in Australia. As was shown in the last chapter, a large number of scholarships are allocated for Pacific students to study in Pacific universities. The Australia Regional Development Scholarships were also part of the rebranding or consolidation that occurred in 2010, and they became known as the Australia Awards Pacific Scholarships.

These numbers do not tell the reader anything about the success of the individuals who made up the numbers, or the impact those individuals were able to have after they completed their studies. In this way numbers can be a misleading way in which to understand scholarship programs, as designers often expect an outsized impact in relation to the number of awards on offer.[20] This period can be particularly misleading if one is to measure

---

20   The South-East Asian Scholarship Scheme is a good example of this issue, with six awards expected to help repair Australia's reputation in South-East Asia in the early 1950s. The expectation is not entirely unfounded – advertising the availability of a scholarship will positively engage a much higher number of people than there are awards available.

it on numbers, given that one of the significant areas of growth during this decade was in short courses. These short courses allowed for a greater number of 'awardees' to be counted, despite the experiences of a PhD or Masters student not being comparable to that of a short course awardee. Again, however, the numbers were part of a broader public diplomacy engagement that was increasingly important to DFAT (under both Labor and Coalition governments), often at the cost of long-lasting or deeper impact. The longer-term outcomes of the switch to shorter programs will take years to be understood.

There was, during this period, some evidence that the scholarships did have development outcomes. An Australian National Audit Office audit in 2010 found that scholarships made a 'tangible contribution to improving tertiary training outcomes, particularly in the Pacific region'.[21] The report did criticise the unpredictability of aid levels in the Pacific region in particular, reflecting the inconsistent numbers of awards being offered each year. The report also highlighted that these scholarships, and other tertiary training support in the Pacific region that made up 60 per cent of the education spending, 'has come from initiatives that are not integrated with the budgets and policies of recipient country governments'.[22] The failure to fully integrate scholarships into the policies of recipient governments was a criticism first levelled at the Equity and Merit Scholarship Scheme (EMSS) in the late 1980s. That it was raised in yet another review nearly 20 years later highlights both the difficulty of integrating scholarships into broader bilateral aid programs, and the desire of successive Australian governments to retain significant control over the scholarship program. It also, again, returns us to the reality that the scholarship programs reflect Australian policy more than they reflect the priorities of the recipients. This includes deciding who the awardees are and what they study, because the scholarship program has purposes and motivations other than aid. The auditors of 2010 clearly understood the multiple motivations behind scholarships, noting that:

> [the] global focus of scholarships to study in Australia reflects, in part, the role they play in Australia's foreign policy agenda, including their role in improving people-to-people links between Australia and its partners.[23]

21　Auditor General, ed., *AusAID's Management of Tertiary Training Assistance* (Canberra: Australian National Audit Office, 2010), 14.
22　Auditor General, *AusAID's Management of Tertiary Training Assistance*, 16.
23　Auditor General, *AusAID's Management of Tertiary Training Assistance*, 18.

The auditors noted that Australian alumni filled senior positions in Indonesia, Fiji and PNG and this was helpful for Australian politicians and diplomats. The move of the aid program into DFAT only served to highlight and entrench these foreign policy goals within the scholarship program.

Despite the significant cuts to aid and scholarships implemented by the Abbott Government, one new scholarship program was able to gain traction and broad support. The New Colombo Plan was championed by Foreign Minister Julie Bishop, who created the program in an effort to encourage Australian students to travel to the Indo-Pacific region.[24] Using the Colombo Plan name was an attempt to borrow from the existing goodwill that had been developed from the original plan in the region that the new plan was focused on. As has been noted in earlier chapters, the Colombo Plan continued to influence policymakers across the decades, and this was continuing into the new millennium.

The New Colombo Plan was largely mobility grant funding, provided to universities who were able to subsidise the cost of student mobility programs such as study tours. A small number of students were able to study on longer-term scholarships, undertaking a semester abroad. These awards were designed, like many of the scholarship programs discussed in this book, to have a much larger impact than the numbers involved might imply. The promotion of the program was huge and encouraged the sense that thousands of students were having transformative experiences in Asia and the Pacific. The program did increase the number of students able to experience study abroad during their universities studies, but recent research by Agnieszka Sobocinska and Jemma Purdey found that the New Colombo Plan study tour model 'facilitate a short-term period of emotional involvement and self-reflection, rather than forging enduring connections'.[25] This is in contrast with the long-lasting connections that the Colombo Plan created, and the name New Colombo Plan was intended to evoke. The New Colombo Plan was also focused on business and corporate outcomes, with a significant focus on internships, which was in line with the private sector focus that had dominated aid design and implementation under the Abbott Government.

---

24 The term Indo-Pacific was favoured by Bishop, widening Australia's area of 'interest' from the Asia Pacific to include the Indian Ocean and the nations that border that ocean, including East Africa and South Asia.
25 Agnieszka Sobocinska and Jemma Purdey, 'Enduring Connections?', *Bijdragen tot de taal-, land- en volkenkunde / Journal of the Humanities and Social Sciences of Southeast Asia* 175, no. 2–3 (2019): 225, doi.org/10.1163/22134379-17502001.

10. DIPLOMACY OR DEVELOPMENT?

Like most of the scholarship and education programs discussed in this book, the design of the New Colombo Plan was not targeted at Pacific countries; the focus remained on East and South-East Asia. Nevertheless, the 2015 iteration included Pacific-based projects and mobility grants.[26] In 2018 the top four destination countries for New Colombo Plan scholarship students were Hong Kong, Singapore, Japan and China. No Pacific nations featured in the top five destinations for mobility grant funding.[27] While the program was not designed around engagement with Pacific nations, the use of the 'catch-all' term Indo-Pacific did allow for Pacific nations to participate. The term is far more inclusive than the 'Asiabound' terminology of the Gillard Government, but the fact that the Pacific does not have the Colombo Plan as part of its history with Australia does demonstrate that the scheme was, at the very least, named without thought of the Pacific. Communities of the Pacific had none of the familiar associations with the Colombo Plan that were present in South-East Asia.

As mentioned earlier in this chapter, during this rebranding of the Australian Development Scholarships to the Australia Awards, the Australian Regional Development Scholarships were renamed the Australia Awards Pacific Scholarships. These continued despite the cuts to aid and scholarships. Some more significant changes were made to some country programs; in PNG, the scholarship design was amended to include a significant number of in-PNG awards, largely for undergraduate study. These scholarships, which continue today, have been targeted to particular sectors such as nursing and midwifery. This scholarship uses a similar rationale to that of the Pacific scholarships, as described in the previous chapter, whereby students were encouraged to use the in-PNG award to complete undergraduate study and the in-Australia awards for postgraduate study. This indirect injection of Australian aid through fees and other supports also helped to meet some of the recommendations of the review of PNG universities completed in 2011.

In 2017 the Turnbull Government launched the Australia Awards Women's Leadership Initiative, with funding of $5.4 million over five years (2017–2022).[28] This was announced after another women's leadership program for

---

26 '2015 Mobility Program Offers', Department of Foreign Affairs and Trade, www.dfat.gov.au/people-to-people/new-colombo-plan/mobility-program/Pages/2015-mobility-program-offers, accessed 20 April 2023.
27 Ly Thi Tran and Mark Rahimi, *New Colombo Plan: A Review of Research and Implications for Practice*, Research Digest 14 (Melbourne: International Education Association of Australia, 2018), 8.
28 Julie Bishop, 'Speech at the Launch of the Australia Awards Women's Leadership Initiative', 8 February 2018, Minister for Foreign Affairs, Canberra, www.foreignminister.gov.au/minister/julie-bishop/speech/speech-launch-australia-awards-womens-leadership-initiative, accessed 24 April 2023.

the Pacific, the Pacific Women Shaping Pacific Development program, was announced in 2012. The Pacific Women's program was far broader, with a significantly larger remit and budget of $320 million over 10 years.

The Australia Awards Women's Leadership Initiative was designed as an 'on-award' enhancement for Pacific students, an experience while they are in Australia. This initiative was part of a broader trend within the AA program more broadly to focus on 'on-award enrichment'. This emphasis saw a significant focus on providing extracurricular activities, such as the Women's Leadership Initiative, for Australia Award scholars while they were in Australia. These activities were often designed to support a particular cohort of students (i.e. those studying in a particular sector), but were often limited by country. These programs help to demonstrate some of the ways in which the scholarship program has changed in the decades since the EMSS.

In the design of the EMSS in the late 1980s, the Australian Vice-Chancellors' Committee International Development Program (IDP) was contracted to support the implementation of the program. By 2018 nearly all of the AA country programs were managed by third parties known as managing contractors. These companies bid for the contracts to run the programs, with each contractor taking a slightly different approach to the way in which the scholarship program was managed, within the overall parameters set by DFAT. This is how the designers of the EMSS envisaged their scholarship program evolving, but just as the granting of decision-making power to the Australian diplomatic posts created tensions and uneven delivery, so did the involvement of managing contractors.

In this structure, students of the Pacific were disadvantaged. Apart from the Women's Leadership Initiative, there were few on-award enrichment activities available to students from the Pacific (outside of PNG). This is in large part because the AA programs in the Pacific were smaller, and it was less cost-effective for the managing contractors to include on-award enrichment as part of their programs.

This serves to highlight the continued uneven application of the scholarship program across countries. This had positive and negative consequences. It allowed for individual countries to tailor aspects of the scholarship program to suit individual country needs, as highlighted in the EMSS example. But for students from the countries of the Pacific, it meant that their access to extension activities was limited.

10. DIPLOMACY OR DEVELOPMENT?

One additional program introduced during the period covered by this chapter aimed to identify and quantify the benefits of the awards investigated by this book: the Global Tracer Facility. This Facility was tasked with identifying contributions to development from the AA. They also assessed the contribution to Australia's 'economic diplomacy' from these scholarships. While the remit of the Tracer Facility was stated as tracing AA students, in reality staffers have traced alumni from a raft of the scholarship schemes discussed in this book, including the Colombo Plan, the EMSS and the Australian Development Scholarships. The Tracer Facility staffers have used a number of methods to approach the large project, including methods more common to market research. The reports produced by the Tracer Facility have covered a number of specific areas across a number of countries and regions (for example, one report focuses on alumni from Fiji over several decades who studied education-related courses).

The existence of the Tracer Facility, and its reporting, have provided successive Australian governments (both the Turnbull and Morrison governments), and specifically DFAT, with significant evidence to support the continued investment in scholarships. The reports point to positive outcomes in development and positive outcomes for Australia.[29]

The outcomes that the Tracer Facility sought to measure are indicative of what the Australian Government wanted from the investment in scholarships:

> Outcome 1: Alumni are using their skills, knowledge and networks to contribute to sustainable development.
>
> Outcome 2: Alumni are contributing to cooperation between Australia and partner countries.
>
> Outcome 3: Effective, mutually advantageous partnerships between institutions and businesses in Australia and partner countries.
>
> Outcome 4: Alumni view Australia, Australians and Australian expertise positively.[30]

---

29 Australian Council for Education Research, 'Australia Awards Global Tracer Facility – Case Study #1: Fiji', (Melbourne: Department of Foreign Affairs and Trade, 2017).
30 *Global Impact of Australian Aid Scholarships: Long-term Outcomes of Alumni*, Australian Council for Education Research, www.dfat.gov.au/sites/default/files/global-impact-australian-aid-scholarships-long-term-outcomes-alumni.pdf, accessed 20 April 2023.

It is difficult to avoid the fact that three of the four desired outcomes are focused on positive outcomes for Australia, either cooperation between Australia and the partner countries, or that alumni view Australia in a positive light. This approach to a program that is, at its core, a foreign aid program represents the view that Jackson put forward in his 1984 report: Australian foreign aid needed to be, foremost, in Australia's national interest. This was also the view of the Howard Government, which put national interest at the forefront of its aid rationale. In provisioning the scholarships, successive Australian governments have been able to focus on the short-term positive outcomes for the recipient nations – scholarships are, after all, extraordinarily popular with recipient nation governments[31] – while the longer-term outcomes that politicians and public servants were interested in are far more focused on Australia. Evidence has been produced by the Tracer Facility that points to the beneficial outcomes of the scholarships to nations, communities and individuals, but the core thrust of the work of the Facility, judging by the measures they used, is how the scholarships can be used to demonstrate outcomes for Australia. In this, the Tracer Facility fits into the broader narrative of Australian Government scholarships over time. They are far more a reflection of Australia and Australian policies than they are a reflection of the needs of the recipient nations and individuals.[32]

As Australian Government scholarships continued into the second decade of the twenty-first century they were first ramped up with new programs and additional funding implemented by the Rudd and then Gillard governments, then pulled back with cuts that were made by the Abbott Government to scholarships and aid more generally. At the beginning of the decade, Jackson's 1984 10,000 scholarship proposal was close to being achieved. In fact, the proposal was that there would be 19,000 scholarships per year. While this may well have involved some creative counting, including short-term awards and fellowships, the ambition was striking. Scholarships formed the majority of Australia's aid to a number of nations, and Africa as

---

31 This has been recently proven, once again, by a request by the prime minister of PNG, James Marape, requesting a new secondary school scholarship program be put in place by Australia for PNG students. The new scheme was due to commence in mid-2020 but was affected by the pandemic.

32 This also applies to broader aid decisions. Research into the motivations of donor countries often points to donor considerations taking prime position when it comes to allocation decisions. See Rukmani Gounder, 'Empirical Results of Aid Motivations: Australia's Bilateral Aid Program', *World Development* 22, no. 1 (1994): 99–113, doi.org/10.1016/0305-750X(94)90171-6, and Charles Hawksley, 'Australia's Aid Diplomacy and the Pacific Islands: Change and Continuity in Middle Power Foreign Policy', *Global Change, Peace & Security* 21, no. 1 (2009): 115–30, doi.org/10.1080/14781150802659473, among others.

a continent. The rebranding of the Australian Development Scholarships into the Australia Awards created the next scholarship to follow the line that began with the South-East Asian Scholarship Scheme in 1948.

With the election of the Abbott Government in 2013 there were cuts in aid, staff and ambitions for scholarships. The numbers plummeted to a low of less than 1,000 scholarships in 2016, with 201 of those from the Pacific. The focus of the Abbott Government on aid supporting private sector development was no disadvantage to the scholarship program, and in some regions was beneficial. But the program was inconsistent across different countries: it was not the same to be an Australia Awards student from Indonesia as it was to be an Australia Awards student from Fiji. Awardees from smaller countries and smaller cohorts were less able to access the enrichment activities that were available to students from larger country programs.

After the focus of the 2000s on security and governance in the aid program and Australian Government policies in the Pacific, there was little policy focus on the Pacific in this period. Governance continued to be a focus of the aid program, and scholarships in particular. However, the proliferation of different 'types' of scholarships in the 2000s that had marked out the foreign policy focus of the Howard Government was much reduced. Perhaps it could be argued that the New Colombo Plan was in part an example of a 'new' scholarship, but while it was named in common with another scholarship program its focus was fundamentally different. It was, however, demonstrative of the centring of Australian interests, especially in the aid program. The New Colombo Plan was also focused on private outcomes for students who wished to have careers in business in the Indo-Pacific region. The people-to-people connections that were sought through the program were for the advantage of private companies, less for governments or public service organisations. It was also a demonstration of an increasing reliance by Australian governments, both Labor and Coalition, on the 'optics' of scholarships over the longer-term outcomes.

This centring of Australian interests in the aid program is also evident in the substantial investment into the Global Tracer Facility, which is focused on understanding the extent of four possible outcomes of the various scholarship programs that have been in place over the decades. Of those four outcomes, three revolved around positive outcomes for Australia, its businesses and community. Fundamentally, by 2018 Australian Government development scholarships had become more focused on diplomatic outcomes and the possible short-term impact of scholarships than on the substantial long-term outcomes the scholarships could achieve. Nevertheless, the scholarships remained in place as a key element of Australian Overseas Development Assistance, perhaps the only aid program to have lasted this long in one cohesive form.

Conclusion

This is the first time that a comprehensive history of Australian Government scholarships to the Pacific has been written. This book has traced the development and implementation of scholarships since the first Australian Government international scholarship, the South-East Asian Scholarship Scheme, in 1948. The scope and timeline of this project, running parallel to the emergence of overseas students as a mainstay on Australian university campuses, allows the book to be more than just a history of scholarships. It is also a history of Australia's international education policies. And because Australian Government scholarships were, over these 70 years, a fundamental element of Australia's aid program, this is also in part a history of Australian foreign aid and foreign policy in the Pacific.

The long timeframe allows us to see patterns over time and connections between scholarships and foreign policy. A focus on the provision of development scholarships in the Pacific has enabled the investigation of Australian governments' international development scholarships that have hitherto been marginalised by interest among scholars in the Colombo Plan. This work does not ignore the Colombo Plan, but it does shift the lens for understanding international development scholarships and international aid away from it. It is clear that the Colombo Plan has influenced the delivery of scholarships from its inception until the present. It has shadowed, and often overshadowed, the scholarship schemes that have been offered in the Pacific. In many ways, it is this limited frame of thinking that has prevented the development and design of solutions more tailored to the needs of the Pacific.

There are a number of clear insights that can be taken from this book. Scholarships have continued with various motivations and designs across the period this book covers, with a changing cast of invested stakeholders who wished to make their stamp on scholarship design and outcomes. Funding and money have been important to various expansions and contractions in scholarship schemes and numbers. This is particularly evident in the late 1980s and then again in the late 2000s and into the 2010s. And as this book makes clear, there are explicit links between scholarships and politics. Scholarships are part of Australia's foreign policy, but they also reflect domestic policy and political imperatives.

Bearing in mind these insights, several clear themes run throughout the work. These are: National interest, and in particular the way in which the malleability of scholarships supported the Australian national interest, which was also far from fixed or singular. In most of its renderings, considerations of the Pacific were relatively insignificant or presumed in relation to Australia's national interest. Decolonisation is another key theme, in particular the decolonisation of territories and colonies in the South Pacific, and the intersection between scholarships and these processes of colonisation and decolonisation. The final theme is the concept of incrementalism, of un-radical, iterative policy change in scholarships over more than 70 years.

Because scholarship designs and approaches reflected domestic policy and domestic needs, they were often more focused on meeting the needs of Australia's interests than they were on meeting the needs of Australia's bilateral aid partners. In addition, scholarships to the Pacific were rarely front of mind for policymakers, even those who were focused on scholarships and education aid. Scholarships designed for other regions were extended, often belatedly, to the Pacific and the one proposed program intended to be specifically for the Pacific never made it past the concept stage. Later schemes with more flexible approaches did allow for regional adjustments to better suit the specific needs of Pacific Island countries, but these adjustments often conflicted with the broader aims of the scholarship schemes.

While the policy focus was rarely trained on the Pacific, when successive Australian governments approached the Pacific they did so with a paternalistic view, seeing the island territories and then states as minor players in broader 'big power' politics. This approach can be seen in the 1960s as diplomats discussed expanding Australia's colonial obligations in the Pacific, despite a global movement towards decolonisation. It can also be seen in the introduction of Australian controlled selection for scholarships, and an overwhelming focus on 'governance' as an area of study in the 2000s. Rather than having the concept of development front of mind when developing and implementing scholarships, often Australia's national interest, again Australian interests, played an overwhelming

CONCLUSION

role. Nevertheless, the adaptability of scholarships to meet the different interpretations and understandings of national interest that were held by different departments and bureaucrats in governments have proved vital to the longevity of scholarships.

Managing and controlling aspects of the scholarship program were colonialist. 'Paternalistic' was how one Fijian academic described the change to Australian-centred selection that was a fundamental part of the Equity and Merit Scholarship Scheme (EMSS) program in 1989.[1] The change gave the Australian Government more power to control the types of students who were coming to Australia. While this decision was always couched in the language of effectiveness and equity, especially given the preference by some governments for specific ethnic groups within their country, it privileged the decisions made by Australian Government representatives and created a controlling, neo-colonial framework for the scholarships.

This book has also highlighted the nexus between decolonisation and scholarships. The role of education and scholarships has been identified as crucial for the development of anticolonial movements in other contexts.[2] On the other side of the coin, as noted in the Introduction, scholarships may not be explicitly a colonial project, but they are certainly influenced by colonial era thinking and the privileging of Western styles of knowledge. Many Pacific Island states had little access to higher education until the late 1960s, so travelling for higher education was the only option for those capable and willing. In the case of Papua New Guinea (PNG), the lack of access to higher education was a direct result of Australian policy inaction and the belief of a number of Australian politicians and bureaucrats, including Paul Hasluck, that the development of PNG would be best served by a slow and gradual movement to educational attainment. This approach did not match the ambitions or desires of many of the people of PNG or the expectations of the United Nations; the Australian Government was forced to establish a university in PNG well before there was broad access to high school. These policy and planning failures had long-term impacts, and still mark the Australian Government's relationship with PNG to the present day. In other territories and nations of the Pacific, using scholarships to develop a cadre of alumni who viewed Australia positively has been an overt

---

1 Tupeni Baba, 'Australia's Involvement in Education in the Pacific: Partnership or Patronage?', *Directions: Journal of Educational Studies* 11, no. 2 (1989): 43–53.
2 Michael Goebel, *Anti-Imperial Metropolis: Interwar Paris and the Seeds of Third World Nationalism* (Cambridge: Cambridge University Press, 2015), doi.org/10.1017/CBO9781139681001.

goal of scholarships since the first scheme in 1948. This was seen as an acute need as those nations gained independence and the influence of colonial powers waned, and the Australian Government feared the influence of other nations such as the USSR and more recently China.

Another important theme within this book is the malleability of the scholarships offered. Scholarships were used by different actors for different purposes. While the Australian Government was the overarching 'actor' providing these scholarships, within that bureaucracy many departments and individuals fought for their goals and aims in shaping the scholarship schemes. Interdepartmental disputes between the Department of External Affairs (DEA), the Commonwealth Office of Education (COE), the Department of Immigration and the Prime Minister's Department marked many of the schemes discussed in this book. For example, in the late 1940s and 1950s DEA staff were keen for Australia to support newly independent states, while the Prime Minister's Department and the COE were more concerned to keep the scholarship bound within the frame of the British Empire. The compromise achieved, the Australian International Awards Scheme, allowed the Prime Minister's Department to trumpet the generosity of Australia at the Montreal Commonwealth Conference in 1958. Australia's participation in the Oxford Commonwealth Education conference of 1959 led to its inclusion in the Commonwealth Scholarship and Fellowship Plan, a program that not only allowed students from developing nations to study in Australia, but also supported Australian students to study across the Commonwealth (usually in the UK). This is analogous to many debates about aid and development assistance at the time, with Australian politicians still believing Australia to be a 'developing country' while wanting to support the development of other developing countries in the region (never for purely altruistic reasons). By joining the Organisation for Economic Co-operation and Development (OECD) Development Assistance Committee in 1961 and conducting a review of Australian aid in 1964, DEA was able to more firmly place Australian aid in its global context, and highlight the diplomatic benefits of a structured and purposeful aid program.

The addition of a bureau focused on aid delivery, and a professionalising of aid policy development in the 1970s added more voices to the debate about the purposes of scholarships. These scholarships, while ostensibly 'development' scholarships aiming to support developing countries to build the skills and knowledge of their citizens, had other goals. Influencing key public servants, promoting Australian higher education, supporting

Australian educational institutions, diplomatic negotiation 'chips' – these were some of the many and varied goals of a single scholarship scheme. This does not diminish the impact on the individuals and communities who benefited from these scholarships. These political aspects of the schemes, while beneficial for the longevity of the scholarship programs, did not necessarily serve the interests of all parties involved.[3] A clear-eyed view of the motivations behind scholarships should be important for all of those involved, but identifying those motivations can be a challenge.

In a finding notable for its potential to influence scholarship design in the future, this research has highlighted another aspect of scholarship delivery in Australia over the last 70 years. Iterative change has marked scholarship design and delivery, with elements of each scheme influencing the next. There have been moments of revolutionary zeal, such as the Whitlam Government's subsidy scheme and the Hawke Government's EMSS, but these are rare. In addition to each scholarship influencing the next iteration, scholarship design was influenced by other government and private scholarship programs. The Rhodes Scholarship had a clear influence on the implementation of scholarships around the world, and in turn so did the Fulbright. The Commonwealth Scholarship and Fellowship Plan development was a chance for many different nations to share their own scheme designs, influencing each other. Aspects of scholarship design were shared across schemes, and many schemes continue to share common restrictions and requirements.[4]

This book also shows that domestic and immigration policies have always had a significant impact on international scholarships, and international education more broadly. This reality is important to understanding how international scholarship programs are perceived within the Australian community. For example, the South-East Asian Scholarship Scheme was created to counter the negative impacts of the White Australia Policy in South-East Asia. Many of the equity elements of the EMSS, including a gender balance target, were influenced by equal opportunity legislation across Australian jurisdictions. The ending of the subsidy scheme was heavily

---

3   Research by Anne Campbell and Emelye Neff points to unresolved conflicts of purpose within scholarship programs leading to 'ambiguous models and inadequate evaluations as well as diffuse programming driven by unclear expectations'. Anne C Campbell and Emelye Neff, 'A Systematic Review of International Higher Education Scholarships for Students from the Global South', *Review of Educational Research* 90, no. 6 (2020) (online publication): 2, doi.org/10.3102/0034654320947783.
4   For example, the requirement of students to return 'home' for two years was common across many schemes but there is no clear reason for this timeframe.

influenced by the introduction of fees for domestic students; charging fees for domestic students while international students were still subsidised was not a sustainable policy position.

Through all these scholarship program evolutions and redesigns, Australia was establishing the role it would take within the decolonising region. This was particularly true in relation to the territories under Australian control, such as the Territory of Papua and New Guinea and Nauru. Debates around citizenship, responsibility and obligation continued well after independence, and in some cases continue into the present day. The focus in this book on the relationship between Australia and the territory and then nation of PNG is fundamental. This research reinforces other work that highlights the failure of successive Australian governments to properly develop the education system in PNG, as was its responsibility as the trustee and colonial power. This failure has reverberated through the decades, and the continuing demand for Australia Awards scholarships and Australian aid funding reflect, in part, a continuing need expressed by the Papua New Guinean Government and population for access to higher education.

This work has been focused on Australian Government scholarships, which have been supported by both major political parties. A clear line can be drawn from the South-East Asia Scholarship Scheme to the Australia Awards, representing a substantial segment of Australia's aid program across decades.[5] The programs have changed in their conditions and terminologies, but the continuity of scholarships for students from developing countries to study in Australian universities has remained. The Australian Government, through these scholarships, sought to train students who would become important and influential on their return home. That influence and importance is intended to lead to development outcomes but is also intended to lead to Australia being in a position to leverage that influence. The balance between these two elements is precarious and shifts further to the side of development outcomes in some schemes such as the EMSS, or in the other direction for others, such as the Australian Leadership Awards.

---

5   Because of the way scholarships were budgeted for differently across this period, the exact proportion of the aid budget can be difficult to calculate. According to the Australian National Audit Office in 1998, the Australian Development Scholarships made up approximately 9 per cent of the total aid budget – *Management of the Australian Development Scholarship Scheme*, Audit Report No. 15 1999–2000 (Canberra: Australian National Audit Office, 1999).

CONCLUSION

As already noted, the period covered by this book parallels decolonisation in the Pacific, which began at the end of the Second World War and continues today. And while other research has found connections between educational opportunities and anticolonial sentiment,[6] this book has not found substantial evidence that a large number of students who studied in Australia developed a sense of nationalism, or anticolonialism, during their time in Australia. This is not to say that it did not occur, but merely to say that this research has not sought nor found evidence to suggest it. This is an area where additional research would be of great utility.

The recording of the stories of alumni has changed significantly over the period this book analyses. This is highlighted in the student stories included in each chapter. The earlier stories are pieced together with the aid of archival documents and newspaper articles. Later stories are oral histories, interviews with alumni, long after they have returned home. For recent alumni, the stories are more prevalent and accessible, although it can be difficult to understand the place that their scholarship will play in their broader life story. This change, however, highlights the desire by governments and universities to use the stories of these students as a marketing and corporate social responsibility tool, and a desire for the scholarships to be measured and quantified for impact and outcomes. The recording and publication of these stories is an area of further research and work that merits attention.[7] The experiences of these students and alumni in Australia provide valuable insight into the nature of Australian society and changes to the community and its attitudes over time. The experiences of alumni after they return home also provide the Australian Government and the public with an understanding of the value of their investment in these scholarships.

This research has also traced the development and growth of the international education sector in Australia, through the lens of scholarships. This element of this book puts forward a more comprehensive and thorough investigation of the history of this sector than has previously been published. In particular, the conventional narrative that focuses on the Colombo Plan as the first point in a timeline is not accurate, nor is the pinpointing of the

---

6   Goebel, *Anti-Imperial Metropolis*.
7   Work done by Julia Horne, David Lowe, Jemma Purdey and Jon Ritchie has provided excellent oral histories recording the experiences of students. Nevertheless, the Australian public continues to misunderstand both Australian Government scholarships and the international education sector more broadly.

Jackson Report as the beginning of the 'trade' approach to education as an exportable commodity. The history of international education in Australia is another area where further scholarly research is overdue.

In essence, this book has found that international development scholarships are more a reflection of Australia, its sense of its role and position in the Pacific, than they are a reflection of the needs and requirements of Pacific Island countries. The Australian Government's relationship with Pacific Island states evolved substantially over the 70-year period this book addresses. The relationships have always been complex and multifaceted, but the power balance has never been equal – Australia has always perceived itself as a leader in the region, either as a colonial power or a 'deputy sheriff'. The scholarship programs, as part of broader aid programs, have encouraged (often unsuccessfully) Australian diplomats and bureaucrats to understand more about the Pacific Islands, but as repeated Senate inquiries have shown, the Australian Government never really came to terms with the bilateral relationships with Pacific nations. Successive governments continued to take Pacific Island nations and their 'allegiance' for granted. Mistakes, problems and stereotyped assumptions have been repeated by Australian bureaucrats over generations. Nevertheless, the provision of scholarships to Pacific Island countries has continued uninterrupted for 70 years. Scholarships remain popular with Australian and Pacific politicians and, on the whole, with alumni. This is unlikely to change in the foreseeable future.

Bibliography

Archival documents

National Archives of Australia

A452, 1958/743: Chan, Cyril – Re scholarship for Papua and New Guinea.

A452 1960/5670: Proposed 'Colombo Plan' for the Pacific under the South Pacific Commission.

A452, 1961/2382: Scholarships or Grants for Native students – Papua and New Guinea.

A452, 1970/2871: Article in The Australian re cancellation of W Kaputin's scholarship - Papua New Guinea.

A452, 1970/3068: Visit to Papua New Guinea by the Prime Minister – July 1970 - briefs and speeches.

A452, 1970/4026: Tertiary Scholarships Papua New Guinea – eligibility of expatriate students.

A463, 1958/4459 Part 2: Commonwealth conference on education – Oxford, United Kingdom, 1959.

A463, 1958/4459 Part 3: Commonwealth conference on education – Oxford, United Kingdom, 1959.

A463, 1958/4459 Part 4: Commonwealth conference on education – Oxford, United Kingdom, 1959.

A463, 1958/4459 Attachment: Commonwealth conference on education – Oxford, United Kingdom, 1959.

A463, 1965/2353: British Commonwealth co-operation in education – Australian assistance to western Pacific territories.

A1209, 1965/6088: Offer of scholarships from iron curtain countries to Papua and New Guinea.

A1209, 1974/6740: Admission to and welfare of overseas students in Australia – Policy.

A1209 1977/609 Part 2: Sponsored overseas students in Australia.

A1361, 53/20/1 Part 1: Commonwealth Educational Co-operation - Pacific Islands - Policy and General.

A1361, 53/20/2 PART 1: Commonwealth Educational Co-operation - Pacific Islands -Scholarships Offered By Australia.

A1838, 561/6/18/3 Part 1: Information – Foreign Affairs Sub Committee – Parliamentary Joint Committee on Aid – Department of Foreign Affairs submissions.

A1838, 2047/1: Economic and Technical Assistance – Australian Government Overseas Scholarships outside the Colombo Plan.

A1838, 3080/10/4/3 Part 1: Papua New Guinea – Australian Relations with Papua New Guinea – Role of the Department of Foreign Affairs – Aid to Papua New Guinea.

A1838, 3080/10/4/3 ANNEX: Papua New Guinea – Relations with Australia – Role of Department of Foreign Affairs – Aid to Papua New Guinea.

A3211, 1960/2725: Commonwealth Conference on education – Oxford 1959 – Proposal for Commonwealth Scholarship Scheme.

A4250 1977/1724: Review of level of services provided for sponsored overseas students.

A4250, 1984/897: Reports Goldring and Jackson Committees DTB training matters.

A4250, 1984/1427: Jackson and Goldring Ministerial Correspondence and Statements on Overseas Students Policy.

A4250, 1984/1428: Jackson and Goldring Ministerial Correspondence and Statements on Overseas Students Policy.

A4250, 1984/1860: Ministerial and other representations about matters raised in the Jackson and Goldring reports.

A4250, 1984/1941: Reports- Goldring and Jackson Committees – Development Training Branch – training matters.

A4250, 1984/2194: Public reactions to the Jackson report.

A4250, 1989/735: AIDAB – Program Equity and Merit Scholarship Scheme.

A4250, 1989/792: Proposed Aid Scholarship Scheme.

A4250, 1990/801: AIDAB OSS – TP Specific – EMSS – History.

A4250, 1990/1349: AIDAB – JCSS review of program.

A4250, 1990/1583: AIDAB – JCSS (John Crawford Scholarship Scheme) - review of program.

A4250, 1990/4203: Australian International Development Assistance Bureau – PAC 2 Tonga tripartite review of scholarship system Australia New Zealand Tonga.

A4250, 1991/2160: AIDAB – EMSS John Crawford Scholarship Scheme Policy.

A4926, 886: Australian international scholarships - Decision 1055(GA).

A8950 5270: Undergraduate and Postgraduate Training for Students from South Pacific Countries – May.

B848, V1984/82: Jackson committee report on Australian Overseas Aid.

B848, V1984/93: Jackson committee report on Australian Overseas Aid.

National Library of Australia

MS9600/11/1, Papers of Sir Donald Cleland, circa 1960–circa 1990 [General letters 1951–57].

National Archives of Papua New Guinea

Box 340, File 6–2, Australian International Scholarship Scheme 1958.

Fiji National Archives

'C.D&W Scholarship – Applications and Recommendations', 28/277/4, 1951.

'Fiji Scholarship – Proposal by Morris Hedstrom | Newspaper Clipping from 26 July 1944', F28/265, 1944.

'Final Report of the Interdepartmental Committee to Consider the Award of Scholarships, 4th October', 25/296/7, 1947.

'Minutes of the Meeting of the Education Advisory Council Held on Friday 1st March 1957 18/57 – Award of Fiji Scholarship', F28/451/1 Education Advisory Council – Minutes of Meetings, 1957.

'Morris Hedstrom Trust Deed Draft', F28/265.

'Non-European Students | Policy Information', F28/7/79, 1951.

'Scholarships and Bursaries – 1957', F28/451/1, 1957.

National Archives and Records Administration (USA)

RG59, Box 1840 – Central Foreign Policy Files 1964–66 1966.

Oral history collection

Lowe, David, Jon Ritchie and Jemma Purdey. 'Scholarships and Connections: Australia, Indonesia and Papua New Guinea, 1960–2010', data set. Deakin University, 2015.

Beatrice Mahuru, interview with Jemma Purdey, 16 December 2015.

Jaking Marimyas, interview with Jemma Purdey, 17 December 2014.

James Kaiulo, interview with Jonathan Ritchie, 12 February 2015.

Lavarah Haihavu, interview with Jemma Purdey, 16 December 2014.

Paulus William Kei, interview with Jemma Purdey, 14 December 2014.

Ray Anere, interview with Musawe Sinebare, 17 December 2014.

Samson Akunaii, interview with Jonathan Ritchie and Musawe Sinebare, 9 July 2014.

Glenbow Museum Archive (Canada)

'Judy Lo Fonds', Glenbow Museum Archive, Calgary, Canada.

Newspaper and magazine articles

'150 Delegates for Oxford: Empire Education'. *Daily Telegraph*, 22 May 1959.

'19 Native Scholars Arrive in Australia'. *Pacific Islands Monthly*, 1 February 1954.

'Aussie Attack on Aid Misuse'. *Niugini Nius*, 8 June 1984.

'Australian Scholarships for Fiji'. *Pacific Islands Monthly*, 1 January 1955.

'CAA Attitude Hardens'. *Community Aid Abroad Review*, September–October 1984.

Conkey, Howard. 'Australia Benefits from Taking Foreign Students'. *The Canberra Times*, 7 June 1984.

Davis, Ian. 'Report Seeks More Foreign Student Aid'. *The Age*, 8 June 1984.

'Don't Blame Native Boys Says Minister'. *Melbourne Herald*, 24 July 1957.

'Dream Has Come True for Papuan'. *The Fiji Times*, 1 August 1967.

Dunstan, Graeme. 'Letter to the Editor: Kaputins Victimised'. *The Australian*, 12 June 1970.

'Fiji Indians Must Accept Reality – Malaysian PM'. *The Fiji Times*, 4 November 1988.

'Fiji Teacher Refused Permission to Enter New Guinea'. *The Fiji Times*, 17 January 1966.

'Fiji's Outstanding Students Win Scholarships'. *Pacific Islands Monthly*, 1 February 1955.

'Fisheries Assistant's Scholarship'. *The Fiji Times*, 6 January 1966.

'Flood of Inquiries on Study in Australia'. *The Fiji Times*, 8 June 1984.

Griffin, JT. 'Letter to the Editor | Reinstated'. *The Australian*, 1970.

'Happy Group of New Guinea and New Britain Secondary Students'. *South Coast Bulletin*, 28 August 1959.

Howard, John. 'John Howard: RAMSI Ends with its Mission Accomplished for Solomon Islands'. *The Sydney Morning Herald*, 28 June 2007.

Inder, Stuart. 'Fiji's Progress Praised'. *The Fiji Times*, 9 June 1984.

Kaputin, John. 'In New Guinea, as Elsewhere "Violence is a Reality Which You Have to Face"'. *Pacific Islands Monthly*, 1970.

Lohr, Steve. 'MX Reversal by Australian Isn't Popular'. *The New York Times*, 24 February 1985.

'Long-Range Planning Urged in Development'. *The Fiji Times*, 26 July 1966.

Mannheim, Markus. 'Doubts Raised over Aid Scholarships'. *The Canberra Times*, 27 April 2011.

'Most Students Now Have Jobs'. *South Pacific Post*, 13 March 1959.

'Natives' Exams to Be Made Tougher'. *South Pacific Post*, 16 September 1958.

'Natives Taken from School'. *Daily Telegraph*, 24 July 1957.

'New Guinea Becomes Battlefield for Australian Party Politics'. *Pacific Islands Monthly*, 1 February 1970.

'Official Australia and Fiji'. *The Fiji Times*, 17 July 1967.

'PNG Hails Its New Ties with Islands'. *The Fiji Times*, 25 March 1974.

'PNG Promised Conditional Aid'. *The Fiji Times*, 5 March 1974.

'Report Does Not Satisfy Director'. *South Pacific Post*, 3 October 1958.

'"Right Calibre Men" – Fiji Politically Ahead of New Guinea Say MPs'. *The Fiji Times*, 21 July 1967.

Rodrigo, Tennyson. 'Building a Life through Studies in Australia'. *Sydney Morning Herald*, 23 November 2012 (online).

'Salary Policy "Based on Skin Color"'. *Post Courier – Port Morsby*, 11 June 1970.

Savva, Niki. 'PNG Aid Should Be Cut, Jackson Tells Gov'. *The Australian*, 8 June 1984.

'Scholarships Replace Subsidies'. *Canberra Times*, 19 December 1988.

'The Sinister Role of ADAB in Overseas Students' Affairs'. *Tharunka*, 24 September 1979.

Spillius, Alex. 'Bush Entrusts "Deputy Sheriff" Howard with Pacific Policing Role'. *The Telegraph*, 15 August 2003.

Tiko, Samisoni. 'Letters to the Editor: Alien System'. *The Fiji Times*, 11 November 1988.

Walters, Patrick. 'Australian Aid Spread Too Thinly, Report Says'. *The Sydney Morning Herald*, 8 June 1984.

'Welcome New Aid Peacock Tells PNG'. *Post Courier*, 9 June 1972.

Zakharov, Jeannie. 'Cabinet Decides to Stop Aid to Fiji'. *Canberra Times*, 30 September 1987.

Government publications and political speeches

'2015 Mobility Program Offers'. Department of Foreign Affairs and Trade. www.dfat.gov.au/people-to-people/new-colombo-plan/mobility-program/Pages/2015-mobility-program-offers, accessed 20 April 2023.

'Annexe Two: Outline of Major Programs by Scheme'. Canberra: AusAID, 2008.

'Annexe Three: Scholarship Programs by Region/Country (Draft)'. Canberra: AusAID, 2008.

Auditor General, ed. *AusAID's Management of Tertiary Training Assistance*. Canberra: Australian National Audit Office, 2010.

Austrade, ed. *Australia Awards Data (2002–2018)*. Canberra: Australian Trade Commission, 2018.

Australian Council for Education Research. 'Australia Awards Global Tracer Facility – Case Study #1: Fiji'. Melbourne: Department of Foreign Affairs and Trade, 2017.

Australian Universities Commission. *Report of the Australian Universities Commission*. Canberra: Australian Government Publishing Service, 1957. nla.gov.au/nla.obj-1363949525, accessed 29 July 2020.

Barnes, CE. 'Report of the Commission on Higher Education for Papua and New Guinea', news release. 30 July 1964.

Bishop, Julie. 'Speech at the Launch of the Australia Awards Women's Leadership Initiative'. 8 February 2018. Minister for Foreign Affairs, Canberra. www.foreignminister.gov.au/minister/julie-bishop/speech/speech-launch-australia-awards-womens-leadership-initiative, accessed 24 April 2023.

Commonwealth. *Parliamentary Debates*. House of Representatives, 7 May 1963, 1071 (Hasluck).

Commonwealth Office of Education Annual Report for 1961. Canberra: Government of the Commonwealth of Australia, 1962.

Commonwealth Office of Education Annual Report for 1966. Canberra: Government of the Commonwealth of Australia, 1967.

The Contribution of Australian Aid to Papua New Guinea's Development 1975–2000. Evaluation and Review Series No. 34. Canberra: AusAID, 2003.

Department of Education and Training. *Higher Education in Australia: A Review of Reviews from Dawkins to Today.* Canberra: Department of Education and Training, 2015.

Department of Foreign Affairs and Trade. *Australian Aid: Promoting Prosperity, Reducing Poverty, Enhancing Stability.* Canberra: Department of Foreign Affairs and Trade, 2014.

Defence and Trade References Committee Foreign Affairs, ed. *Economic Challenges Facing Papua New Guinea and the Island States of the Southwest Pacific.* Canberra: Parliament of Australia, 2009.

Defence and Trade Senate Standing Committee on Foreign Affairs, ed. *A Pacific Engaged: Australia's Relations with Papua New Guinea and the Island States of the Southwest Pacific.* Canberra: Parliament of Australia, 2003.

Downer, Alexander. 'Inaugural Lecture on National and International Security: 16 May 2006, Wollongong'. 2006. webarchive.nla.gov.au/awa/20060601232535/http://pandora.nla.gov.au/pan/25167/20060602-0000/www.foreignminister.gov.au/speeches/2006/060516_national_international_security.html, accessed 28 July 2020.

'FOI Disclosure Log – Australian Aid Related Requests (before 1 November 2013)'. Department of Foreign Affairs and Trade. www.dfat.gov.au/about-us/corporate/freedom-of-information/Pages/foi-disclosure-log-australian-aid-related-requests.aspx, accessed 26 May 2016.

Garnaut, Ross and Rabbie Namaliu. *PNG Universities Review – Report to Prime Ministers Somare and Rudd.* Canberra: AusAID, 2010.

Global Impact of Australian Aid Scholarships: Long-term Outcomes of Alumni. Australian Council for Education Research. www.dfat.gov.au/sites/default/files/global-impact-australian-aid-scholarships-long-term-outcomes-alumni.pdf, accessed 20 April 2023.

Goldring, John, *Mutual Advantage.* Canberra: Australian Government Publishing Service, 1984.

Gosling, Margaret. 'Scholarship Effectiveness Review Part 1'. Edited by AusAID. Canberra: Commonwealth of Australia, 2008.

Gosling, Margaret. 'Scholarship Effectiveness Review Part 3'. Edited by AusAID. Canberra: Commonwealth of Australia, 2009.

Hasluck, Paul, *Australian Policy in Papua and New Guinea: Statement in the House of Representatives.* Canberra: Government Printer, 1960.

Jackson, R Gordon. *Report of the Committee to Review the Australian Overseas Aid Program*. Parliamentary Paper No. 206 of 1984. Canberra: Australian Government Printing Service, 1984.

Joint Australia/New Zealand Pacific Scholarships Review: Final Draft Report. Canberra: Department of Foreign Affairs and Trade (Aus), Ministry of Foreign Affairs and Trade (NZ), 2010.

Management of the Australian Development Scholarships Scheme, Audit Report No. 15 1999–2000 (Canberra: Australian National Audit Office, 1999).

'PNG's Jakapi Arigo on IT, Masters, Queensland and Rugby League'. Australia Global Alumni, Department of Foreign Affairs and Trade (Australia), 2019. www.globalalumni.gov.au/alumni-stories/pngs-jakapi-arigo-on-it-masters-queensland-and-rugby-league, accessed 28 March 2023.

Ryan, Susan. 'Changes to Overseas Student Arrangements', news release. 19 August 1986. parlinfo.aph.gov.au/parlInfo/download/media/pressrel/HPR09022017/upload_binary/HPR09022017.pdf;fileType=application%2Fpdf#search=%22media/pressrel/HPR09022017%22, accessed 22 July 2020.

'Submission to the Standing Committee on Foreign Affairs, Defence and Trade by the Acting Fiji High Commissioner to Australia: Mr Kamlesh Kumar Arya'. Canberra: 2008.

Secondary sources

Books

Banivanua-Mar, Tracey. *Decolonisation and the Pacific: Indigenous Globalisation and the Ends of Empire*. Critical Perspectives on Empire. Cambridge: Cambridge University Press, 2014.

Browne, Stephen. *Aid and Influence: Do Donors Help or Hinder?* London: Earthscan, 2006.

Burchill, Scott. *The National Interest in International Relations Theory*. New York: Palgrave MacMillan, 2005. doi.org/10.1057/9780230005778.

Corbett, Jack. *Australia's Foreign Aid Dilemma: Humanitarian Aspirations Confront Democratic Legitimacy*. Routledge Humanitarian Studies. Abingdon, Oxon: Routledge, 2017. doi.org/10.4324/9781315523491.

Davis, Dorothy and Bruce Mackintosh, eds. *Making a Difference: Australian International Education*. Sydney: University of New South Wales Press, 2011.

Doran, Stuart Robert, ed. *Australia and Papua New Guinea, 1966–1969*. Documents on Australian Foreign Policy. Canberra: Department of Foreign Affairs and Trade, 2006.

Eldridge, Philip J. *The Politics of Human Rights in Southeast Asia*. Politics in Asia Series. Routledge, 2002.

Garner, Alice and Diane Kirkby. *Academic Ambassadors, Pacific Allies: Australia, America and the Fulbright Program*. Manchester: Manchester University Press, 2019. doi.org/10.7228/manchester/9781526128973.001.0001.

Gaunder, Padmini. *Education and Race Relations in Fiji 1835–1998*. Fiji: Padmini Gaunder, 1999.

Goebel, Michael. *Anti-Imperial Metropolis: Interwar Paris and the Seeds of Third World Nationalism*. Global and International History. Cambridge: Cambridge University Press, 2015. doi.org/10.1017/CBO9781139681001.

Howie-Willis, Ian. *A Thousand Graduates: Conflict in University Development in Papua New Guinea 1961–1976*. Edited by EK Fisk. Canberra: Pacific Research Monographs, Australian National University, 1980.

Humphrys, Elizabeth. *How Labour Built Neoliberalism*. Leiden, The Netherlands: Brill, 2018. doi.org/10.1163/9789004383463.

Immerwahr, Daniel. *How to Hide an Empire: A History of the Greater United States*. London: The Bodley Head, 2019.

Kelly, Andrew. *ANZUS and the Early Cold War*. Cambridge: Open Book Publishers, 2018. doi.org/10.11647/OBP.0141.

Kokoda Initiative. *Voices from the War: Papua New Guinean Stories of the Kokoda Campaign, World War Two*. Canberra: Government of Papua New Guinea and Government of Australia, 2015.

Lal, Brij V, ed. *Politics in Fiji: Studies in Contemporary History*. Sydney: Allen & Unwin, 1986.

Oakman, Daniel. *Facing Asia: A History of the Colombo Plan*. Canberra: Pandanus Books, 2004.

Perraton, Hilary. *Learning Abroad: A History of the Commonwealth Scholarship and Fellowship Plan*. Revised edition. Cambridge: Cambridge Scholars Publishing, 2009.

Thompson, Roger C. *Australia and the Pacific Islands in the Twentieth Century*. Australian Scholarly Publishing, 1998.

Unger, Corrina R. *International Development: A Postwar History*. London: Bloomsbury Academic, 2018.

Viviani, Nancy. *Nauru, Phosphate and Political Progress*. Canberra: Australian National University Press, 1970.

Book chapters

Dassin, Joan and David Navarrete. 'International Scholarships and Social Change: Elements for a New Approach'. In *International Scholarships in Higher Education: Pathways to Social Change*, edited by Joan Dassin, Robin Marsh and Matt Mawer, 305–27. New York: Palgrave Macmillan, 2017. doi.org/10.1007/978-3-319-62734-2_15.

Dassin, Joan, Robin Marsh and Matt Mawer. 'Introduction: Pathways for Social Change?'. In *International Scholarships and Higher Education: Pathways for Social Change*, edited by Joan Dassin, Robin Marsh and Matt Mawer, 3–21. New York: Palgrave Macmillan, 2017. doi.org/10.1007/978-3-319-62734-2_1.

Dobel, Graeme. 'The "Arc of Instability": The History of an Idea'. In *History as Policy: Framing the Debate on the Future of Australia's Defence Policy*, edited by Ron Huisken and Meredith Thatcher, 85–104. Canberra: ANU Press, 2007.

Dong, Lili and David W Chapman. 'China's Scholarship Program as a Form of Foreign Assistance'. In *Crossing Borders in East Asian Higher Education*, edited by DW Chapman, WK Cummings and GA Postiglione, 145–66. CERC Studies in Comparative Education, vol 27. Dordrecht: Springer, 2010. doi.org/10.1007/978-94-007-0446-6_7.

Dunstan, Paula. 'Beyond the Campus: Students Engagement and Community Responses'. In *Making a Difference: Australian International Education*, edited by Dorothy Davis and Bruce Mackintosh, 338–64. Sydney: UNSW Press, 2011.

Herrera, Linda. 'Higher Education in the Arab World'. In *International Handbook of Higher Education*, edited by JJF Forest and PG Altbach, 409–21. Springer International Handbooks of Education, vol. 18. Dordrecht: Springer, 2007. doi.org/10.1007/978-1-4020-4012-2_20.

Hessler, Julie. 'Third World Students at Soviet Universities in the Brezhnev Period'. In *Global Exchanges: Exchange Programs, Scholarships and Transnational Circulations in the Modern World*, edited by Ludovic Tournes and Giles Scott-Smith, 202–15. Oxford: Berghahn Books, 2017. doi.org/10.1007/978-1-4020-4012-2_20.

Johnson, Lonnie R. 'The Fulbright Program and the Philosophy and Geography of US Exchange Programs since World War II'. In *Global Exchanges: Exchange Programs, Scholarships and Transnational Circulations in the Modern World*, edited by Ludovic Tournès, and Giles Scott-Smith, 173–87. Oxford: Berghahn Books, 2017. doi.org/10.2307/j.ctvw04fqt.16.

Kent, Anna. 'Recent Trends in International Scholarships'. In *International Scholarship in Higher Education: Pathways to Social Change*, edited by Joan Dassin, Robin Marsh, and Matt Mawer, 23–42. New York: Palgrave Macmillan, 2017.

Lal, Brij V. 'Politics Since Independence: Continuity and Change, 1970–1982'. In *Politics in Fiji: Studies in Contemporary History*, edited by Brij V Lal, 74–106. Sydney: Allen & Unwin, 1986.

Lee, David. 'Australia's Ambassadors in Washington, 1982–89'. In *Australia Goes to Washington: 75 Years of Australian Representation in the United States*, edited by David Lowe, David Lee and Carl Bridge, 183–207. Canberra: ANU Press, 2016. doi.org/10.22459/AGTW.12.2016.10.

MacWilliam, Scott. 'Papua New Guinea in the 1940s: Empire and Legend'. In *Australia and the End of Empires: The Impact of Decolonisation in Australia's near North*, edited by David Lowe, 25–42. Geelong: Deakin University Press, 1996.

Meadows, Eric. 'From Aid to Industry: A History of International Education in Australia'. In *Making a Difference: Australian International Education*, edited by Dorothy Davis and Bruce Mackintosh, 50–80. Sydney: UNSW Press, 2011.

Pietsch, Tamson and Meng-Hsuan Chou. 'The Politics of Scholarly Exchange: Taking the Long View on the Rhodes Scholarships'. In *Global Exchanges: Exchange Programs, Scholarships and Transnational Circulations in the Modern World*, edited by Ludovic Tournes and Giles Scott-Smith, 33–49. Oxford: Berghahn Books, 2017. doi.org/10.2307/j.ctvw04fqt.7.

Tournes, Ludovic and Giles Scott-Smith. 'A World of Exchanges: Conceptualizing the History of International Scholarship Programs (Nineteenth to Twenty-First Centuries)'. In *Global Exchanges: Exchange Programs, Scholarships and Transnational Circulations in the Modern World*, edited by Ludovic Tournes and Giles Scott-Smith, 1–30. Oxford: Berghahn Books, 2017. doi.org/10.2307/j.ctvw04fqt.7.

Waters, Chris. 'Official Influence in the Making of Foreign Policy: The Washington Study Group on the South Pacific, 1962.' In *Australia Goes to Washington: 75 Years of Australian Representation in the United States, 1940–2015*, edited by David Lowe, David Lee and Carl Bridge, 105–22. Canberra: ANU Press, 2016. doi.org/10.22459/AGTW.12.2016.06.

Journal articles

Ang, Ien and John Stratton. 'Asianing Australia: Notes Towards a Critical Transnationalism in Cultural Studies'. *Cultural Studies* 10, no. 1 (1996): 16–36. doi.org/10.1080/09502389600490441.

Auletta, Alex. 'A Retrospective View of the Colombo Plan: Government Policy, Departmental Administration and Overseas Students'. *Journal of Higher Education Policy & Management* 22, no. 1, (2000): 47–58. doi.org/10.1080/713678129.

Baba, Tupeni L. 'Academic Buccaneering Australian Style: The Role of Australian Academics in the South Seas'. *Directions: Journal of Educational Studies* 9, no. 1 (1987): 3–11.

Baba, Tupeni L. 'Australia's Involvement in Education in the Pacific: Partnership or Patronage?'. *Directions: Journal of Educational Studies* 11, no. 2 (1989): 43–53.

Banivanua-Mar, Tracey. 'Shadowing Imperial Networks: Indigenous Mobility and Australia's Pacific Past'. *Australian Historical Studies* 46, no. 3 (2015): 340–55. doi.org/10.1080/1031461X.2015.1076012.

Bray, Mark. 'Decolonisation and Education: New Paradigms for the Remnants of Empire'. *Compare: A Journal of Comparative and International Education* 24, no. 1 (1994): 37–51. doi.org/10.1080/0305792940240104.

Bray, Mark. 'Education and the Vestiges of Colonialism: Self-Determination, Neocolonialism and Dependency in the South Pacific'. *Comparative Education* 29, no. 3 (1993): 333–48. doi.org/10.1080/0305006930290309.

Byrne, Caitlin and Rebecca Hall. 'Realising Australia's International Education as Public Diplomacy'. *Australian Journal of International Affairs* 67, no. 4 (2013): 419–38. doi.org/10.1080/10357718.2013.806019.

Campbell, Anne C and Emelye Neff. 'A Systematic Review of International Higher Education Scholarships for Students from the Global South.' *Review of Educational Research* 90, no. 6 (2020) (online publication). doi.org/10.3102/0034654320947783.

Cassity, Elizabeth. 'Cast the Net a Little Wider: Australian Aid in the South Pacific'. *International Journal of Educational Development* 28 (2008): 246–58. doi.org/10.1016/j.ijedudev.2006.12.003.

Corbett, Jack and John Connell. 'All the World is a Stage: Global Governance, Human Resources, and the "Problem" of Smallness'. *Pacific Review* 28, no. 3 (2015): 435–59. doi.org/10.1080/09512748.2015.1011214.

Crocombe, Ron and Malama Meleisea. 'Higher Education in the Pacific Islands: Spheres of Influence, Trends and Developments'. *International Journal of Educational Development* 9, no. 3 (1989): 163–73. doi.org/10.1016/0738-0593(89)90044-8.

Davidson, James W. 'The Republic of Nauru'. *The Journal of Pacific History* 3, Issue 1 (1968): 145–50. doi.org/10.1080/00223346808572131.

Dinnen, Sinclair. 'RAMSI Ten Years On: From Post-Conflict Stabilisation to Development in Solomon Islands?'. *Journal of International Peacekeeping* 18, Issue 3–4 (2014): 195–213. doi.org/10.1163/18754112-1804005.

Eldridge, Philip. 'The Jackson Report on Australia's Overseas Aid Program: Political Options and Prospects'. *Australian Outlook* 39, no. 1 (1985): 23–32. doi.org/10.1080/10357718508444868.

Elvin, H Lionel. 'First Commonwealth Education Conference Oxford, July, 1959'. *International Review of Education* 6, no. 1 (1960): 79–82. doi.org/10.1007/BF01416669.

Ferns, Nicholas. 'Colonialism as Foreign Aid: Development Policy in Papua New Guinea, 1945–75'. *Australian Historical Studies* 51 (2020): 459–76. doi.org/10.1080/1031461X.2020.1808689.

Fraser, Stewart E. 'Australia and International Education: The Goldring and Jackson Reports—Mutual Aid or Uncommon Advantage?'. *Vestes* 27, no. 2 (1984): 15–29.

Fraser, Stewart E. 'Overseas Students in Australia: Governmental Policies and Institutional Programs'. *Comparative Education Review* 28, no. 2 (1984): 279–99. doi.org/10.1086/446435.

Goldsworthy, David. 'Australian External Policy and the End of Britain's Empire'. *The Australian Journal of Politics and History*, no. 1 (2005): 17–29. doi.org/10.1111/j.1467-8497.2005.00357.x.

Goldsworthy, David. 'British Territories and Australian Mini-Imperialism in the 1950s'. *Australian Journal of Politics & History* 41, no. 3 (1995): 356–72. doi.org/10.1111/j.1467-8497.1995.tb01266.x.

Gounder, Rukmani. 'Empirical Results of Aid Motivations: Australia's Bilateral Aid Program'. *World Development* 22, no. 1 (1994): 99–113. doi.org/10.1016/0305-750X(94)90171-6.

Hawksley, Charles. 'Australia's Aid Diplomacy and the Pacific Islands: Change and Continuity in Middle Power Foreign Policy'. *Global Change, Peace & Security* 21, no. 1 (2009): 115–30. doi.org/10.1080/14781150802659473.

Jinks, Brian. 'Australia's Post-War Policy for New Guinea and Papua'. *The Journal of Pacific History*, 17, no. 2 (1982): 86–100. doi.org/10.1080/00223348208572438.

Keenleyside, Hugh L. 'U. N. Technical Assistance Programme'. *Pakistan Horizon* 5, no. 1, (1952): 33–38.

Kent, Anna. 'Overseas Students Coordinating Committees: The Origins of Student Support in Australia?'. *Transitions: Journal of Transient Migration* 4, no. 1 (2020): 99–114. doi.org/10.1386/tjtm_00015_1.

Kramer, Paul A. 'Is the World Our Campus? International Students and U.S. Global Power in the Long Twentieth Century'. *Diplomatic History* 33, no. 5 (2009): 775–806. doi.org/10.1111/j.1467-7709.2009.00829.x.

Laifer, Natalie and Nicholas Kitchen. 'Making Soft Power Work: Theory and Practice in Australia's International Education Policy'. *Politics and Policy* no. 5 (2017): 813–40. doi.org/10.1111/polp.12219.

Lake, Marilyn. 'The Australian Dream of an Island Empire: Race, Reputation and Resistance'. *Australian Historical Studies* 46, no. 3 (2015): 410–24. doi.org/10.1080/1031461X.2015.1075222.

Lee, John Michael, 'On Reading the Morris Papers: 1959 Revisited'. *Round Table* 98, no. 405 (2009): 767–76. doi.org/10.1080/00358530903371445.

Lim, David. 'Jackson and the Overseas Students'. *Australian Journal of Education* 33, no. 1 (1989): 3–18. doi.org/10.1177/000494418903300101.

Lowe, David. 'The Colombo Plan: Modernisation and Memory and Cultural Engagement in Australia and New Zealand'. *Journal of Australian Studies* 28 (2015): 142–53. doi.org/10.20764/asaj.28.0_142.

Lowe, David. 'Percy Spender and the Colombo Plan 1950'. *Australian Journal of Politics & History* 40, no. 2 (1994): 162–76. doi.org/10.1111/j.1467-8497.1994.tb00098.x.

Maddocks, Ian with Seumas Spark. '"Taim Bilong Uni": Ken Inglis at the University of Papua New Guinea'. *History Australia* 14, no. 5 (2017): 545–60. doi.org/10.1080/14490854.2017.1389233.

Marginson, Simon. 'National and Global Competition in Higher Education'. *The Australian Educational Researcher* 31, no. 2 (2004): 1–28. doi.org/10.1007/BF03249517.

Matsuda, Matt K. 'The Pacific'. *The American Historical Review* 111, no. 3 (2006): 758–80. doi.org/10.1086/ahr.111.3.758.

McDougall, Derek. 'Edward Gough Whitlam, 1916–2014: An Assessment of His Political Significance'. *Round Table* 104, no. 1 (2015): 31–40. doi.org/10.1080/00358533.2015.1005360.

Megarrity, Lyndon. 'Indigenous Education in Colonial Papua New Guinea: Australian Government Policy 1945–1975'. *History of Education Review* 34, no. 2 (2005): 41–58. doi.org/10.1108/08198691200500009.

Megarrity, Lyndon. 'Regional Goodwill, Sensibly Priced'. *Australian Historical Studies* 38, no. 129 (2007): 88–105. doi.org/10.1080/10314610708601233.

Mohok McLaughlin, Juliana and Anne Hickling-Hudson. 'Beyond Dependency Theory: A Postcolonial Analysis of Educating Papua New Guinean High School Students in Australian Schools'. *Asia Pacific Journal of Education* 25, no. 2 (2005): 193–208. doi.org/10.1080/02188790500338187.

Moore, Clive. 'Helpem Fren: The Solomon Islands, 2003–2007'. *The Journal of Pacific History* 42, no. 2 (2007): 141–64. doi.org/10.1080/00223340701461601.

Nelson, Hank. 'Liberation: The End of Australian Rule in Papua New Guinea.' *Journal of Pacific History* 35, no. 3 (December 2000): 269–80. doi.org/10.1080/00223340020010562.

Oakman, Daniel. 'The Politics of Foreign Aid: Counter-Subversion and the Colombo Plan, 1950–1970'. *Pacifica Review: Peace, Security & Global Change* 13, no. 3 (2001): 255–72. doi.org/10.1080/13239100120082710.

Oakman, Daniel, 'The Seed of Freedom: Regional Security and the Colombo Plan'. *Australian Journal of Politics & History* 46, no. 1 (2000): 67–85. doi.org/10.1111/1467-8497.00086.

Oakman, Daniel, '"Young Asians in Our Homes": Colombo Plan Students and White Australia'. *Journal of Australian Studies* 26, no. 72 (2002): 89–98. doi.org/10.1080/14443050209387741.

O'Brien, Patricia. 'Remaking Australia's Colonial Culture? White Australia and Its Papuan Frontier 1901–1940'. *Australian Historical Studies* 40, no. 1 (2009): 96–112. doi.org/10.1080/10314610802663043.

Papoutsaki, Evangelia and Dick Rooney. 'Colonial Legacies and Neo-Colonial Practices in Papua New Guinean Higher Education'. *Higher Education Research and Development* 25, no. 4 (2006): 421–33. doi.org/10.1080/07294360600947434.

Perna, Laura W, Kata Orosz, Bryan Gopaul, Zakir Jumakulov, Adil Ashirbekov and Marina Kishkentayeva. 'Promoting Human Capital Development: A Typology of International Scholarship Programs in Higher Education'. *Educational Researcher* 43, no. 2 (2014): 63–73. doi.org/10.3102/0013189X14521863.

Pietsch, Tamson. 'Many Rhodes: Travelling Scholarships and Imperial Citizenship in the British Academic World, 1880–1940'. *History of Education* 40, no. 6 (2011): 723–39. doi.org/10.1080/0046760X.2011.594096.

Ramesh, Sanjay. 'Reflections on the 1987 Fiji Coups'. *Fijian Studies: A Journal of Contemporary Fiji* 5, no. 1 (2007): 164–78.

Riley, Charlotte Lydia. '"Tropical Allsorts": The Transnational Flavor of British Development Policies in Africa'. *Journal of World History* 26, no. 4 (2015): 839–64. doi.org/10.1353/jwh.2016.0065.

Rosewarne, Stuart, 'Australia's Changing Role in the South Pacific: Global Restructuring and the Assertion of Metropolitan State Authority'. *Journal of Australian Political Economy*, no. 40 (1997): 80–116.

Skilbeck, Malcolm and Helen Connell. 'Commonwealth Education in Its Changing International Setting'. *The Round Table* 98, no. 405 (2009): 687–09. doi.org/10.1080/00358530903371395.

Sobocinska, Agnieszka and Jemma Purdey. 'Enduring Connections?'. *Bijdragen tot de taal-, land- en volkenkunde / Journal of the Humanities and Social Sciences of Southeast Asia* 175, no. 2–3 (2019): 225–51. doi.org/10.1163/22134379-17502001.

Sukma, Rizal. 'Indonesia and the Tsunami: Responses and Foreign Policy Implications.' *Australian Journal of International Affairs* 60, no. 2 (June 2006): 213–28. doi.org/10.1080/10357710600696142.

Waters, Chris. 'The MacMahon Ball Mission to East Asia 1948'. *Australian Journal of Politics & History* 40, no. 3 (1994): 351–63. doi.org/10.1111/j.1467-8497.1994.tb00109.x.

Waters, Chris. 'Macmillan, Menzies, History and Empire'. *Australian Historical Studies* 22, no. 119 (2002): 93–107. doi.org/10.1080/10314610208596203.

Waters, Chris and Garry Woodard. 'Macmahon Ball's Goodwill Mission to Asia 1948'. *Australian Journal of International Affairs* 49, no. 1 (May 1995): 129–34. doi.org/10.1080/10357719508445151.

Waters, Christopher. '"Against the Tide": Australian Government Attitudes to Decolonisation in the South Pacific, 1962–1972'. *The Journal of Pacific History*, no. 2 (2013): 194–208. doi.org/10.1080/00223344.2013.794576.

Weisbrot, David. 'In Memoriam: Judge John Goldring (1943–2009)'. *Australian Law Reform Commission Reform Journal* 63, no. 94 (2009): 63–64.

White, Carmen M. 'Affirmative Action and Education in Fiji: Legitimation, Contestation, and Colonial Discourse'. *Harvard Educational Review* no. 2 (2001): 240–68. doi.org/10.17763/haer.71.2.p1057320407582t0.

Other published works

Anderson, Kent and Joanne Barker. 'Vale Endeavour, Long Live the New Endeavour: The End of Australia's World Leading Commitment to Internationalism and the Opportunity to Reassert Ourselves'. *Australian Policy History* 28 May 2019. aph.org.au/2019/05/vale-endeavour/, accessed .

Anere, Davidson. 'The Spirit of Brotherhood: A Tribute'. *My Land My Country* (blog). mylandmycountry.wordpress.com/2016/10/08/the-spirit-of-brotherhood-a-tribute-by-davidson-anere/, accessed 22 July 2020 (site discontinued).

Baba, Tupeni. *The Business of Australian Aid: Education, Training and Development – The Marjorie Smart Lecture for 1989: Tupeni Baba; and a Summary of the Proceedings of a Subsequent Panel Discussion Edited by D.R. Jones, V.L. Meek and J. Weeks*. Edited by David R Jones, V Lynn Meek and J Weeks. Melbourne: St Hilda's College, University of Melbourne, 1989.

'Chapter XII: International Trusteeship System'. In *Charter of the United Nations*. New York: United Nations, 1945. www.un.org/en/sections/un-charter/chapter-xii/index.html, accessed 26 September 2020.

Daniels, Dale. 'Student Income Support: A Chronology'. Research Paper Series, 2017–18. Canberra: Parliamentary Library, 2017.

Davis, Thomas. 'Does Australia Have an International Development Assistance Policy? National Interest and Foreign Aid Policy Making'. In *Proceedings, Second Oceanic Conference on International Studies*. Australia: University of Melbourne, 2006.

Dobell, Graeme. 'Australia, Solomon Islands and RAMSI'. *The Strategist*, 13 October 2017. www.aspistrategist.org.au/australia-solomon-islands-and-ramsi/, accessed 26 July 2020.

Dobell, Graeme. 'The South Pacific: Policy Taboos, Popular Amnesia and Political Failure (Speech)'. Part of the Menzies Research Centre Lecture Series: Australian Security in the 21st Century. Canberra: The Menzies Centre, 2003.

Fisher, Denise. 'New Caledonia's Independence Referendum: Local and Regional Implications'. *The Lowy Institute* (blog), 8 May 2019. www.lowyinstitute.org/publications/new-caledonia-s-independence-referendum-local-regional-implications, accessed 31 March 2023.

Henningham, Stephen. 'No Easy Answers: Australia and the Pacific Islands Region'. *Parliamentary Research Service,* no. 5 (1995).

Hughes, Helen. 'Aid Has Failed in the Pacific'. Submission to the Inquiry into Australia's Relationship with Papua New Guinea and Other Pacific Island Countries, submission no. 61, 2002, www.aph.gov.au/Parliamentary_Business/Committees/Senate/Foreign_Affairs_Defence_and_Trade/Completed_inquiries/2002-04/png/submissions/sublist, accessed 28 March 2023.

Lee, David. 'Jackson, Sir Ronald Gordon (1924–1991)'. *Australian Dictionary of Biography*. Canberra: National Centre of Biography, Australian National University, 2016. adb.anu.edu.au/biography/jackson-sir-ronald-gordon-23122, accessed 19 April 2023.

Lehr, Sabine. 'Cuba's Scholarship Tradition: The Perspective from Ghana'. *NORRAG News* 45 (April 2011): 89–91. www.researchgate.net/publication/256375092, accessed 24 April 2023.

Lowe, David. 'The Colombo Plan and "Soft" Regionalism in the Asia-Pacific: Australian and New Zealand Cultural Diplomacy in the 1950s and 1960s'. Alfred Deakin Research Institute Working Paper Series 1, 2010.

McMaster, Morgan, Alejandra Guevara, Lacey Roberts and Samantha Alvis. *USAID Higher Education: A Retrospective 1960–2020*. Washington DC: United States Agency for International Development, 2019.

Negin, Joel and Glen Denning. *Study of Australia's Approach to Aid in Africa: Commissioned Study as part of the Independent Review of Aid Effectiveness*. Canberra: Department of Foreign Affairs and Trade, 2011.

Purdey, Jemma. 'Scholarships and Connections: Australia, Indonesia and Papua New Guinea'. Alfred Deakin Research Institute Working Paper Series Number 46, 2014.

Tran, Ly Thi and Mark Rahimi. *New Colombo Plan: A Review of Research and Implications for Practice*. Research Digest 14. Melbourne: International Education Association of Australia, 2018.

United Nations Visiting Mission to the Trust Territories of Nauru and New Guinea, 1962 – Report on New Guinea. New York: United Nations Trusteeship Council, 1962.

Weeden, William J, interview by Tony Ryan. 'Jock Weeden Interviewed by Tony Ryan in the Conversations with Australian Educators Oral History Project' [sound recording]. 22 March 1995. nla.gov.au/nla.obj-217270737.

Wesley, Michael. 'Australia's Poisoned Alumni: International Education and the Costs to Australia'. Policy Brief. Sydney: Lowy Institute for International Policy, 2009.

'The World Bank Data – Fiji'. The World Bank Group. data.worldbank.org/country/fiji, accessed 19 April 2023.

'The World Bank Data – PNG'. The World Bank Group. data.worldbank.org/country/PG, accessed 19 April 2023.

Unpublished theses

Chhoeun, Kongkea. 'Australian and Chinese Scholarships to Cambodia: A Comparative Study'. PhD thesis, Australian National University, Canberra, 2019.

Ferns, Nicholas. 'Beyond Colombo: Australian Colonial and Foreign Policy in the Age of International Development, 1945–1975'. PhD thesis, Monash University, 2017.

Kent, Anna. 'Australian Development Scholarships and Their Place within Diplomacy, Development and Education'. Masters thesis, University of Melbourne, 2012.

Sebastian, Eugene F, 'Protest from the Fringe: Overseas Students and Their Influence on Australia's Export of Education Services Policy 1983–1996'. PhD thesis, University of Sydney, 2009.

Index

Note: page numbers in *italics* indicate information found in tables or other illustrations.

AA. *see* Australia Awards (AA)
Abbott Government, 203–204, 206–207, 216, 217
ACIAR John Allwright Scholarships, 187
ADAA. *see* Australian Development Assistance Agency (ADAA)
ADAB. *see* Australian Development Aid Bureau (ADAB)
ADCOS. *see* Australian Development Cooperation Scholarship (ADCOS)
ADS. *see* Australian Development Scholarships (ADS)
Africa, 205–206
aid relationships
    private sector focus, 212, 217
    recipient state, 162–164, 166, 169–171
Akunaii, Samson, 121–122
ALAS. *see* Australian Leadership Award Scheme (ALAS)
Allison Sudradjat Awards, 187, 188
ANAO. *see* Australian National Audit Office (ANAO)
Anere, Ray, 119–120
ANZUS (Australia, New Zealand and United States) treaty, 30, 151–152
Aoae, Joseph Stanislaus, 53
ARDS. *see* Australian Regional Development Scholarships (ARDS)

Arigo, Jakapi, 175–176
ASTAS. *see* Australian Sponsored Training Assistance Scheme (ASTAS)
AusAID, 190, 196
    audit of scholarship programs, 183–184
    dissolution, 206
    executive agency status, 177
    outsourcing scholarship management, 186
Australia
    citizenship, 50, 53
    as colonial power, 4, 23, 25, 30, 43–50, 224
    as middle power, 5, 93
    relations with Pacific region, 2, 4, 57, 75, 147, 226
    reputation, 37
    role in the Pacific region, 27, 96, 188–189, 200–201, 224
    seat on United Nations Security Council, 203, 205
    security, 178–179, 191–192
    self-interest, 45, 135–137, 216
    Trusteeship of Nauru, 31–32
Australia Awards (AA), 204–206, 209, *210*
    Pacific Scholarships, 210, 213
    Women's Leadership Initiative, 213–214

Australia in Papua and New Guinea
   Australian administration, 2, 43–48, 74, 79–87, 221
   delays in independence, 23, 109–110
   education, 29, 48–49, 79, 80–81, 85–86, 91
Australia–IMF Scholarship Program for Asia, 187
Australian aid, 132–133. *see also* scholarships as Australian aid
   and education, 105–106, 124, 129, 193
   effectiveness, 181–182
   following Fijian coups, 151
   measurability, 180
   motivations, 205, 211–212
   to Pacific nations, 82, 189–190
Australian Council for Overseas Students, 129
Australian Development Aid Bureau (ADAB), 95, 104, 129–130, 138, 139–141. *see also* Australian International Development Assistance Bureau (AIDAB)
Australian Development Assistance Agency (ADAA), 93, 95, 105–106, 113
Australian Development Cooperation Scholarship (ADCOS), 165, 168, 182. *see also* Australian Development Scholarships (ADS)
Australian Development Scholarships (ADS), 179–180, 182–184
Australian government. *see also* bureaucracy
   departmental tensions, 41, 75–76, 112–113, 222
   education policy, 50
   instability, 204
   Oxford Commonwealth Conference, 62–66
   policymaking, 94, 115, 123–124, 142, 144–147, 194, 201–202
Australian International Award Scheme, 34, 39, 40, 46–47, 72
Australian International Development Assistance Bureau (AIDAB), 152, 169, 170
   Equity and Merit Scholarship Scheme (EMSS), 154–156, 165
   scholarships management, 165–166
Australian Leadership Award Scheme (ALAS), 187, 188, 193–194
Australian National Audit Office (ANAO), 183–184, 211
Australian Pacific Technical College Scholarships, 187
Australian Partnership Scholarship Program, 188
Australian Regional Development Scholarships (ARDS), 187, 197, 210, 213
Australian Sponsored Training Assistance Scheme (ASTAS), 166. *see also* Australian Development Scholarships (ADS)
Australian universities
   Dawkins Reforms, 126, 144–147
   fee structures, 145, 160–161
   Higher Education Contribution Scheme (HECS), 144
   student support, 182

Barnes, Charles, 82
Bishop, Julie, 207, 212
brain drain, 164
British Empire, 56–57. *see also* decolonisation
   Commonwealth Scholarship and Fellowship Plan (CSFP), 59–62, 64–66
   decline, 41
   and education, 70, 76–77
   Oxford Commonwealth Conference, 67–68

bureaucracy. *see also* Australian government
  Australian Administration in the Territory of Papua and New Guinea, 43, 46–47
  Australian Development Assistance Bureau (ADAB), 140–141
  Australian International Awards Scheme, 72–73
  Equity and Merit Scholarship Scheme (EMSS), 154–156, 171
  scholarships in aid programs, 196
  stability, 177
Bush, George W, 178

Carnegie Mellon University Awards, 187
Casey, Richard, 37
CD&W. *see* Colonial Development and Welfare Scholarships (CD&W)
Centre for Transnational Crime Prevention Scholarships (CTCPS), 187, 191–192
Chan, Cyril, 20–25
China, 9, 36, 131, 180
  Chinese-heritage students, 21
Cleland, Donald, 24, 47
Cocos Islands, 22
Cold War, 11–12, 29–30, 150
Colombo Plan, 4, 9, 19, 28–29, 35–38, 76
  and Commonwealth Scholarship and Fellowship Plan (CSFP), 61, 62–64, 66
  impact, 219
  New Colombo Plan, 213
  Papua New Guinea participation, 111
Colonial Development and Welfare Scholarships (CD&W), 9, 12, 38, 69

colonialism. *see also* Australia in Papua and New Guinea
  colonial administration, 4–5
  and education, 8, 13–14, 38, 76–77, 96, 116, 221
  paternalism, 3, 5, 82
Commonwealth of Nations, 56, 68, 75
Commonwealth Scholarship and Fellowship Plan (CSFP), 51
  Australian commitment, 69–70
  based in UK, 57–58
  and Colombo Plan, 61, 62–64, 66
  introduction of, 55
  origins, 58–61, 71
  Oxford Commonwealth Conference, 64–66, 67–70, 76
  in Pacific region, 71–72, 73, 79
  purpose of, 71, 76
Commonwealth Scholarships, 22, 49–50
Commonwealth Trade and Economic Conference, 58
communism, 29–30
  fears of, 36
  scholarships, 83
CSFP. *see* Commonwealth Scholarship and Fellowship Plan (CSFP)
CTCPS. *see* Centre for Transnational Crime Prevention Scholarships (CTCPS)
Cuba, 181

decolonisation, 6–7, 80, 220, 221–222
  British Empire colonies, 41, 67–69
  Commonwealth of Nations, 56, 68, 75
  dangers of, 27, 30–31, 90
  Pacific region, 29, 75, 93–94, 95–97, 107, 224
  postcolonial development, 6
  and scholarships, 13–14
Department of External Affairs (DEA)
  Australian International Award Scheme, 40–41

Colombo Plan, 36–37, 38, 66
  scholarships, 3, 34–35, 56–57
  Territory of Papua and New
    Guinea, 33, 46–47
Department of Foreign Affairs (DFA),
  95, 102, 112–113, 141
Department of Foreign Affairs and
  Trade (DFAT), 203, 205–206
Department of Immigration (and
  Ethnic Affairs), 8, 55, 114, 141
development
  Commonwealth Scholarship and
    Fellowship Scheme (CSFP),
    69–70, 76
  and education, 130
  educational needs in Papua New
    Guinea, 47–48
  national self-interest, 133–134,
    135–137
  Papua New Guinean
    independence, 23, 85–86
  scholarship alumni, 52, 84, 122
Development Training Scholarships,
  95, 100, 101, 116, 166
diplomacy, 171, 203–218, 223
  goodwill development, 103,
    153–154
  role in scholarship selection,
    156–157, 159
  scholarships as, 28–29, 37, 70,
    195, 203, 212
Downer, Alexander, 178–179, 190,
  191

education
  brain drain, 164
  equity of access, 158–160, 199
  gender and sex discrimination,
    213–214
  and mobility, 6, 8–10
  Pacific scholarships, 33–34
  secondary school, 52
  as trade, 124, 135, 149
  Western values, 36, 40

Equity and Merit Scholarship Scheme
  (EMSS), x–xiv, 126, 149–150,
  154–156, 165, 221. *see also* John
  Crawford Scholarship Scheme
  (JCSS)
  background, 152–155
  equity as principle, 158–160
  impact on Pacific relations,
    162–164
  number of scholarships offered,
    161–162
  program selection, 156–158,
    163–164
  review, 164–165

fee subsidy scheme
  ending, 154
  international students, 97–100,
    104–106, 114, 125–126,
    143–144, 145
  Overseas Students Charge, 95,
    97–98, 105, 128, 129, 137,
    143
  tertiary study fees, 94
Fiji, 11–12
  coups, 150–151, 192
  diaspora, 198
  independence, 55, 93–94, 95–96
  Morris Hedstrom Scholarship
    Scheme, 11–12
  opposition to Australian
    scholarships, 13–14
  racial tensions, 150–151, 156–157
  relationship with Australia, 75,
    195, 198
  scholarship recipients, 33, 34,
    38–40, 52–53
  scholarships offered, 181
  subsidised students, 98, 99, 156
Fiji Scholarships, 38
Foot, Hugh, 80–81
foreign policy. *see also* Colombo Plan
  aid, 206–207
  development, 129

immigration, 22, 84, 223–224
international relations, 27,
    162–164, 166, 169–171
leadership and governance, 194
and scholarships, 141
Fraser Government, 97, 101, 131
Fulbright Scholarship, 11

Garnaut, Ross, 207–209
Global Tracer Facility, 215–216, 217
Goldring Report, 127–131
    compared with Jackson Report,
        124–126, 130, 137, 146
    Overseas Student Task Force, 130,
        138–144
    policy impact, 143
    reaction to, 139, 146
Goldring, John, 124, 127
Gopal, Uttaman, 52–53
Gosling Review, 187–188, 194–197, 202

Haihavu, Lavarah, 175
Hasluck, Paul, 22, 23–24
    education in Papua and New
        Guinea, 48, 73, 81
    as Minister for Territories, 45–46,
        50, 82, 221
Hawke Government, 125, 127, 128,
    144, 147, 169
    nuclear testing, 151–152
    response to Fijian coups, 151
HECS. *see* Australian universities
Holt, Harold, 59, 71
Howard Government, 177, 178–179,
    190–191

India, 30, 60, 64, 70
Indonesia, 30, 98, *99*, 104, 162, 186
international students, 55
    Australian Council for Overseas
        Students, 129
    bridging studies, 159, 169
    diversity of cohort, 185–186

full-fee positions, 135, 142
numbers, 209–211
Overseas Student Task Force, 130,
    138–144
policy review, 123, 124–125,
    128–129, 138–144
Review of Private Overseas Student
    Policy, 128
services review, 101–103
subject choice, 99–100, 106, 179
support for, 22, 24–25, 37, 103,
    159, 169
iterative policy development, 5, 147,
    153, 183, 220, 223

Jackson Report, 131–138
    compared with Goldring Report,
        124–126, 130, 137, 146
    criticism of, 136–138
    Overseas Student Task Force, 130,
        138–144
    policy impact, 143–144, 155–156
    reaction to, 139–140, 142–143,
        146
Jackson, Gordon, 131
John Crawford Scholarship Scheme
    (JCSS), 165–168
Joint Australia/New Zealand Pacific
    Scholarships Review (JPSR),
    199–200

Kaiulo, James, 120–121
Kaputin, William, 90
Kei, Paulus William, 174–175

Latin America, 204, 205

MacMahon Ball, William, 28
Mahuru, Beatrice, 121, 122
Malaysia, 99, 142, 149, 153, 157, 162,
    167
Marimyas, Jaking, 91
McEwen, John, 65
Menzies Government, 49, 59, 64

Menzies, Robert, 56, 57, 59, 65
Morris Hedstrom Scholarship Scheme, 11–12
Mutual Advantage. see Goldring Report

Namaliu, Rabbie, 207–209
nation-building, 179, 190–191, 194. *see also* development
national interest, 2, 45, 216, 220
Nauru
    independence, 75
    phosphate exploitation, 31–32
New Caledonia, 151, 167, 196
New Colombo Plan, 212–213
New Zealand, 61
    joint review of scholarships, 199–200
    nuclear ban, 152
    role in Pacific, 200
    scholarship programs, 199

Overseas Student Task Force, 130, 138–144

Pacific Islands Plan, 73–74
Pacific region, xvii–xviii, 204
    and Australian policy, 4, 220
    coups, 150–151
    French Pacific integration, 195–196
    New Colombo Plan, 213
    nuclear testing, 151–152
    relations with Australia, 2, 4, 57, 75, 147, 226
    security, 178–179
    South Pacific Forum, 96
    stability, 178, 188–189
    trustee territories, 31
    universities, 197, 198–199
Pacific Women Shaping Pacific Development program, 214
Papua New Guinea
    aid to, 111–113, 116–117
    Australian administration, 2, 43–48, 79–87, 221
    Bougainville conflict, 110, 151
    education, 48–49, 79, 80–81, 85–86, 91
    independence, 85–87, 109–117
    residents' eligibility for scholarships, 20–22, 46–48, 79–80, 104
    role in Second World War, 44–45
    students in Australia, 48, 49–50, 114–115, 137
    subsidised students, 98, *99*
    universities review, 207–209
    University of Papua New Guinea (UPNG), 81, 221
policy review, 201. *see also* Goldring Report; Jackson Report
    Australian National Audit Office (ANAO), 183–184, 211
    Gosling Review, 187–188, 194–197, 202
    international students, 123, 124–125, 128–129, 138–144
    joint review of scholarships, 199–200
    Senate inquiries, 179, 188–190, 192–193

race and racism, 5, 110
    'racial' mixing, 49
    access to education, 150–151
    immigration policy, 21
    in scholarship selection, 39–40, 53, 156–157
Regional Assistance Mission to Solomon Islands (RAMSI), 178, 191, 204
Rhodes Scholarship, 11–12
Rudd Government, 192, 203, 205, 207
Russia. *see* USSR (Union of Soviet Socialist Republics)

INDEX

Scholarship Effectiveness Review. *see* Gosling Review
scholarship experiences, 7, 225
    Akunaii, Samson, 121–122
    Anere, Ray, 119–120
    Aoae, Joseph Stanislaus, 53
    Arigo, Jakapi, 175–176
    Chan, Cyril, 20–25
    Gopal, Uttaman, 52–53
    Haihavu, Lavarah, 175
    Kaiulo, James, 120–121
    Kaputin, William, 90
    Kei, Paulus William, 174–175
    Mahuru, Beatrice, 121, 122
    Marimyas, Jaking, 91
    Papua New Guinean students in Australia, 48, 49–50, 114–115, 137
    records, 174
    Wong, Judy Annemarie, 52–53
scholarship programs. *see also* Commonwealth Scholarship and Fellowship Plan (CSFP); Equity and Merit Scholarship Scheme (EMSS); South-East Asian Scholarship Scheme
    ACIAR John Allwright Scholarships, 187
    Allison Sudradjat Awards, 187, 188
    Australia Awards (AA), 204–206, 209, 210, *210,* 213–214
    Australia–IMF Scholarship Program for Asia, 187
    Australian Development Cooperation Scholarship (ADCOS), 165, 168, 182
    Australian Development Scholarships (ADS), 179–180, 182–184
    Australian International Award Scheme, 34, 39, 40, 46–47, 72
    Australian Leadership Award Scheme (ALAS), 187, 188, 193–194
    Australian Pacific Technical College Scholarships, 187
    Australian Partnership Scholarship Program, 188
    Australian Regional Development Scholarships (ARDS), 187, 197, 210, 213
    Australian Sponsored Training Assistance Scheme (ASTAS), 166
    Centre for Transnational Crime Prevention Scholarships (CTCPS), 187, 191–192
    Colonial Development and Welfare Scholarships (CD&W), 9, 12, 38, 69
    Commonwealth Scholarships, 22, 49–50
    Development Training Scholarships, 95, 100, 101, 116, 166
    Fiji Scholarships, 38
    Fulbright Scholarship, 11
    John Crawford Scholarship Scheme (JCSS), 165–168
    Morris Hedstrom Scholarship Scheme, 11–12
    New Colombo Plan, 212–213
    outsourcing of, 186, 214
    records, 179
    Rhodes Scholarship, 11–12
    Secondary School Students' Project (SSSP), 168–169
    Sponsored Training Program (STP), 166
scholarships. *see also* selection of scholarship candidates
    benefits to recipient countries, 186
    design of, 58
    as diplomacy, 28–29, 37, 70, 195, 203, 212
    domestic policy, 220
    eligibility, 20–22, 46–50

evaluation, 165, 186, 211–212, 215–216
funding, 8, 35, 213
history, 10–11
inconsistent impacts, 214–215, 217
means testing, 111, 167
outsourcing management, 186
Pacific region, 73–74, 160, 167
policy focus, 194, 223–224
public scholarships, 182
purposes of, 222–223, 224, 226
requirement to return, 110–111, 184–185, 187, 200–201
review, 187
scope, 55, 63, 185
and security, 83
scholarships as Australian aid, 1, 58–59, 216
  Australian Development Scholarship Scheme (ADS), 184
  Australian Overseas Development Assistance, 218
  Colombo Plan, 65, 111
  Equity and Merit Scholarship Scheme (EMSS), 162
  Gosling Review, 196
  international students' fees, 94–95, 97
  recipient states, 169–171
  requirement to return, 110–111, 184–185, 187, 200–201
  selection, 33–34, 100–101
  Territory of Papua and New Guinea (TPNG), 82
Second World War, 44–45
secondary school scholarships, 20–25, 86–87, 101, 110, 115–116, 121
Secondary School Students' Project (SSSP), 168–169
security in Pacific region, 191–192, 201
selection of scholarship candidates
  discrimination, 106–107, 156–157, 199–200
  donor country, 155, 182, 221

Equity and Merit Scholarship Scheme (EMSS), 156–158, 163–164
means testing, 111, 167
nepotism, 134, 159
outsourcing process, 186
recipient country, 38–40
Solomon Islands, 190–191
  Regional Assistance Mission to Solomon Islands (RAMSI), 178, 191, 204
Somare, Michael, 96, 113, 115, 207
South Pacific Forum, 96
South-East Asian Scholarship Scheme, 5, 9, 19, 28, 35, 38–39, 223. *see also* Australian International Award Scheme
  extension to Pacific students, 33–34
  history, 3–4
Spender, Percy, 36
sponsored student scheme
  ending, 154
  international students, 97–100, 104–106, 114, 125–126, 143–144, 145
  Overseas Students Charge, 95, 97–98, 105, 128, 129, 137, 143
  tertiary study fees, 94
Sponsored Training Program (STP), 166

Taiwan, 180–181
Tonga, 98, *99,* 163
Turnbull Government, 213
Tuvalu, 96

United Nations Security Council, 203, 205
United Nations Technical Advice Administration, 38
United Nations Trusteeship System, 31–33, 45
  Trusteeship Council, 80, 86

university education. *see also* Australian universities; fee subsidy scheme
   in Australia, 59
   fee structures, 94, 95, 97
   Higher Education Contribution Scheme (HECS), 144
   Papua New Guinea, 207–209
USSR (Union of Soviet Socialist Republics), 30, 150

Weeden, William, 34, 72
White Australia Policy, 2–3, 8–9, 22, 84
   end of, 99
   impact on Australia's reputation, 27, 39–40, 53
Whitlam Government
   education policy, 93–95
   equal rights policy, 106–107
   immigration policy, 99
   Papua New Guinean independence, 117
   tertiary education fees abolition, 97, 110, 112, 126
Wong, Judy Annemarie, 52–53

www.ingramcontent.com/pod-product-compliance
Lightning Source LLC
Chambersburg PA
CBHW071737150426
43191CB00010B/1612